ANSTRUTHER

A HISTORY

ANSTRUTHER

A History

STEPHANIE STEVENSON

JOHN DONALD PUBLISHERS LTD
EDINBURGH

ISBN 0 85976 234 3

Phototypeset by Burns & Harris Ltd., Dundee
Printed in Great Britain by Bell & Bain Ltd., Glasgow

Acknowledgements

This book began as a series of talks for the Anstruther Improvements Association's 'Anster Nichts'. In preparing the talks, title deeds proved a most useful source of local information, and I am grateful to the National Trust for Scotland and many local friends who made their deeds available to me; and to David Cook, Neil Anderson, Paul Denholm, solicitors, and William Motion and Colin Sutherland, bank managers, who let me study the deeds in their offices. The Customs Officers in Kirkcaldy were equally helpful. In answer to my hopeful queries, I received invaluable information from R. A. Langdon, Executive Officer of the Research School of Pacific Studies of the Australian National University, Canberra, from Professor Hans Chr. Johansen of Odense University and Dr Thomas Riis from Copenhagen. I am indebted to Robert Smart, Keeper of Muniments at St Andrews University, I. C. Copland, Head Librarian of the North East Fife District Library and Mrs N. Blair of the Murray Library, Anstruther, and must also thank the many Anstruther folk who have shown such interest in my researches, have answered my questions and have told me more delightful stories than I have been able to include in this book. Finally I must say how grateful I am to Harry Watson, who while researching his own book on Kilrenny and Cellardyke sent me gems of information that I would never have found on my own.

For the photographs I must thank the following: John Doig and the Scottish Fisheries Museum on pages 23, 27, 31, 49, 81, 87, 101, 103, 105, 109, 129, 131, 133, 135, 137, 203, 209, 211, 213, 215, 221; Bill Flett, 15, 139, 145, 227, 229; Dr John Henry, 19, 195; David Thomson, Kilrenny, 33; Anstruther Church, 53; Mrs Brown and Matt Armour, 91; Capt. Robert Reekie, 95; Mrs G. Clarke, 110; and Mrs L. Cronsberry, 163.

Stephanie Stevenson

Contents

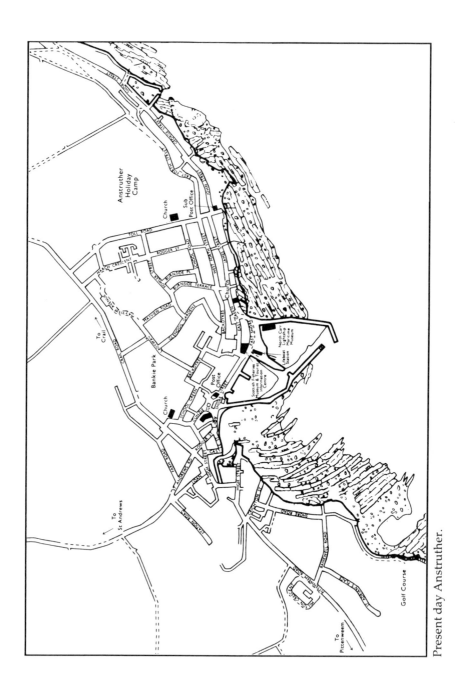

Present day Anstruther.

Part I

West Anstruther

1
Early History

The Fife coast is the product of two geological periods, one very distant and one comparatively recent. The rocks which make the shore so hazardous were laid down while Britain made a slow (sixty-five million years!) voyage from 15′ south to 10′ north of the equator. The arid conditions of the preceding Old Red Sandstone continent were followed by a tropical climate and the area consequently had variable sea levels in which deltas, estuaries and lagoons were from time to time replaced by deeper seas, so that a complicated sequence of sandstones, fossil soils, thin coals and shales was occasionally interrupted by limestones and marine clays. The hardness of sandstone in comparison with the more easily eroded shales left narrow slots in which sand collected, and these slots or inlets provided the first havens for boats along the shore. Innergellie Creek is a nearby example of an unimproved natural haven, and Randerston Creek, to the east of Fife Ness, shows signs of simple development.

The feature which influenced the shape of the East Neuk towns is a legacy of the more recent Ice Age. The removal of water from the oceans, in the formation of ice, lowered the level of the sea by a maximum of about 300 feet, but the falling surface of the sea was offset by the depression of the land under the immense weight of the ice. During warmer periods, as the ice cap melted, the seas refilled more rapidly than the land could rise and temporary shore lines were formed. The last recession of the ice cap left Anstruther with a beach about ten feet above the level of the sea. Close behind this is another beach at about fifty feet.

The early history of Anstruther is not as cleary defined as its geological formation. Aerial photographs of the district show prehistoric enclosures near Easter Grangemuir and dwelling sites near Pittenweem. In 1938 an exceedingly fine specimen of a stone axe cut from a piece of red granite, oval in shape, 4″ by 3″, 1¼″ thick and weighing 15 ounces, was found by Mr Robert Brown of Shore Street, Cellardyke, in the vicinity of the bathing pool (it is now in the Royal Museum of Scotland, Queen Street,

Edinburgh) and another prehistoric stone tool was found in 1956 near the Marches. If the stone implements belonged to the sites where they were found they indicate ancient settlements and an ancient trade, since no red granite occurs in East Fife.

Two names, however, tell us something about the early days. The name Anstruther is from the Gaelic *sruth* or *sruthair* meaning a stream or place of streams. The name occurs on the west coast of Scotland: Reisa *an t-Sruith*, an island in the tidal streams at the head of the Sound of Jura. The earliest written form in which the name occurs is Aynstrother, a dash over the first syllable indicating a contracted word. In a charter of 1587 the name appears in full as Athernynstruther, the streams of Ethernan, a Celtic saint who studied in Ireland and was consecrated bishop there, returning to what may have been his native country to devote his life to missionary work. An altar was dedicated to him on the Isle of May and a chapel at Kilrenny, anciently Kilretheni: *kil* or chapel of Ethernan. The 'Annals of Ulster' record the death of Ethernan in 699 AD 'among the Picts'.

Above the west end of the town there was once a large mound called Chesterhill Knowe, which implies a Roman presence. Names are not always reliable in deducing the history of a site and the name Chesterhill may not be ancient, although it was in use in the late sixteenth century many years before the discovery of what might have been a Roman well. A small portion of the town's lands at Chesterhill were feued in 1782 to John Finlayson, officer of excise, and in digging a foundation for his house a fine well was found and two skeletons enclosed in a kind of coffin consisting of a large stone at each end. George Gourlay, in his book on Anstruther, published in 1888, adds some Roman coins, and bones that 'lay all about as of men slain in battle'.

There is a reference in 1590 to the 'mothlaw', *motte*, a mound forming the site of a castle or camp, and *law*, a hill or mound. It was not a burial mound as according to the Rev. James Forrester the well was in the middle and the two graves in the side of the mound. There seems to be no reason, however, to doubt that, as either name, mothlaw or Chesterhill suggests, there was a camp on the hill between the burn and the west haven, and why not a Roman camp? A Roman camp is marked on the Ordnance Survey map to the south-west of Boarhills above the Kenly Burn.

The Roman historian Tacitus tells how in the summer of 83 AD Agricola sent ships and troops to explore the regions beyond the

Firth of Forth. Temporary or marching camps of leather tents, erected quickly and always to the same drill and lay-out, would have been necessary for the troops as they followed the coast keeping in touch with the fleet. Frequently, Tacitus writes, cavalry, infantry and marines, gathered in the same camp to celebrate their achievements. It is not difficult to picture such a scene on a long summer evening on the high ground above the Dreel. The native tribes did not wait for a declaration of war, Tacitus writes, but stormed the Roman camps and forts, but the bones lying around Chesterhill, 'as of men slain in battle', belong to a later date.

Apart from the advent of Christian missionaries from the fourth century onwards and the commemoration of the Celtic saint Ethernan, nothing more is known for certain about the early Anstruthers, but numerous graves of a similar construction to those at Chesterhill were found along the shores of Fife in the eighteenth and nineteenth centuries. After the great storm of October 18th 1898 James Smith, sailmaker, walking along the shore of the Billowness the next day came across a number of leg, arm and jaw bones and part of a skull on the surface of the beach to the west of Johnnie Doo's pulpit rock, together with some large stones, 'which had evidently formed a coffin'.

This report in the *East of Fife Record* prompted two other recollections of bones and burials at the Billowness. M. Cockbain from Birkenhead remembered that fifty years before there were low grassy mounds in the little amphitheatre to the west of Johnnie Doo's Hole which were known locally as 'the graves of the Pecks' [Picts]. Twenty years later they had disappeared under sand. R. Robertson from Edinburgh recalled that some twenty years before, several boys, of whom he was one, found 150 yards to the east of Johnnie Doo's pulpit a number of human bones 'resting on and covered with long slabs of stone'. The boys took their 'gruesome find' to George Gourlay, the local historian, who concluded that the bones were of an aboriginal chief who had fallen either in internecine strife 'or in open combat with a foreign foe'.

In Easter Anstruther in 1871 two coffins were found, one under the back premises of a house in Shore Street, and the other in the garden ground of a house on the west side of Rodger Street. Both graves were made of slabs of stone about a foot square, set on edge to make a cavity the size of a body, with no covering or base. The bones found in the Shore Street grave were pronounced by the local doctor to have belonged to a female, and from the worn appearance of the teeth and other indications 'it was surmised that they were those of an elderly person'. The Rodger Street grave was about six feet in length and along with the human remains was a piece of deer's horn or antler. These graves within sound of the sea, like those found at Chesterhill, were attributed in the last century to North Sea Raiders, but now they are thought to be early Christian and Pictish. Whether or not the graves were Danish, many of the raiders must have been killed and some may have settled around the coast of the East Neuk, and it would be safe to say that over the several hundred years of their raids up until the tenth or eleventh centuries, many of these expert sailors and navigators would have come into the sheltered haven of Anstruther.

2

The Maritime Tradition

There was probably some settlement at the mouth of the Dreel from the earliest times. There was a fertile hinterland, rich fishing off the coast, a natural haven at the mouth of a freshwater stream with the shelter of raised beaches to the west and north, a sandy shore on which to anchor and careen sea-going vessels and upstream a ford across the burn. Around these two natural features of ford and haven grew two small hamlets.

Our earliest written knowledge of Anstruther comes from the Records of the Priory of May, a monastery founded on May Island by King David I (1124-1152). His grandson William I (1165-1214) granted the monks of May 'four pence from all ships having four hawsers coming to the ports of Pittenweem and Anstruther for the sake of fishing or selling fish, and in like manner boats with fixed helms'. He reserved for his own use the can, or duty, collected at these ports and directed his officers to pay the tenth penny or tithe to the monks. Clearly many of the ships using the haven of Anstruther were larger and more elaborate than the open boats used for inshore fishing and there was evidently a worthwhile trade in fish from the haven.

Before long the canons of Dryburgh, to whom the parish church of Kilrenny belonged, were complaining that the monks of May were taking the whole tithe while they themselves, they claimed, were entitled to one half of the tithes since Kilrenny boats were moored on their side of the stream and were thus within the bounds of Kilrenny parish, which at that time encompassed the entire shore of Anstruther Easter. The argument was settled before the Papal Commissioners at Melrose in 1225.

The monks of May were to pay yearly one merk of silver within the parish church of Kilrenny to the canons of Dryburgh, in compensation no doubt for the share of the tithes that they had been denied in the past. The canons were also to receive full tithes from their own parishioners using the Kilrenny shore; the monks of May were to receive the full tithes 'from all coming from other quarters and using the said shore', that is the Kilrenny shore. If

The sheltered haven at the mouth of the Dreel. The Castle stood near the rocks on the right. On 'the Shore', opposite, at the foot of the Wester High Street, the White House replaced a much older house in 1765. The seventeenth-century house, centre, was once an inn.

this division of tithes was equitable, it suggests that there were as many vessels coming from other quarters as there were local boats. The biographer of St Kentigern, writing in the twelfth century, wrote of such an abundance of fish around the Isle of May that Angles, Scots, Belgian and French men came for the fishing and were all sheltered in the havens of the island — and evidently in the haven of the Dreel.

The next recorded mention of Anstruther's haven is in the early sixteenth century in the Accounts of the Lord High Treasurer of Scotland:

> 1503. Item, the third day of Junij . . . to the bote that landit the king in Anstrother that day .... vij s
> 1503 3 June Item, that samyn day quhen the king com on land to the preistis of Anstrother to say ane trentale of messes of Sanct Nicholas .... xx s
> 1508 [8 Mar.] Item, that day to ane bote of Anstrother that hed the king to Maj and agane to Pettinweeme .... xxviij s

A 'staple' or market for goods from eastern Scotland was created in the Low Countries in the early years of the fourteenth century, first at Middelsburg, then in 1359 at Bruges. From the mid-sixteenth century to the end of the eighteenth, the Scottish staple was at Veere, in Zeeland, where the handsome Scottish merchant house still stands. In 1380 the municipal authorities of Rheims passed an ordinance regulating the sale of salmon, herring and cod imported from Scotland, all three of which could have come from Anstruther. In 1498 James IV (1478-1513) in a seven-year truce with England issued a writ that Englishmen coming with merchandise to the ports or havens of Pittenweem, Anstruther, Earlsferry and Crail, should be given safe conduct.

From the mid-1500s a Convention of Royal Burghs met annually to supervise and regulate everything that would affect the prosperity of Scotland and benefit the commerce and trade of Royal Burghs, a system, Daniel Defoe commented in 1706, that was taken from the union of the Hans-Towns in the Baltic. In 1600, when skippers and owners of ships were concerned about the number of mariners who were leaving their ships in foreign countries for better pay elsewhere, both the Anstruthers were among those east coast burghs which were asked to bring to the next convention with their commissioners 'ane meister and skipper or twa' to devise and set down new regulations regarding the signing on and payment of sailors in foreign trade. At this time, the east coast burghs were trading with England; with France at Calais, Dieppe, Caen, Rouen, Rochelle and Bordeaux; with Spain and Portugal; and with the countries of the 'Eister Seas' [the Baltic].

The natural haven at the mouth of the Dreel probably assumed the appearance of a regular harbour sometime in the sixteenth century before the grant of a Royal Charter in 1587. A drystone rubble-filled bulwark, perhaps reinforced with baulks of timber, would have been constructed along the natural line of a sandstone ridge to give added protection to the sheltered sandy beach. Such bulwarks or piers offered limited resistance to the constant battering of winter storms and were a continual drain on the financial resources of the coastal burghs. In 1613, 1615 and again in 1619 there were supplications from Anstruther Wester's commissioners craving support for the reparation of the harbour. In July 1620 the Convention:

> considering the necessitie of the sed herberie and how commodious the same is to the haill ships resorting within this Firth for safetie both of ships and guids, hes grantit and gevin . . . to the sed burgh, for help to the reparatioun of thair sed herberie, the somme of twa hundreth pundis money of this realme.

The money was to be paid in two instalments 'provyding always that the sed burgh be comptabill thereof to the burrowis [the Convention] and bestow the same upon the reparatioun of the sed herberie and no otherways'. There was to be no cheating with the funds.

At a meeting at Dumfries in July 1605 the commissioners met to discuss an 'artickle recommendit to the estaitis be his maieste anent the tred of fisching', the 'grittest benefit this cuntrey does effoord', and to report to the next session of Parliament 'quhat number of buschis thai will furneis and send forth to the said fisching'. The 'buschis' or busses were half-decked, single-masted herring boats and the proposal concerned a second attempt to colonise the island of Lewis. Most of the principals in the venture were Fife lairds, among them Sir James Anstruther, but a previous expedition in the autumn of 1598, which almost certainly sailed from Anstruther, was a failure. The commissioners nevertheless were willing to support another giving as their reason that though they already fished in the open sea [as far as Orkney and Shetland] 'the maist profitabill and easie fishing at all tymeis is to be haid in the ileis and lochs' of the Western Isles — after a hazardous journey through the Pentland Firth and round Cape Wrath. The expedition was a failure, as was a third attempt in 1609.

After Lammas [August 1st] 1657, John Lamont wrote in his *Diary*, 'ther was few or none hearing gotten ether in Fife or at Dunbar . . . so that the like of this dreave was not for many yeares past, vizt for badnesse'; and again the following year 'there was few or none herring gotten . . . 1662 and 1663, there was no harring gotten in likemaner'. A *Compt of the Iles Fishing* in the burgh's records shows that in the season 1658-1659 about a dozen local boats were fishing in the Western Isles. Among the skippers was a 'Martt Gairdiner'. Martin Gardners have long been fishermen in Cellardyke and there are still Martin Gardners in Anstruther still at the fishing, but now it is for lobsters, partans and prawns, not white fish and herring.

As five local burghs were granted Royal Charters in the previous century [Earlsferry, Pittenweem, the two Anstruthers and Kilrenny] it must have been a prosperous period on the whole, but the seventeenth century was one of misfortunes. War was declared on Spain in 1625 and two years later Charles I declared war on France, both countries with which the east coast burghs traded. The burghs were instructed to give their best advice to their commissioners 'anent the number of schips that may suffice for defence of the cuntrey' against a foreign invasion. Ten years later Covenanters were expecting an English invasion so in March 1639 'burgesses and gentlemen' in East Fife, which was strongly Covenanter, met at Anstruther to consult 'anent ye mutual defence on this coast'. Ships' cannon were mounted on batteries around the burghs and beacons of tar barrels on iron branders were to be set up in eminent places so that any danger that appeared at sea might be made known along the coast. The 'wind-miln' at Crail, the 'castell of Caiplie', the Law of Kellie and the Toft hill at Pittenweem were selected and Anstruther Wester was to erect a beacon at Rennyhill. A nightly watch was to be kept from the first of April 'until God send a happy success to the business of the Kirk'.

A decade later the burghs again met at Anstruther to consult 'how that the coast sall be keipit fra ye invasion of ye ennemie' — not Charles I this time but the forces of Oliver Cromwell — 'and that they may try for powder and ball to be in reddiness'. But the Parliamentary army had already invaded Scotland and a year later on July 17th 1651, 'being Thursday, a pairtie of the English army invaded the shyre of Fife'. On August 7th, Lamont writes, 'Enster was very ill spoyled by them and several of the town's people taken prisoners'.

Cromwell set up a Council of State in 1655 'to give all due encuragement to the trade and commerce of that nation [Scotland] and to advance manufactures and fisheries there'. Thomas Tucker, Registrar to the commissioners for Excise, was sent into Scotland the following year. He described the coastal towns of East Fife as 'all pitiful small towns', and commented on the 'smallnesse and fewnesse of the shipping and the greatnesse of the poverty of the countrey' of Fife. Trade both inwards and outwards, he reported, 'was at all times very small and worth little'.

To compound the problems of war the winter of 1655 was a season of exceptional storms. There were excessive rains in October and on December 10th 'ther fell extraordinaire mutch snow, and all that night ther blew a great wynde, which occasioned great loss and damage to the shyre of Fife by sea and land'. And the sea 'it did flow far above its ordinair limits and banks and there were many small barkes and other vessells that perished', even those lying in harbours as at 'Enster . . . also piers

The parapet of the Dreel Bridge with Anstruther Wester's arms on the left and the Anstruther family arms on the right. The path to the ford came down through the gap in the wall on the left.

were doung doune in severall places, as in St Andrews, Enster, Craill . . .' and 'severall small houses of the meaner sort of peopell did fall doune to the ground'.

In pursuance of an act of the General Convention at Edinburgh in July 1716, a commissioner from Crail and another from Pittenweem were appointed to visit West Anstruther 'and to report the case and condition thereof'. They found:

> several large preatches particularly three lately the sea has made on the wear [guard] walls of the said burgh on the west shore which are walls fronting to and for keeping of the sea off the burgh and streets and houses of the town whereby the streets interveening betwixt the said Sea wall and the houses are not only inteerly washed away but also some houses opposite to the saids breatches are beat doun and demolished as that belonging to Philip Brown and others washin down to the very walls of the standing habitable houses That every high tyde and storme there they are likely of being sapped in the foundation and ruined and to be made to fall not only to ruin of the houses themselves but also to the hazard of the lives of the Inhabitants as the Alexr Todys if they do not desert them timeously or that they be not repaired so that Philip Brown has

relinquished if not disclaimed his and seems under no concern about it And Alexander Tody and his family seems in imminent danger from the case of his whereby from these and severall others in the like case and in all probability as appears by occular inspection many other houses all along that part of the town threatened from the great decay of their wear or sea walls the particular heritors and Inhabitants houses are not only likely to be ruined But also the said burgh and streets and territorys thereof mightly impaired . . . and will be much more if not speedy prevented . . .

Philip Brown was a wealthy skipper and was clearly not living in the street by the sea if he could show such unconcern about his house there. It was probably a simple house of the kind described by Lamont.

At the meeting of the Convention at Edinburgh in January 1661 the commissioners of Anstruther Wester represented the 'sad condition of their burgh occasioned through the loss of trade and their whole shipping, the onlie meanes of thair subsistance, and uther sad calamities of these distractit times' and asked for exemption from payment of its taxes 'until it sall pleas the Lord they come to some treading quhairby they may be in capacitie to beare burthen with the rest of the burrowis'. Understanding from the neighbouring burghs the condition of West Anstruther to be 'most deplorable', the Convention 'unanimouslie condiscend to be assisting them in their supplication'.

Crail, Anstruther Easter and Kilrenny also craved exemption from payment of their public burdens because of 'the Inglisch plundering of thair burghis and away taking of thair whol schippis and barkis and boatis'. Four years later Anstruther Wester was allowed to 'abide from all conventions for the space of five years' and after some years of deliberation the missive dues owed by the burgh to the Convention were apportioned among the other burghs who, persuaded of Anstruther Wester's distressed condition 'and that the town was past all hopes of having trade in time coming', were willing to clear them of all bygone taxes since 1672. Its annual tax, formerly five shillings, was reduced to one. Conditions gradually improved and by an Act of Parliament of July 1690 Anstruther Wester's privileges as a Royal Burgh were restored.

All the coastal burghs of Scotland were called upon in 1672 to furnish their proportion of 500 seamen for His Majesty's service for the third war against the Dutch which Charles II declared that year. Anstruther Easter was to send 8, Kilrenny including Cellardyke 8, Crail 7, Pittenweem 6, Anstruther Wester 3, Elie 3, 'St Minnince' 2, Earlsferry 2, Largo 1. The numbers required were presumably proportional to the numbers of sailors in each burgh, so that during its worst years Anstruther Wester still had men at sea.

An account of the burgh prepared by the Magistrates and Town Clerk for the *Report on the State and Condition of the Burghs of Scotland* in September 1691 declared that the burgh had no ships 'except the fourt pairt of ane bark and one other of four last . . . no fish boats, no merchants, noe trade'. But the Poll or Tax Roll of 1695 shows that the sea was providing a profitable livelihood for some of its inhabitants. The three largest groups of employment that year were eight female and three male servants, six weavers, and five mariners and two skippers. The two skippers were among the five burgesses paying tax of over £2 Scots. Apart from a maltmaker who paid £1 16s and a smith and a wright who paid 18s, the mariners paid the next highest tax at 12s, along with six weavers, three tailors, a glover, a dyer, and a shoemaker. All the other assessed inhabitants paid six shillings, so the seamen were comfortably off and the skippers evidently prosperous.

In this Roll of 1695 no fishermen are named, just 'seamen' and 'mariners'. The fishing boats probably had part-time crews: William Brown, skipper of a dreave boat in 1716, was a blacksmith, and weavers often turned to fishing in slack times, but fishing was important to the burgh. When John Lyall was chosen commissioner in 1711 he was sent to the Convention 'sufficiently instructed anent the state and the present condition of the fishing on their coast', and in 1720 John Cunningham was to go as Commissioner providing always that acts of the Convention 'be noways Exclusive of nor prejudicial to our present fishings and way and manner thereof'.

A general list in 1708 of 'white herrings, salmond, codfish etc exported and to be exported cured with foreign salt' shows Anstruther Wester as lowest on the list of the East Fife burghs. Crail was the highest exporter of fish, with 292 lasts 6½ barrels, followed by Anstruther Easter with 253 lasts 7 barrels, then Elie, Pittenweem, St Monance, and finally Anstruther Wester with 37 lasts 1½ barrels. [A last of herring was usually twelve barrels.] While this was a special list it probably shows the comparative extent of the burghs' trade in fish.

The earliest surviving figures of Anstruther Wester's annual roup of the teinds of the white fish and herring are those of 1741 when they were bought for £36 Scots money [one pound Scots was equal to 1s 8d sterling and one shilling was equal to one penny sterling]. From 1745 the sum paid was for the teinds of both Lammas and winter draves and the highest sum was £39 Scots in 1746. From 1752 when £1 12s sterling was the highest offer there was an almost steady decline until 1850. The Rev. James Forrester stated in the *Statistical Account of Scotland (1791-8)* that cod, ling, turbot, 'hollybut', haddocks, herrings, flounders and lobsters were caught by West Anstruther men and sent to Cupar, Edinburgh, Stirling and Glasgow (the lobsters were sent to London) and he continued:

> What the state of the fisheries once were and how much they have declined, will appear from the following facts, which are either taken from the records, or related on undoubted authority. The minister drew the teinds (i.e. tythes) of fish as part of his stipend; the town generally farmed them at the rate of ten, twelve, or sometimes fifteen pounds a year. In these last twenty years they have never let for more than 13s and have sometimes been as low as 5s.

In 1799 the teinds were 2s and in 1850, the last year of the public roup of the fish teinds, the highest offer was 1s.

The Rev. James Forrester commented that at that time there was not a single person in the parish who could properly come under the denomination of a fisherman, 'yet in the herring season', he writes, 'there are four boats, which are manned by the tradesmen of the place and some mariners, and fitted out for the fishing'. They used the West Haven which was 'singularly useful in the herring season'. Before the Union of 1707, he wrote, Anstruther Easter and Anstruther Wester had 30 boats employed in the fishery, but in 1764 Anstruther Wester had only two.

To make up for the loss of income from the teinds the Town Council in the 1850s encouraged fishcurers to use the empty pier. Mr Birrell of Liverpool and John Bonthron of Anstruther Easter took the two curing-stations in 1854 and the following year Thomas Napier, fish-curer from Montrose, took them for £15. In 1856 he paid £15 sterling for the east station and £19 for the west, which more than made up for the loss of the teinds and shore

High seas at Anstruther, October 1979.

dues. In 1859, a poor year for the fishing, only one station was let and in July the town treasurer had to dispose of the other 'for such rent as he can obtain therefor'. Thomas Napier continued to rent the pier until 1864, but the following year only £4 was offered for the two stations and that was the last recorded roup of the curing-stations on the pier.

The Town Council accepted 25s from Messrs Thomas Brown and Sons of Lowestoft in May 1875 to dry fish on the pier, and two years later David Kidd of West Anstruther, for 12s 6d, was allowed the use of the harbour parapet walls for the drying of fish during the season. In 1896 Robert Cuthbert dried fish on the pier

'as formerly' for 7s 6d and that was the burgh's last income from
the white fish and herring.

Anstruther Wester's early prosperity derived from salmon
fishing — its coat of arms is three salmon fretted in triangle — but
it declined in the eighteenth century. The Convention declared in
1711 that Scotland's salmon fishing was a very valuable branch of
trade which had of late years decayed exceedingly, 'partly
because of the non execution of laws against the killers of
salmond in forbidden time, and the destroyers of the fry or smolts
of salmond'. In 1806, however, George Willis, town clerk of
West Anstruther, offered the Council every twentieth salmon for
a lease of the fishing for five years. Twenty years later James Clark
and James Birrell from Largo took the lease until 1858 when James
Henderson from Crail paid £5 for the salmon fishing 'in front of
the burgh lands'.

The slipway at the West Haven was built for the flat-bottomed
cobles of the salmon fishers. Their poles and standing nets were
set 'beyond the Green Craig' at the west end of the Haven and the
nets were hung to dry near what is now the first tee of the golf
course. After the death in 1871 of James Henderson the lease was
taken by Joseph Johnston & Sons of Montrose who fished the
salmon round the east coast of Fife. For some years the firm
rented the tall house in the High Street to the west of the *Dreel
Tavern* and it is still known as the 'Salmon-fishers' House'. It also
rented from the owner of *Chesterhill Cottage* a shed and office in
the Pittenweem Road. The firm gave up the salmon fishery in
September 1930, but the salmon still come to these waters. A
Royal Navy Fisheries Protection vessel was frequently seen in
front of the burgh lands in the early 1980s and a man from the
district was subsequently prosecuted for fishing salmon illegally.

The sums offered for the customs, anchorages and shore dues
in the eighteenth century were lower than the offers for the fish
teinds. To boost the receipts the Town Council in 1746 included
the let of the flesh shambles [slaughter house] in the High Street,
and offers increased over the next four years by an average of £3
Scots a year. Then in 1750 the 'causeway mealls' [a tax on traffic]
were included and the highest offer increased from £12 12s Scots
[£1 1s sterling] to £1 8s 6d sterling, but the increase was not sustained: by 1763 offers for the customs and shore dues were down
to 8s sterling. The next year, 1764, the 'sea stones' or 'iron stones'
were included and boosted the town's income for a few years.

Ironstones occur locally as nodules of ferrous carbonate embedded in shale, and were particularly numerous on the shore to the west of the Billowness; when split open they show characteristic nuclei which are thought to be fragments of shark. The best stones must have been exhausted by 1839 when the Town Council remitted their claim on James Pringle for the shore dues as all the stones shipped by him to Newcastle for smelting were of poor quality and he got nothing for them.

In 1764 Forrester wrote in the *Statistical Account*, West Anstruther had one ship of 20 tons. Four years later a visitor to the town observed that 'some years ago the burgh enjoyed a considerable trade and was in a more flourishing condition than it is at present . . . The vestige of trade is now scarcely subsisting in this Burgh'. By the 1790s, however, the staple export commodities of the burgh, Forrester wrote, were herring and cod, and since the opening of the Forth-Clyde canal in 1790, wheat, barley and beans were sent to the Glasgow market. The only manufactures exported were Osnaburgs [heavy linens] and green [unbleached] linen. By then Anstruther Easter and Wester together had 20 ships, 6 in foreign trade, 13 in coasting and 1 in the fishery trade. Eight of these, probably coasters, belonged to Anstruther Wester. The larger vessels must have used the Easter harbour as Forrester wrote that the peculiar disadvantages of the Wester Parish were the encroachment of the sea 'and the harbour not admitting ships of burden'. He thought the 'creek called Westhaven' might at no great expense 'be made an excellent harbour. Nature seems to have fitted it for that purpose, as boats can come in almost at low water'. But such expenditure was beyond West Anstruther's means.

Pigott's Directory of 1837 makes no mention of any fishing or trading activity in the Wester harbour: 'The inhabitants are principally employed in agricultural pursuits'. The anchorage and shore dues averaged 20s sterling a year in the early years of the nineteenth century but after 1850, like the teinds, the dues were no longer rouped. Sea traffic to the ancient haven of Anstruther Wester had finally ceased, but this did not prevent a divisive argument in the town in 1860 over the proposed Union Harbour.

The three neighbouring burghs agreed in October 1857 to unite in promoting the improvement of Anstruther Easter's harbour but when the limits of the new harbour, from Caddie's Burn to the Billowness, were published two of the town's three managers objected to the inclusion of Anstruther Wester 'as prejudicial to the rights of the Burgh'. Edward Ellice, M.P. for the St Andrews Burghs, explained that the extended limits were to prevent vessels evading their legitimate dues but he secured a reserve clause to protect the town's rights. The managers, James Brydie and George Dishington, nevertheless persisted in their opposition and carried their protest to the House of Lords.

The appeal against the Union Harbour Bill was heard before a Select Committee on July 9th 1860. Edward Ellice thought that the new harbour would be an immense gain to West Anstruther which was 'quite a place of decadence', its harbour 'a creek running up a sort of ditch or drain'. The third manager, George Darsie, a member of the deputation to London, explained that the quay was hardly a harbour but 'an extension of the street', and to a question on trade at the pier he replied: 'I have been in Anstruther all my life and all that time I do not think I have seen twenty decked ships'. Darsie was then 52 years of age. There had been no direct revenue from the harbour in anchorage and shore dues, he said, for a number of years; in 1853 £2 11s had been received and in 1854 £1 11s, but thereafter no dues had been charged. He did not believe that any boats had entered the harbour in the previous year.

Thomas Stevenson, engineer of the new harbour works, explained that the planned breakwater would afford shelter for boats going into West Anstruther. If the limits set for the new harbour were more circumscribed vessels would anchor in front of the harbour and when the tide came in they would run into West Anstruther and deliver their fish without paying their dues to the new harbour authority. This had probably occurred to the two dissenting managers.

The Select Committee unanimously approved of the harbour limits as fixed by the Bill, which was passed that same week. The objectors had tried to retain the independence of Anstruther Wester's ancient harbour but in view of its revenue it was a vain hope. Towards the end of the century, however, many thought that the West Sands would have been a far better site than the east for a deep-water harbour and they had a scheme drawn up taking in the Billowness. It would have cost between £45 and £50,000 and would have afforded a depth of eleven feet in more than half of the harbour at low tide but no financial help could be obtained and the project was abandoned.

Anstruther Wester's High Street from the Buckie House corner. The path to the ford, to which the Dreel Tavern (right of the white house) is aligned, goes off to the right, behind the houses in the foreground. The white house was the salmon-fisher's house.

No financial help was available to repair the damage to the harbour caused by the great storm in the winter of 1898. When repairs were required after a storm in November 1750 the Town Council employed a mason and an assistant each at a shilling a day 'in this short day' and recommended that the inhabitants should assist as ordinary workmen or barrowmen. They were to have a 'chopin of ale and a halfpenny worth of Bread each day they should work'. [A chopin was equal to a Scots pint which was more than an imperial quart.] Provost Porter organised a Grand Bazaar after the storm of 1868 but in 1898 an appeal was made to the public for voluntary contributions. The response was of a 'gratifying nature' and by February of the following year £300 had been promised and £280 paid. There were contributions from Captain Keay and his sons, from Stephen and John Williamson, John Darsie, John Black and A. Dishington, all in Liverpool; from Charles Gray and William Murray in London, J. J. Watson in Dundee and John Simpson in Australia, and donations from Edinburgh, Glasgow, Grimsby and Kilmarnock. John Currie, architect in Elie, offered to do the work of reconstruction free of charge. The response showed great public spirit but as Provost Porter pointed out West Anstruther imposed no taxation in spite of Acts of Parliament allowing them to do so. The heritors clearly preferred the occasional voluntary contribution to a regular rate on the town.

The pier was let for some years to fishermen for laying up their boats; seven shillings was collected in 1866. In 1874 small boats belonging to West Anstruther residents were to be charged 2s 6d a year, those of parties residing elsewhere 5s, and larger boats 10s. There was no charge on residents engaged in fishing 'excluding parties engaged in salmon fishing', so there must still have been some part-time fishermen in the burgh. The Council ordered in 1899 that boats were no longer to lie on the pier and the pawls were to be removed. The last we read of the pier before it became a car park was a letter to the Council in February 1901 from several inhabitants objecting to the vacant ground at the harbour being let to showmen.

The harbour came into its own again on a misty July morning in 1984. Captain Anderson's *Hilda Ross* and several other small boats brought thirty-five Spaniards of the *Tercio Viejo Del Mar Oceano*, the Ancient Order of the Ocean Sea, to West Anstruther to commemorate the arrival of survivors from the Spanish Armada in 1588. In authentic uniforms and costumes with weapons of the period and a replica of a cannon the Spaniards were received with pageantry and ceremony as inhabitants of Anstruther re-enacted the charitable welcome given to the men in the past. As before, the Spaniards were received by the Minister of the Parish and the Lord of the Barony of Anstruther.

3

Shipmasters and Mariners

The harbour of West Anstruther is only once mentioned specifically in the Kirkcaldy customs records. On July 22nd 1681 'The *Tryall of Whitbie*, Edward Readman master, loaded with kelp for Whitby to the value of 144 pounds Scots at Anstruther Wester'. Otherwise the port stated is 'Anstruther' or 'Enstruther' but the wester burgh had its own shipmasters.

One of the earliest named was William Dairsie or Darsie who lived in a house on the Shore [Esplanade]. He owned drave boats and in 1597 a trading vessel, the *Jonas*. The Kirk Session records that in 1602 he gave 40s to the church 'when he cam from Norroway'. In May 1618 he is recorded at Elsinore in Denmark passing through the Sound on his way to Konigsberg at the eastern end of the Baltic Sea, and five years later he again sailed through the Sound. He must have been a merchant as well as a shipmaster, a usual thing in those days, as in 1606, 1610 and 1629 he was a commissioner for West Anstruther at the Convention of Royal Burghs, as was a neighbour in 1621, Thomas Richardson, shipmaster, who also sailed through the Sound.

Two of Darsie's contemporaries were mariners named Wad or Waid, one of whom, unlike a distinguished descendant of the family, brought little credit to his home town. In 1601, John Bowsie, skipper burgess and elder of Anstruther Wester church, was in Bordeaux when an English ship, the *Nicolsoun of Newcastle*, David Smyth, master, and David Waid, mate, arrived in the river. The fathers of both men were burgesses of Anstruther Wester and 'men of good fame'. A Frenchman chartered the ship to take a cargo of wine to St Malo and John Bowsie was asked by Smyth and Waid to become surety for the owner and themselves. 'Being moved with a favourable consideration of thame, in respect they were his countriemen and townis bairnis', Bowsie agreed. But when the Frenchman had put his wine and his factor on board and the ship was past the river of Bordeaux:

the said Scottismen and Inglischmen, concurring togidder in counsall and actioun, maist cruellie and traiterouslie conspirit the death of the factor, quha wes lyand sleipand in his bed, tuik him out of his bed, kaist him overbuird and drownit him, and careit the schip with hir laidning of wyne to Ireland, where they sold the same.

It was 'bruitit' that the two Scotsmen were the authors of this villainy, 'to the grit reproche of this natioun', and John Bowsie as their cautioner was immediately searched for. 'Be the providence of God' he escaped, but his whole goods and gear were confiscated 'to his utter wrack, miserie and undoing'. When he returned home he applied for a summons against Waid, who was apprehended in the town of Anstruther-bewest-the-burn and committed to the Tolbooth, where 'he being pricked in conscience, hes, in presence of minister, bailyeis and clerk of Anstruther, maid ane confessioun of the said murthour'. Bowsie was to take David Waid first to Newcastle to be confronted with the owner of the ship, and then to the magistrates of Bordeaux where the Scots, not surprisingly, were 'verie far discredited and mislykit' for the affair.

The other contemporary was George Waid, no doubt a relation of the offending David whose fate is not reported. He must have had some local standing or reputation to have had the following appeal so sympathetically considered by the Convention of Royal Burghs; few such personal cases appear in the records. At St Andrews on July 7th 1615 the commissioners reviewed the supplication given in by George Waid, mariner burgess of Anstruther Wester:

> deploring his depauperat estait, pairtlie be lose of his sicht, pairtlie be the raging of the tempestuous seas that daylie menasas to bring doun in his house standing most opposeit thairto, to his utter ruine, and thairfor craving thair supplie for remeid thairof in tyme, the saids commissioners of burrowes having sein and considerit his said supplication hes grantit to him the soum of twa hundreth punds and ordanit the samyne to be ingatherit according to the extent roll.

The skipper Henry Beattie in the 1695 Tax Roll was also shipmaster and merchant. In May 1685 he took coal from Dysart to Holland and loaded provisions for 'Norroway', and at the end of

One of the last boats to be launched at Anstruther, from Smith and Hutton's yard, Harbourhead, in the early 1970s.

the year took Dunbar herring to St Malo and brought back salt. As a prosperous merchant he was chosen commissioner for Anstruther Wester in 1697, 1706 and 1707. The other skipper in the Tax Roll, Philip Browne (who in 1707 bought number four Castle Street in Anstruther Easter), may also have engaged in foreign trade; his sons Philip and Robert were both shipmasters.

Another shipmaster was William Bytter or Boyter — there are still seafaring Boyters in Anstruther and Pittenweem. In the 1660s he was master of the *Christian of Enstruther*, the *Philip of Enstruther*, and the *Providence of Kilrenny*, but after 1685 it is 'William Bytter his ship'. He took Dunbar herring to Newcastle and in March 1667 brought back for himself a mixed cargo which included iron and 'drawen lead', 'sterch', two barrels of galls, probably oak galls used in dyeing, gray paper and pressing paper, lint [prepared flax ready for weaving], twenty firkins or barrels of glass and one of 'shott', English hops, raisins, aniseed, and playing-cards. For a merchant in Elie he brought back a similar cargo with the addition of cut glass, currants, and indigo for dyeing. He sailed to London and Newcastle, and to Norway for timber; he took provisions to Holland and Dunbar herring to St Malo, returning with cargoes of French wine and casks containing 140 pounds of raisins and 100 pounds each of 'figges', prunes, and six pounds of capers.

In the 1680s Robert Boyter, shipmaster, took Dunbar herring to Gothenburg for Robert Lyall, the wealthy merchant of Anstruther Wester, and brought back for him rough hemp and cordage. Thomas Waterston, shipmaster, sailed to Norway and the Low Countries for William Anstruther and brought back deals and barrels of tar, iron and hogsheads of vinegar. Thirty years later there was a James Waterston, shipmaster, in West Anstruther and two hundred years later a Thomas Waterston, shipmaster, in Anstruther Easter.

The eighteenth century shipmasters were among the wealthier inhabitants of the burgh, and they and mariners often served on the Town Council. George Smyth, shipmaster, was a baillie in the 1720s, and John Reid, shipmaster, was elected councillor in 1749. In September 1750 William Thomson, mariner burgess, and brother-in-law of John Reid, was elected on the same day councillor and baillie, but 'being absent at sea his acceptance as Baillie is delayed until he return'. Similar phrases occur at subsequent elections: 'he at the time of his election being absent at sea' or he was 'necessarily absent at sea', or he accepted office 'having only arrived yesterday'.

Another William Boyter, shipmaster, was elected a councillor in September 1754, and accepted office the following January 'he being on a voyage beyond the seas when he was elected'. Ten years later he was elected baillie 'he having been absent at sea for some months past'. In 1766 he was again absent at sea in September and was admitted to the Council in October. Alexander Boyter, mariner, was elected councillor 'while absent at sea' and in 1768 Andrew Barnet, mariner, was elected councillor. Captain Kyd was a councillor in the 1770s and William Adamson, shipmaster, who first appears as 'ship carpenter', was a councillor in the 1780s.

In the Sound Toll, a list of ships sailing through the narrow straits between Denmark and Sweden, William Adamson is recorded in July 1793 sailing from Anstruther to Memel in Lithuania in ballast and from Memel back to Anstruther with oats and barley. In May of the following year he sailed from Gothenburg to the Baltic with barrels of herring, returning in June from Dantzig to Amsterdam with rye, and there he probably picked up another cargo for another destination. In July 1795 he again passed through the Sound with coal from Kirkcaldy for St Petersburg and returned in September to Leith with a cargo of wheat. Adamson lived at 13, Esplanade, until he went as shipbuilder to Sunderland in 1811.

Two sailors, John Wilson and John Meldrum, were members of the Town Council in 1798 and the early 1880s, John Meldrum not accepting office as councillor in 1804 until July of the following year. At the time of the elections of 1813 and 1814 he was absent at sea, and in the 1816 election he took his oath for the previous year 'not having been present since last Michaelmas'.

William Miller, wright, accepted office as councillor in December 1765 'he being absent at sea in the last election'. He is described as mariner for the next few years, in 1770 as shipmaster, and in 1776 as shipbuilder. In October of that year he asked the Town Council for permission to build a ship 'upon the Shoar or Pier' and to feu a piece of ground to build a house to hold his tools and lumber. This is the first mention in the records of shipbuilding on the pier. The Town Council gave their permission, obliging him 'to make good and upbuild any Breatch or down falling of any of the Bullworks belonging to the said Pier . . .' He was permitted to build a temporary house for his tools and lumber for the next thirty years, a lease which seems to imply an expectation of further shipbuilding on the pier.

Twelve years later John Durie, wright, applied for permission to build a vessel on the pier, and in January 1877 J. A. Millar, boat-builder at Cellardyke, asked for building ground at the harbour for which he paid a yearly rent of £5 sterling. On a day in February 1882 when Councillor Jarvis of Anstruther Easter launched a new fishing boat at the Middle Pier, Councillor Millar launched from his yard at Anstruther Wester 'a handsome new boat for Skipper James Smith (Brown), the *Agnes Brown*, 50' 4" in length. His business did not prosper, however, and in 1886 the Town Council agreed to reduce the rent of the building ground at the pier 'on the understanding that it may be increased if trade improved'. In the spring of 1888 Millar removed from the pier and it was let for the next ten years to William Kirkaldy at the *Commercial Hotel* in Anstruther Easter but there was no mention of boat-building.

William Miller, son of the shipbuilder, was described in 1777 as 'carpenter', but three years later he was a shipmaster, and in 1783 was elected baillie. Throughout the 1780s Baillie Captain Miller

B

was absent at sea at the time of the Council elections, and on two occasions he did not appear until the following February and March to accept office and take the oath. In 1790 there was an Alexander Millar, shipmaster, and his brother, John Millar, planned to take his burgess oath 'when he returned from sea'. Both William and Alexander Miller are recorded in the Sound Toll in the 1780s and '90s.

In April 1784 William Miller sailed through the Sound on his way from Alloa to Copenhagen in ballast; in June he sailed from Libau in Latvia to Anstruther with lasts of barley, oats and peas and 29 calf skins — for George Darsie, tanner in Anstruther Easter, perhaps; in July he sailed from Anstruther to St Petersburg in ballast and in September returned to Dunbar with a mixed cargo of iron bars, hemp, flax, tallow, tow; barrels of peas, barley, and wheat; shipsplanks, ordinary deals and 25 rix-dollars [units of account] of unspecified goods, probably luxury goods. The following year he sailed in June from Anstruther to Copenhagen with coal and in July from Skagen, at the north-east tip of Denmark, to Dantzig. When he returned to Anstruther in August his cargo included 3500 wooden nails. In August 1786 he sailed from Anstruther to Memel in ballast and returned the next month with 220 balks of squared timber, and 600 staves; in July 1788 he sailed from Middelburgh in Zeeland to St Petersburg in ballast and to Leith in September with agricultural produce. He made two journeys from Anstruther to Memel and Memel back to Anstruther in the following year with balks of timber, laths and Prussian deals, and returned to Dunbar the next year with a similar cargo. In the summer months of 1792, '93, '94 and '95 he sailed from Memel in ballast from Anstruther, Dundee and St Andrews, making the journey twice in 1794, and returning each time with balks of timber, Prussian deals, laths and staves. William Miller senior died in 1798, but his son continued at sea, certainly until 1816. In that year he took his seat on the Burgh Council in September, having been absent since the previous Michaelmas.

Alexander Miller made seven voyages to Memel between 1784 and 1795 including one from Middelburgh and one from St Andrews, returning to Anstruther in May 1784 from Konigsburg with a cargo of oats. Twice he returned to St Andrews and on the other occasions to Anstruther, each time with the usual cargo of timber. In 1790 he sailed from Gothenburg to Pillau in Lithuania

John Keay, captain of the
tea-clipper *Ariel*.

with herring and from Pillau to Liverpool with wheat and barley.
Some of the voyages of these shipmasters were to and from their
home port, but on many occasions they would have had to pick
up and deliver cargoes where they could find them, hence the
many long absences.

During the latter half of the eighteenth century the burgh had
one excise officer and two customs officers. On several occasions
in the 1760s Robert Hunter, Surveyor of Customs at the port of
West Anstruther, was elected to the Town Council 'while absent
at sea upon the Revenue business', as likely as not chasing
smugglers as attending to legitimate trade.

Shipmasters were attracted to the Wester Burgh even when
there was little or no activity at its harbour. Archibald Williamson,

shipmaster and shipowner, who in the 1841 Census is modestly described as a merchant seaman, was born in Cellardyke in 1787, the fourth surviving son of Stephen Williamson, farmer, maltster and shipowner. He served his apprenticeship on one of his father's ships, the *Barbara and Mary*, David Fowler, master. (Barbara was his youngest sister and Mary was his mother, Mary Grieve.) On the death of his father in 1813 he inherited his considerable shipping interests but gave up an active career at sea when he married Isabella Lawson of Kettle in 1826 and shortly after moved from Cellardyke to West Anstruther, to *Marsfield House* where his two youngest daughters were born. About ten years later he built *Bellfield* in Anstruther Easter. Williamson was admitted a member of the Anstruther Easter Sea Box Society in 1815, and was boxmaster at his death in 1847, which was much regretted by the masters and managers 'from the long and constant attention he paid to its interest'. (Anstruther Wester had its own Sea Box Society until the early 1720s when John Lyall was factor.) At a meeting of the heritors of Anstruther Wester in 1829, Archibald Williamson, representing the Sea Box Society, which owned land in the Wester parish, was appointed to the committee called to discuss the building of a new school, which may have attracted him to the burgh in the first place.

His two eldest sons, Stephen and John, both made their names and fortunes in shipping, though neither were professional seamen. John Williamson was a director of the Cunard Shipping Company from the time of its foundations as a public concern in 1880 until his retirement in 1902. He followed the sea-going tradition of Anstruther in a small way throughout his working life: from his home in Birkenhead he always took the ferry to his office in Liverpool and was never known to make the journey by train.

Captain John Keay, one of the most famous masters of the tea clipper ships, came to live in the burgh in 1869. He was born in East Green, Anstruther Easter, in September 1828, the son of Captain Thomas Keay, who was for many years master of the brig *Medium of Anstruther* 'employed in the foreign trade'. John served his apprenticeship with his father and then sailed with the notable master, Captain Robert Fowler of Cellardyke. In 1859 he commanded his first tea clipper, the *Ellen Rodger*, owned by Captain Alexander Rodger, a native of Cellardyke. In three successive years, 1859, '60 and '61, in the *Ellen Rodger*, reputed to be one of the fastest ships ever in the China trade, Captain Keay was home in first, second and third places in the races from China to London with the season's first cargo of tea, but the ship most closely associated with his name was the *Ariel*, launched in 1865, with John Keay as first master.

One of the most exciting races in the history of the tea clippers was that between the *Ariel*, Captain Keay, and Captain Rodger's *Taeping*, Captain MacKinnon. On May 29th 1866, within a few hours of each other, eleven clippers left the port of Foochow for London. *Ariel* as the largest and newest was the favourite to win. Of four vessels running neck and neck the whole way, *Taeping* was first on the fourth and fifth legs and *Ariel* was first on the sixth and seventh. Both ships came up the English Channel together, with another Scottish clipper, the *Serica*, Captain Innes, and reached Gravesend on the same tide, 99 days out on a voyage of 16,000 miles. *Ariel* was ten minutes ahead of her rival at the Downs, but *Taeping*, drawing less water, tied up at the London dock twenty minutes ahead of *Ariel*, winning the bonus of 10s a ton for the first cargo to reach the home port, and a £100 bounty for the winning captain. So close was the race, however, that Captain MacKinnon shared the bounty and the bonus with Captain Keay and his crew. An unforeseen result of the race was that with so many clippers arriving in port within a few days the price of tea fell heavily. The excitement of the 1866 race was perhaps equalled in our own day by the America's Cup of 1983 when *Australia II*, the first challenger ever to succeed against American yachts, clinched the event in the final race.

Captain Keay remained master of the *Ariel* for the next three years. Captain Edwards in the *Sunday Express* in May 1986 described the 853-ton, 197-foot long *Ariel*, carrying 25,451 square feet of canvas, as having such fine lines 'that she was reputed to be able to glide through the water without a breath of wind to urge her on'. John Keay was noted for his iron discipline. In a heavy southerly gale off Cape Agulhas in 1868, Captain Shewan wrote, Captain Keay, knowing that *Taeping* and other clippers were close on her heels, kept the *Ariel* going through a tearing gale and a high-confused sea. Everything moveable was swept from the decks 'and it became a question whether the wheel itself would survive the gale'. With the opening of the Suez Canal in 1869 the heyday of the superb China clippers was over, and Captain Keay transferred to steam, taking command in 1871 of a steam trader, the *Vixen*, sailing between London and Calcutta.

In 1851 Captain John Keay was admitted a member of the Sea Box Society and in April 1862 was elected deputy boxmaster. Two years later he was admitted a burgess and freeman of Anstruther Wester, and in 1869 bought his father-in-law's house in the High Street. He made his home in the burgh for almost ten years but moved to Liverpool in the late '70s when he was appointed manager of a steamship line there. Until two years before his death in Liverpool in 1918 in his ninetieth year he returned every summer to *Fernbank*. He married Helen Dishington, second daughter of George Dishington and Ann Rodger, 'daughter of a sailor in Kilrenny'. Their eldest son, Thomas, died of diphtheria at West Anstruther in 1863 at the age of six; the second son, George Dishington, the only son to go to sea, married Jessie Tosh of *High Cross* in 1891; John was a banker in Liverpool, as was his brother-in-law, and Robert Dishington Keay, born in Anstruther Wester in 1869, was an engineer. He was educated at Liverpool College, where he distinguished himself in athletics and was head boy of the school. He was largely responsible for the building of the great Scotstown works at Glasgow and in 1914 was sent to Esquimault, Vancouver Island, as manager of a shipyard for Yarrows Ltd, with whom he had worked for twenty years. He died in Victoria two years later at the early age of 49.

A steamboat manager lived in Anstruther Wester in the 1870s, a John Ker, who stood for the Town Council in 1872, but the burgh was still home to captains of sail until 1949, among them James and David Thomson. James was born in 1836 in St Andrews, where his father was a miller, and came to work at Anstruther Mill, but he served for two years with David Mitchell, sailmaker, in Rodger Street, and at the age of 18 went to sea. He showed great natural ability, rising quickly in his profession, and for thirty years was master of vessels of large tonnage, principally in foreign trade. An obituary in the *East of Fife Record* in March 1899 stated that shipowners had the highest regard for his great business qualities (an important factor in a master's career), his honesty, and his administrative ability with various crews, 'controlling men without being tyrannical'. In 1881 James Thomson took command of a new ship, the *Euphrosyne of Greenock*, a steel full-rigged main skysail ship of which he remained master until he retired from the sea in 1896. He died three years later in his 64th year at his home, *Wellpark*, in Pittenweem Road, and was

Rodger Street in 1905: David Mitchell, sailmaker, in the house (beyond the railings) on the left, his sign below the first-floor windows, and Miss Tosh with her bicycle, opposite.

buried in the churchyard of West Anstruther.

Three of his four sons, two of whom lived in Anstruther Easter, had successful careers at sea. In the eighteenth century ship-masters often began their careers as ship carpenters, but in the great days of sail in the nineteenth century an apprenticeship to a sailmaker was usual and David the second son served, like his father, in the Rodger Street sailmaker's loft. At the age of fifteen David Thomson went to sea under his father in the barque *Hannemann* and remained with her for four years before joining the *Golden Fleece*, an iron full-rigged ship. In 1885 David Thomson joined his father on the *Euphrosyne* as sailmaker. He qualified as a master in about 1890 and when his father retired David, at the age of 29, took command of the ship until she was sold in 1909. In her twenty-four years under the British flag *Euphrosyne* had only two masters, the Thomsons, father and son. The *Record* recounted on August 16th 1907 Captain Thomson's 'thrilling experience' rounding Cape Horn in *Euphrosyne* in a violent storm which with brief intervals lasted a fortnight. He ordered all sails and gear to be cut away and as the vessel ran under bare poles heavy seas swept the deck carrying away the bridge and standard compass. Four of the ship's boats were lost overboard and the only one left for the crew was a small dinghy which could only carry a few

men, but the battered *Euphrosyne* eventually reached Queens-
town in Ireland:

> Captain Thomson by his intrepid conduct and the encouraging
> words addressed to his crew inspired them with confidence even at
> times when the ship was in the most critical condition and the
> praise extended to him by all on board for his splendid services
> during an anxious and wearisome struggle with the elements is the
> best proof of his qualities as the average sailor is not given to praise
> unless it is richly deserved.

Alfred Smith, son of W. Smith in East Green, was a member of
the crew. Other thrilling experiences were to be shipwrecked in
the *Golden Fleece* on the island of Sandalwood in the East Indies,
and to be torpedoed in 1917 on the *Hinemoa*, thirty miles west of
the Scilly Isles.

At the beginning of 1921 Captain Thomson was offered the
command of one of Sir William Garthwaite's sailing ships and in
1926 took command of the big four-masted barque the *Garthpool*,
built by W. B. Thomson of Dundee in 1891. On October 3rd 1929
Captain Thomson with an experienced crew embarked on a
ballast passage to Australia, but on the night of November 8th the
Garthpool struck the outer reefs of Bonavista Island, Cape Verdes.
(Abnormal magnetic variation was the probable cause of the
calamity.) It was the end of the last big sailing vessel to fly the
British flag, and it was the end of Captain Thomson's career. He
had spent forty-eight years at sea, all in sailing ships, and had
commanded big deep-water ships for thirty-three years. Until the
loss of the *Garthpool*, he had never had a serious accident and yet,
as Captain Clark writes in *Four Captains*, right at the end, on a fine
clear night, in an area not usually associated with navigational
hazards, his ship became a total wreck: 'It was a cruel blow for
such a fine record'.

Captain Thomson, 'a strongly-built man of medium height with
a quiet reserved manner', retired to Anstruther Wester. He and
his wife, a lively Cape Horner from Aberdeen who often sailed
with him, celebrated their golden wedding anniversary in 1947,
two years before his death at *Millbank* at the age of 83, 'almost
certainly the last of his type in Britain, a shipmaster who had
spent his entire career in sailing ships' (apart from a working-
passage of two weeks across the Atlantic on an American steamer
in 1920). His son, William, who lives in Crail, went to sea with his

Captain David Thomson by the wheel of the *Garthpool*, May 1927.

father as a cabin boy but decided that a career at sea was not for him, although he served for six years in the Royal Navy during the Second World War. But the tradition of the sea lingered on at *Millbank*.

From the late 1950s it was the home of another fine sailor until his death in 1975 at the age of 77: skipper James Muir, formerly of Cellardyke. He was born into a family who had been fishermen for generations and at the age of thirteen went to sea in his father's boat, the *Ebenezer* KY 36, a Fifie with a three-cylinder paraffin engine. He was mate for his father until at the age of twenty-four he became skipper of the *Twinkling Star* KY 347 where he remained until war was declared in 1939. As a Royal Naval Reservist he was posted to Gosport in the south of England

to the *Ocean Swell* on anti-submarine net-laying duty and was subsequently stationed at various ports around the British Isles from
Falmouth to Scapa Flow. He was awarded the MBE in 1944 and
after some convoy duty he ended the war as a lieutenant at
Genoa.

Jimmie Muir returned to the fishing after the war and for five
years was skipper of the *Wilson Line* KY 322. When the boat was
sold at Yarmouth he bought the *Silver Cord* KY 124, a motor diesel
for both herring and line fishing, in which in 1957 he won the
Prunier Trophy, an award first presented in 1936 by Madame
Prunier, owner of a famous fish restaurant in London, to the boat
making the biggest single catch in one night off the coast of East
Anglia, the award alternating between the English and Scottish
fishing fleets; he had been runner-up in the 1948 season. Jimmie
Muir married Catherine Reekie Mathers from a St Monans fishing
family and both their sons went to the fishing. The elder, who still
lives at *Millbank*, went with his father to the fishing for about
twelve years and gained his skipper's certificate, but then
transferred to the Merchant Navy, thus combining both of the
burgh's maritime traditions.

4

The Royal Charter

The Dreel, a small but effective barrier between the two
Anstruthers, formed the western boundary of the parish of
Kilrenny, in which Anstruther Easter was situated, and the
eastern boundary of the Lands of Pittenweem, which encompassed Anstruther Wester and were given to the monks of May
by David I in the twelfth century. The monks, under the aegis of
the Convent of St Andrews, eventually moved their monastery
from the May to Pittenweem to be safe from attacks from English
pirates and in 1540 James V incorporated the Lands of Pittenweem
into a lordship and free barony in which the monks had
jurisdiction. At the same time the two settlements of Pittenweem
and 'Litell Anstruther' were made Burghs of Barony with a
measure of self-government and the right to hold markets and
fairs. For taxation purposes Anstruther Wester, 'ane pendikill of
Pettinweeme', was still conjoined with Pittenweem but its rights
as a free Burgh of Barony were confirmed by charter in 1554.

'From which time the said burgh [of Anstruther west the burn]
has been greatly augmented, as well in population as in policies
and edifices, and its bounds extended by the concourse of
merchants and others, lieges and strangers, who have come to
the Town and harbour of Anstruther'. (There never was a time
when strangers were not coming to Anstruther.) The 'new
edifices' probably included the Church Tower and that substantial stone house by the path to the ford. The Preamble of the Royal
Charter, which was granted to the Burgh of Anstruther west the
burn on October 21st 1587 under the Great Seal of James VI [1566-
1625], then states that lately the Town of Anstruther on the east
side of the said burn belonging to the laird of Anstruther had
been erected into a Royal Burgh and it continues:

> Therefore . . . the King has ratified all infeftments made by his
> predecessors, and the Priors and Convents of St Andrews and
> Pittenweem, relating to the said burgh of Anstruther, and further
> has created the said burgh of Anstruther west the burne, with the

harbour and haven thereof, together with all lands belonging thereto, into a free royal burgh, with all privileges etc.

One privilege was the power to make 'Brethren of the Guild' whose dean and court would regulate the trade of the burgh and settle mercantile and marine disputes. These courts eventually came to oversee building operations within the burghs, a kind of town planning authority, for which purpose they were revived in the late nineteenth century. Another privilege was the power to make artificers and merchants 'freemen of the burgh'. When a man became proficient at his trade or craft he was expected to become a burgess of the town by paying a composition or fee for his burgess ticket. As a freeman the burgess had rights within the burgh denied to a stranger or unfreeman. Only a burgess, for instance, could serve on the Town Council. When outsiders were elected to the Council, usually for their own political purposes, they were obliged to pay their burgess composition and take their burgess oath before taking their seat on the Council. Burgesses were granted power to *pak and peill*, that is to engage in wholesale and retail trade, and to 'buy and sell, etc, with weights and measures'. Each burgh had its own set of measures and Anstruther Wester's last set, bought in 1826 from Leith at a cost of £27, is now in the Burgh Room in the Scottish Fisheries Museum.

The charter gave the burgesses power to elect a provost and baillies, to hold burgh courts, and to hold two weekly fairs 'on Monday and Sabbath'. This seems surprising, fairs on the Scottish Sabbath, but Sabbatarianism had not yet taken over Scottish society in 1587. The burgh was permitted to erect a market cross — an old law required that all goods for sale in free burghs should be presented 'at the mercat and mercat cross' which in Anstruther Wester stood in the High Street near the *Buckie House* — and to hold annually two public fairs, on St Nicholas Day in December and on St Mary day, March 25th. Fairs were still being held in the burgh in 1837 on the first Tuesday after April 11th, on July 5th, and November 12th.

Finally the charter lists the sources of the burgh's income, its 'Common Good', a feature of burgh finance peculiar to Scotland. The burgh was granted the right of 'crying and rouping their Common Good . . . and making set and let thereof'. All Town Council announcements were 'cried' through the town by the town officer with his handbell or by 'tuck [beat] of drum'. The 'set

The Dreel Burn, ancient boundary between the burghs of Anstruther Easter and Anstruther Wester.

and let' were the conditions of lease drawn up by the town clerk before the public roup. The highest offerer 'at the outrunning of the [hour]glass' was declared the tacksman, but by the end of the eighteenth century the highest bidder was to be preferred 'on the Judge of the Roup pronouncing the word Thrice'. Each tacksman or lessee was bound to provide a cautioner to guarantee payment of the dues.

The Common Good included the power of levying all customs, tolls, anchorages and harbour dues, and in addition the right of:

> having, using and possessing the common pasture above the rocks lying out from the Burgh, below the arable Lands producing grain, and the sea shore, in length and breadth, according to the circuit of the walls of the Monastery of Pittenweem, to the north muir commonly called Elvands fauld, to the Mylton, and thence along the straight road leading down to Anstruther, according to the tenor of the old infeftments granted to them.

The Billowness and the Burn Braes were let for pasture. The Commonty lands on the Pittenweem road and down by the shore on either side of the Billowness were for arable farming and were rouped in September for a yearly rent in produce which the town sold at public roup between Yule and Candlemas [February 2nd]. The tacksmen were not to sub-let the arable land without permission from the magistrates and over and above their rent they were to pay one half of the minister's stipend, which in 1788 was measured at '2 bolls, 2 firlots, 2 pecks and 2 lipes bear' [barley].

The 'Billiness' and Milntoun Muir or 'whinny muir' were exposed to public roup in 1753 for a rent in money not crops and Alexander Bisset in the Milntoun was the highest offerer at £1 8s sterling. The minute of the roup confirmed that:

> The Inhabitants of this Burgh are to have the privileges as formerly of grazing their Beasts . . . As also the Lint holes for steeping Flax are reserved as they stand to the Inhabitants.

The magistrates reserved power to themselves to ditch, enclose and plant the north side of the Billowness if they should think necessary for the good of the burgh:

> reserving likewise to the Inhabitants the privilege of casting Tairff for their houses and digging whins as used and wont.

Whatever their trade or profession most of the burgesses and indwellers would have kept a cow. The Town Council enacted on April 18th 1627 that unfreemen were to pay £1 Scots for pasturing a cow on the town's common and freemen 1 merk Scots. The charges from the beginning of the nineteenth century were 2s 6d sterling for each beast belonging to a burgess and freeman, and 3s for that of an unfreeman. (As late as 1884 it was reported to the Town Council that a party in the town was 'in the way of keeping a cow in the same apartment as the family sleep in' and pigs were kept in the town into the 1920s.)

The privilege of 'casting Tairff' illustrates the kind of house in which in the past the majority of the inhabitants lived: simple erections of stones from the shore with turf from the Billowness for roof: Lamont's small houses 'that did fall doune to the ground' in severe winter storms. The young shoots of the whins, which the inhabitants had a right to dig, made a nutritious fodder for cattle and horses when bruised and chopped with hay or straw, and the bushes served as fuel, the ashes of which made a useful fertiliser.

The production of linen was an old-established industry in Fife. Flax and lint were brought from the Baltic countries by Anstruther shipmasters, as we have seen, and some flax was grown locally. The Tax Roll of 1695 shows six weavers, all men, and all assessed at 12s Scots, which was not the lowest rate of tax. Throughout the eighteenth century more weavers are named among town councillors and tacksmen than any other trade, but by the time of the 1841 Census there were only five handloom weavers in the burgh and four of them were over the age of fifty-eight. In the 1851 Census only one weaver remained, John Brown, aged 67.

More of the whinny muir was cleared in 1755 for arable farming and leased as the West Milton Muir; the land taken into tack two years before became the East Milton Muir. Part of it was to be reserved 'as shall be thought necessary for the use of the Inhabitants for Fail and Divots for their Houses'. *Fail* was the turf used for walls of houses and *Divots* the turf used for roofs. Thatch later replaced the divots.

The Common Good lands at the Burn Braes were let for pasture and being so close to the burgh always commanded a good rent — and were probably taken for horses rather than cattle. At the roup it was always declared that 'liberty shall be reserved to the Inhabitants to Bleach their Cloaths on the said Braes as usual' and the right was jealously guarded. The town's weavers complained in 1815 that persons not paying burdens in the burgh were bleaching strangers' cloth on the Braes and when challenged abused the tax-paying inhabitants. The town officer was warranted to seize the strangers' cloth 'upon the complaint of any of the Burgesses', and the Bleaching Green was subsequently rouped separately with only inhabitants of West Anstruther permitted to bid. That weaving ceased in the mid-nineteenth century is confirmed by the erection in 1847 of posts at the Green for domestic washing.

Also reserved from the Burn Braes was the town's boiling house, built in 1822 down by the burn at the foot of the Braes, probably for the making of soap or candles. By the 1860s it had become the town's washing house though it may not have been a particularly salubrious place to do the family washing. An 1860s' guide book to Fife described the 'brook Dreel' as a 'melancholy rivulet trickling down through a sad coloured chasm which it has eroded for itself by process of time. It is densely inhabited by water rats'. The ground and boiling house was leased to a fishcurer from 1892 but seven years later it was decided to sell the boilers, ropes and tubs 'for what they were worth', which was probably not very much. From 1901 the old building was rented by carters for stables. The drying green continued in use until after the First World War and carters continued to tether their work horses at the foot of the Braes until they too passed into history.

A name that occurs more frequently than any other among the tacksmen of the Commonty lands is that of Bisset. The death of an Andrew Bissie 'in the Milntoune of Anstruther Wester' is recorded in the parish register in December 1592. A mid-seventeenth century tax roll shows David Bissie and Andrew Bissie among the twelve tax-paying inhabitants in the Mylnetoun and in the roll of 1695 Thomas and William Bisset both 'landlabourers' or farmers are among the fifteen tax-payers in the hamlet. Many other Andrew, Alexander and Robert Bissets appear in the burgh records, frequently as town councillors though never as baillies. Between 1741 and 1853 there were often two Bissets on the Council at the same time, and three Bissets among the stentmasters. Even more consistently than the Boyters, the Bissets all follow one trade, that of farmer. A Robert in 1763 was described as a weaver, but as he was taking the tack of the West Muir he was probably also a farmer. In the Census of 1841 there is a John Bisset mill master of Milton Mill, Alexander an agricultural labourer, and Andrew a farmer at Milton Muir who suffered great loss by the failure of his potato crop in 1845 and '46 and was granted an abatement of rent. The Census of 1851 shows an Alexander Bisset in Milton aged 70 farming six acres. An Alexander Bisset was married in 1892 by the Rev. Mr Bisset of the United Presbyterian Church of Buckhaven to Mary Bruce Bisset of Largoward. The last Bisset to appear in the burgh records, four hundred years after the first, was Alexander Bisset in Arncroach, builder of the coastguard station in Shore Road in 1894.

By the grant of the sea shore in the charter of 1587 the town was provided with two other sources of income, the sea ware and the sea stones. (There was also the 'midden muck' or street dung to be rouped each year. The tacksman was obliged to take off the dung in the principal street once every fortnight during the winter and once a month in summer. The inhabitants put their beasts out to pasture in the summer but during the winter the animals remained in byres and stables in the town with a consequent accumulation of dunghills, often 'obnoxious'. The street dung was never taken at public roup at less than 10s and rarely

Anstruther from the Waid Tower, c. 1930, Adelaide Lodge in the foreground, Chalmers Memorial Church on the left.

more than £2 sterling. Without exception the tacksmen were farmers from Milton, Kilrenny, Pitkierie, Clephanton, Grange-muir or Bonerbo.) The sea ware consisted of driven ware, loose seaweed or tangle driven on to the shore by heavy seas, and kelp ware cut from the rocks for processing.

Kelp ware seems to have been rouped from the late seventeenth century until the second quarter of the nineteenth. The banking, drying and burning of the kelp was allowed on the town's Commonty land at the west end of the town but 'only when the wind blew from the east'. The residue, which contained potassium and iodine, was used in the making of hard soap. All the tacksmen between 1742 and 1824 were from outwith the burgh; in 1817 the tack was taken by James Tod, candlemaker in Anstruther Easter. The last recorded roup was in 1845 when two farmers took the tack, probably for manure as by this time the household production of soap and candles had largely given way to a manufacturing industry.

'From time immemorial' sea ware cast ashore within the

41

boundary of the burgh was under the control of the magistrates. It was customary for indwellers and tenants of the Commonty lands to take what they required for their gardens and crofts, and the surplus was not available to others until they had been allowed forty-eight hours 'or whatever the Town Council considered a reasonable time to remove it after it had been cast ashore'. The charge for removing the surplus sea ware was for a long time 4d a cart load. It provided the town with a steady income — and constant controversy.

Two ancient rights to the sea ware were claimed, one in 1765 by the Earl of Kellie which was successfully defended by the town, and the other by the Andrew Johnstons, owners since 1762 of Rennyhill. This claim went back to a charter of 1500 (extended in 1605) granted to John Strang of the Skeith Quarter of Kilrenny [Rennyhill] 'for the Allowing of them and the Heirs to Drive Sea Ware from the Shore of our Burgh (with the "midden muck") for the yearly payment of Eight Pound Scots To our Town they Allowed to Drive said Ware with ten Horses'. Andrew Johnston of Rennyhill wanted to resume the contract in 1824 and asked for a receipt for £20 'being forty years arrears', but the Council could not comply as the privilege had not been exercised 'within the memory of man'. Johnston threatened legal proceedings but the Town Council unanimously resolved that if Mr Johnston were to raise any action against the town 'the Town shall defend their right to the last'.

A running battle for payment for the driven ware continued almost to the end of the nineteenth century. As the magistrates explained to counsel, the sea ware was a valuable manure and as the price of it had risen from 4d a cart load to 2s, 'which was no inconsiderable addition to the small revenue of the Burgh', the right of taking it away free of charge 'had come to be a matter of some importance'. There is no mention of driven sea ware after 1891. By this time nitrates from South America were available and there was no longer much demand for it. Keen gardeners still collect the tangle and some farmers sometimes take it when cleared from the old harbour beach by the District Council, but mostly it is deposited on the refuse dump at Pittenweem. In the late summer of 1987, however, so much seaweed was left on the beach by exceptionally high seas that the Council had almost to beg farmers to take this once much-prized organic fertiliser.

Clay was sold from the shore from time to time and round blue stones for ballast were rouped in the late 1870s. The inhabitants in difficult times were permitted to dig coal 'below the sea-mark' for which in 1878 they were to pay 8d a cartload for any coal sold, but it was the gravel and sea stones that provided the town with its best income from the shore.

Sand and gravel from the raised beach was in great demand during the nineteenth century for field drainage, roads and footpaths. The Town Council was always concerned about its indiscriminate removal and in 1837 prohibited all persons from taking sand near the sea dykes belonging to the inhabitants 'as the safety of their property was endangered'. The town officer was directed to 'intimate this resolution to Jean Pringle and others and to seize the picks and hammers of offenders . . . and to lodge them in jail for the disposal of the Magistrates'. From the late eighteenth century to the mid-nineteenth the Council provided gravel for the new Turnpike Trust of the St Andrews District but towards the end of the century and into the twentieth tons of road stones for the burgh's own streets had to be ordered from Queensferry and Newburgh.

Sea stones for building were rouped as part of the town's Common Good but after the building of the new town hall in 1795 the stone was sold by private bargain. In the summer of 1824 Robert Wilson, mason in Anstruther Wester, asked permission to quarry about 300 loads of rubble [undressed] stones from the shore to build *Crowhill Toft*. The Council consented 'at the West March only at the usual dues': the charge for building and drain stones was 8d a cartload and hewn stone 3d a foot. As the demand increased the Council decided to open a quarry at the 'Rock of the Billowness' on the west side of the East Commonty. Strangers as well as inhabitants were permitted to quarry stones on satisfying the town that the quarry 'was not to extend to the south so as to allow any encroachment of the sea', and always on the understanding that the quarries were to be refilled.

Anstruther Easter applied for stones for metalling part of East Green in 1847, and the following year was granted gravel from the West Commonty for the Ladywalk 'now undergoing repair'. In 1854 David Brown, farmer and millmaster at Anstruther Easter Mill, took stones to build a house at the east end of the Dreel bridge. Two years later stones were requested for the National Bank in the Easter High Street, and a letter was received from a Donald Horne, WS, questioning the burgh's right to quarry stones below the high tide mark but with no indication on whose behalf the query was made. The baillies' instruction to the town clerk was sufficiently terse: 'Refer him to the Charter of the Burgh'. In June 1864 Philip Oliphant, on behalf of the congregation of Anstruther Easter Parish Church, asked for quarry-stones for raising the height of the manse 'at as moderate a rate as possible'; permission was granted 'at the usual rate'. The next year William Murray, draper, asked for stones for his new house, *Adelaide Lodge*, in St Andrews Road. Requests came from Cellardyke, which in a period of prosperity was filling in gaps in the lower town and building new streets on the braes above, from Pittenweem and Largo, Pathhead and Elie: in 1864 the price of stone was reduced for parties building in Anstruther Wester, but the usual custom was retained on stones 'drove out of the town'. In 1890 the quarry committee offered 200 loads of stone, 'if they can get 7d or 8d a load', for the new church at Anstruther Easter, but unfortunately the offer of local stone for the Chalmers Memorial Church was not accepted.

Stones were taken for the widening of Anstruther Easter's east pier in the mid-1850s — at 2d a cartload or 2d a ton if taken away by lighter — and from 1866 thousands of loads were taken for the new Union Harbour, mostly for infilling; the outer stones were brought from Fifeness. The Billowness was quarried again in the 1930s for further improvements to the harbour but by that time Anstruther Wester was no longer rouping its Common Good.

By its Royal Charter Anstruther Wester was entitled to send a commissioner to the Convention of Royal Burghs. He was required to be a 'merchand trafficquer' and residenter who could bear loss and gain in the concerns of the burgh, and a man fearing God 'of the true protestant religion publicly professed and authorized by the Laws of this Kingdom without suspision in the contrair'. Although the trades and professions of West Anstruther's commissioners are not always given it is nevertheless clear that in spite of this directive the burgh did not always send, and most of the time did not have, merchants, in the strictest sense, to represent its interests. Commissioners in the eighteenth and nineteenth centuries included a baxter, a surveyor of customs, a revenue officer, a writer, a tailor, a farmer, a tanner and a wright, all members of the Town Council, which allowed the commissioner a guinea 'to carry his charges'.

Anstruther Wester was soon finding it hard to keep up with the expense of being a Royal Burgh. Already in 1594 the burgh was fined £20 Scots for 'non-compeirance' at the Convention at Stirling, and another £20 for failing to pay its share of a £200 levy. Exemption from attending Conventions was frequently asked for and granted, with the proviso that expenses saved were spent upon its 'brigis, herbereis, tolbuiths, kirkis, or any other most necessar commoun warkis', and an account sent to the Convention. And so it went on until the difficult times of the late seventeenth century when neither of the two Anstruthers could afford to attend Conventions and in August 1672 Anstruther Wester resigned its privileges as a Royal Burgh.

Even after the restoration of its privileges in 1690 the burgh needed to be exempted from attending Conventions in 1695 and again in 1697 for three more years. In the ten tax rolls between 1594 and 1707 Anstruther Wester vies with Kilrenny for the lowest assessment among the five local burghs. It was usually assessed at just over a third of that of the Easter burgh. Once the difficult years at the end of the seventeenth century were passed, however, the Royal Burgh of Anstruther Wester regularly sent a commissioner and assessor to the Conventions until the amalgamation of the three burghs in 1929.

5

The Town Council

In the *Report on the State and Condition of the Burghs of Scotland, 1692,* John Cunningham, town clerk, wrote:

> The oldest records and registers I have seen . . . of the way of electing magistrates and councillors in this burgh is in the year one thousand and six hundred and fourty four, by which the old baillies and councillors first choses the new councill and then both new councillors and also the old . . . choseth the baillies . . . The number of baillies ordinarily three, the number of councill, consisting of baillies and councillors, variable. I see sometimes tuenty, tuenty two, tuenty four, and sometimes ten, eleven, or nine.
>
> In 1663 their [Anstruther Wester's] election of magistrates then seems to admitt burgesses to vote, and doun to 1671 . . . in which time I find their number of councillers frequently very small, particularly 1668 I find only nine in all, baillies and councill, and them they then continue, by which it appears they have had but few inhabitants to chose on . . . Betwixt 1671 and 1689 I find no records, thirteen years at least of that time this burgh having been out of magistracy . . . occasioned by the low condition it had been reduced to and the heavy burdens lying thereupon.

He then recounts how the Convention of Royal Burghs in July 1689 eased the burgh of its public burdens 'upon condition the inhabitants would meet and make ane new election of magistrates for ruleing and governing of the same'. The late baillies, burgesses and inhabitants 'by some degrees got some [to] ventur upon their offices and accept, and then gives their oaths *de fideli administratione,* out of whom was made a leit of nine for baillies and three for treasurer; and so they go on yearly, the old councill chosing the new councill'.

The Burgh Reform Act of 1833 provided that in Royal Burghs the councils were to be chosen by persons qualified to vote in parliamentary elections, but there was not a sufficient number of qualified voters in Anstruther Wester so the old method of election continued until 1868.

The date of the election and of the roup of the Common Good (usually the third Wednesday in September) was fixed by the Council and the Minute signed by the chief magistrate (the title of provost for the senior baillie was not used in West Anstruther until the late nineteenth century). On the appointed day, the roup being concluded, the town officer would verify on oath that he had personally summoned the Council to meet that day. The Act anent Bribery and Corruption would then be read and the oaths taken of allegiance and abjuration [a disclaimer of the Stewarts' right to the Crown]. The question would then be put 'to continue or alter'. If the vote was for continuing, the three baillies and treasurer were elected as in Cunningham's day. If the vote was to alter, a further vote would be taken as to how many councillors were to go out, and as each was voted off another was voted in his place. As in the past 'none are admitted and chosen councilers untill first they be burgesses'.

In 1750 eight residenters were summoned to be burgesses but only three would consent to be admitted. One as a burgess heir paid £4 Scots and the other two £6 Scots each; the counsel ordained that all 'the aye [other] persons' were to be double cessed 'on account of their disobedience'. The last burgess composition was paid in Anstruther Wester in 1887. Thereafter three years' residence as a householder and payment of all rates levied in the burgh was sufficient entitlement.

The only paid member of the Council was the town clerk who on appointment was granted 'all fees duties and Emoluments belonging to the said office' but towards the end of the nineteenth century he was paid a yearly salary: that of Matthew Conolly's successor in 1878 was fixed at £25. There was muttering in the Council about the clerk's salary in the late '80s. These were difficult years for the district with low prices, Norwegian competition in the fishing, and a country-wide agricultural depression. So bad was trade that in 1890 the town clerk of Pittenweem suggested a conference of the local burghs to inquire into the opening of local coalfields 'as a means of allaying distress'. In these circumstances both the town clerk and the auctioneer of the roup offered to take a reduced fee.

There was one other indispensable official, the town officer. He was originally little more than a town crier, his job being to 'cry' the public roup of the Common Good through the burgh and announce public meetings called by the magistrates. He was warranted to: 'call advertisements through the Town for the inhabitants and strangers by the bell and tuck of drum as required at the rate of two pence for the bell from freemen and three pence from unfreemen and sixpence for the Drum for both indiscriminately'; affix public notices, and private at a small charge, on the burgh cross and on that public noticeboard, the church door; ring the church bell every night at eight o'clock in the evening and half past five in the morning; keep the town clock; and have a yearly salary and a new suit of clothes every three years, 'which he shall always wear on duty'.

The first named town officer, in the early years of the eighteenth century, was Thomas Mitchell, glover, with a salary of £6 Scots. Fifty years later a landlabourer, David ffogo, was town officer, but as time went on the job became a full-time occupation so that by the mid-nineteenth century it was stipulated that applicants for the post were to take on no other work.

One of the first additional tasks assigned to the town officer was to put the 'burning mark' upon the casks of herring designed for export in 1710, and to 'pitch upon any barrel after it is made up and cause break open the same and raise the herrings (If he thinks fit from the very bottom)' and if there were 'broken bruised split or not gutted herrings' among them he was to secure the whole cask until the owners paid the stipulated penalty. He was later to warn people that they were not to carry away sea ware without permission and to report to the baillies any who persisted, and he was authorised to seize cloth bleached illegally at the Burn Braes. The town officer became in effect a local policeman, as is clear from a revised list of instructions given in 1847 on the appointment of a new officer:

> He shall endeavour to suppress all riotous and disorderly conduct and pilfering and stealing within the Burgh seize the picks and hammers and sacks of persons digging sandstone opposite the sea dykes of the Burgh conduct beggars and vagrants out of it as soon as possible stop Carters from riding on their carts and boys from riding horses furiously to water or otherwise within the same and shall endeavour to maintain peace and good order within the town at all times but particularly upon the Lord's Day visit the Lodging and see that no improper persons are lodging therein and also to see that there be no tipling in Public Houses after 11 o'clock on Saturday night and in general shall discharge all the duties which were in use to be performed by former Town Officers within the Burgh.

One of the traditional occupations of old Anstruther: Charles Ingram's fish-curing yard in East Green. *Harbourlea* sheltered housing occupies the site now.

In 1844 the town contributed £5 towards obtaining the services of the newly formed County Police 'when required for one year'. A further £5 was paid to the Police Fund in 1847 but the magistrates decided to dispense with the services of the constabulary for the ensuing year: they had after all the services of an all-purpose town officer. In 1849, however, the Town Council provided a lock-up and accommodation for a regular police officer in the old school below the Town Hall.

David Balfour, appointed town officer in October 1853, was to keep the streets clean and clear the street dung twice a week; light the street lamps and keep them burning until eleven o'clock at night; superintend the sea ware; collect the customs, for which he was paid 10s; and keep the key of the boiling house. A local newspaper gradually superseded his task of crying notices but his duty as lamplighter continued until the late 1920s by which time his office had become almost entirely ceremonial.

The burgh was 'out of magistracy' for a second time in its history in the 1850s. Andrew Gilchrist of Milton farm refused to pay for sea ware he had driven and the Town Council resolved in 1851 to seek legal redress but David Kidd, millmaster at Milton Mill, took the part of his neighbour and dissented, and the following year was voted off the Council. In retaliation he proposed to take legal action in respect that the previous Council election had been null and void: 'Daniel Conolly not having attained the age of twenty-one years and was therefore disqualified for electing or being elected a Councillor'. Daniel Conolly, surviving son of the town clerk, was admitted a burgess and was unanimously elected to the Town Council in 1849 at the age of 19. Baillie Young pointed out that David Kidd had sat for two years with Daniel Conolly on the Council without objection. Either the contentious issue of the sea ware was the cause of the dispute or David Kidd had begun to think that no Town Council was better than an undemocratically elected one. Daniel Conolly in his letter of resignation suggested, 'with a view to making up differences and restoring peace', that the Council should re-elect David Kidd, which they agreed to do, but this did not deter David Kidd from submitting his petition of complaint to the Lords of Council and Session.

The 1851 election was set aside in 1853 and in June three interim managers were nominated to conduct the affairs of the burgh until its corporate rights should be restored. They were David Kidd of Milton Mill, George Darsie, tanner in Anstruther Easter, and Thomas Williamson, farmer at Easter Grangemuir. In the winter of 1856 Thomas Williamson died at the age of 78 and David Kidd died suddenly in November at the early age of 41. They were replaced by James Brydie, a small farmer, formerly a carter, and George Dishington, wright, and the administration carried on as smoothly as before, until the summer of 1860.

From the time that Messrs Dishington and Bridie decided to go ahead with their protest against the Anstruther Union Harbour Bill in June 1860, against the advice of George Darsie and most of the inhabitants, relations between the three managers became strained. At first it was Dishington and Brydie against Darsie, but before the end, Darsie and Brydie against Dishington, who never formally resigned but attended meetings intermittently and for the last twelve months of the administration never appeared at all. Dishington's own business affairs at this time were in serious straits. It must have been with some feelings of relief that the managers handed over to a properly elected Town Council on December 4th 1868.

The first public election of the Town Council of Anstruther Wester took place in the Town Hall at eight o'clock on the morning of December 1st 1868. The day before, the town officer declared, he had proclaimed the election through the streets of the burgh after sound of bell and affixed on the parish kirk door a printed notice to the same effect. The qualified electors of the burgh, about 65, voted 'by openly giving in to the Town Clerk Depute signed Lists containing the names of the persons for whom they respectively intended to vote as Councillors' [the secret ballot was not introduced until 1872], and the following were declared elected:

John T. Darsie, fishcurer	62
John Dougall, schoolmaster	61
John Brown, stationmaster	48
David Culbert, farm servant	44
James Brown, millmaster	43
Andrew Wilkie, mason	42
Thomas Gilmour, slater	40
James Budge, wright	37
William Wood, gardener	36

The trades and professions of these publicly-elected members of Council were not very different from many of those chosen by the old method over the previous two hundred years.

The councillors, 'all residing or carrying on business in Anstruther Wester' and all admitted burgesses, accepted office and the next day at 11 forenoon elected John Thomson Darsie first magistrate, John Dougall second baillie, James Brown treasurer and James Budge procurator fiscal. The new Town Council on the motion of the chief magistrate unanimously agreed to record a vote of thanks to the late managers for their services in conducting the affairs of the burgh 'and more especially for the energetic steps recently taken by them in endeavouring to get the corporate rights of the Burgh restored'.

There had been a possibility earlier in the year that small burghs like Anstruther Wester and Kilrenny (which had been disfranchised forty years before) would not be reinstated by the Municipal Bill for Scotland. However, a petition from the inhabitants, 'numerously signed', was taken to London by a deputation which in the absence of Edward Ellice, MP, received 'valuable assistance' from the MP for the County of Fife, Sir Robert Anstruther. When the deputation left at the beginning of July the editor of the *East of Fife Record* questioned whether the burgh could furnish as many men as would form a legitimate Town

Council, even under the new Reform Bill. An infinitely more desirable improvement, he thought, would be the union of the three closely contiguous burghs.

The new Council had nine members, three of whom had to retire in rotation each year for public re-election; Council officials were re-elected annually by the whole Council. Political conspiracies and internal squabbles no more threatened the now largely routine administration of the modern burgh.

In the first half of the nineteenth century a standing committee of three or four members of Council had been sufficient to attend to the Council's practical concerns. In September 1844 the committee was to superintend 'Roads, Harbour Buildings, Lamps, Wells, and other public works of the Burgh with power as formerly to keep them in good order'. In October it inspected the town's reservoir and was to order such repairs as seemed fit. The next year's committee was to examine streets and roads, and repair them and 'inspect the dyke before Mr Bisset's door and get the same repaired, and to place a ladder at the Back of the Sea Wall near Thomas Young's house and employ a plumber to overhaul the town's well and put the pump in order'. The three managers during their period of office acted as the committee, meeting at the West Port to inspect the sea paths, and at the bleaching green to order what repairs were necessary. It was all very simple and direct.

During the latter half of the nineteenth century, however, the provision of urban amenities, street lighting, paved streets, piped water, drainage and sanitation, became considerably more elaborate and expensive. As central government concerned itself through the century with social reform and public health so more sub-committees became necessary to put into effect new legislation and other paid officials joined the town clerk and the town officer.

Any work that was required to be done was paid for out of the town's income from the Common Good and from the tax assessed and collected each year by the stentmasters who ever since the institution of burgh councils had been appointed each year by the Council from among the responsible male inhabitants of the town. The last stentmasters were appointed in 1860. Thereafter assessments for specific public undertakings were made on a valuation roll of all property in the burgh.

Street lighting with oil lamps was introduced in the 1820s and

Stephen Williamson (1827-1903), businessman, philanthropist, Gladstonian Liberal MP for the St Andrews Burghs from 1880 to 1885.

in 1841 four gas lamps were placed at places pointed out by the magistrates. In September 1858 three more lamps, at the burgh's expense, were put up in the shore road, but the following month when Matthew Conolly at *Chesterhill* wished to have lights they were fitted in his dyke at his own expense. Several other inhabitants paid for the installation of their own street lights over the next few years and the Council from time to time added others as they could afford them.

The water supply was simple and inexpensive enough at the beginning of the century. There was a common well on the Chesterhill, which was reported in 1792 to be in bad repair and in a 'dangerous situation for passengers, being near the road side and no ledging about it'. There was also a reservoir, of a kind. It consisted of a tank above the Burn Braes with pipes laid down to the public pumps and was frequently out of repair with water running to waste. It suffered an 'un-looked for complication' in October 1862 when on the 13th it was reported that some of the town's wells were dry that night because the drain was cut through by the parties engaged in building the railway bridge at the Milton road. The cost of this rather elementary water supply was paid by the town, and again when Conolly of *Chesterhill* and Jamieson of *Marsfield* wanted water carried to the west end of Shore Road, they had each to pay £5 for the work to be done.

Leaking reservoirs, broken pipes and the occasional flooding added to the expense and inconvenience but in 1881 the Council turned down an invitation to join a water scheme proposed by the neighbouring burghs. Over the next few years they considered in turn getting water with Pittenweem, Anstruther Easter, or Elie. A public meeting of ratepayers — heritors and tenants who paid the statutory school and road rates — was called by tuck of drum and advertisement in the *East of Fife Record* to discuss the matter but no decision was reached and nothing was done. Finally in February 1886 the Town Council held a plebiscite of ratepayers: 28 voted in favour of an additional supply of water, 70 voted against, and 75 were neutral or did not reply.

The result was sent to the Board of Supervision in Edinburgh [the later Local Government Board]. Its reply was unambiguous: 'a supply of wholesome water must be introduced' and its provision was the responsibility of the local authority not the ratepayers. At the end of the year the Council was warned by the Board that if nothing was done an action would be brought against them at the Court of Session. The town thereupon joined Anstruther Easter and Pittenweem, and secured a loan of £1,800 from the Public Works Loan Board to cover its share of the new joint water scheme which was estimated at £4,096 11s 9d. On November 23rd 1887 the Town Council attended the opening of the Ovenstone Water Works, which were enlarged in 1926. A new reservoir at Kellie Law was finished two years later at about the time that the last public street pump was removed from the High Street near the Session House. The first water rate was collected in March 1888, but as far as the streets and footpaths within the burgh were concerned there was no compulsion to fix a rate.

A motion put to the Town Council by Baillie Robert Hunter in

1750 reveals the then state of the burgh's main street. The types of vehicles may since have changed, but not apparently their profusion:

> That by the frequency of heavie wheel carriages passing and re-passing the publick streets of the Burrow often suffers and as their present Common Good is otherwise appropriated than for mending such Breaches in the Street and that their is no fund for such up and that it is very hard for the streets of this Burgh to suffer by carriages passing and re-passing, they [the Town Council] doe therefore enact and ordain that in all time comeing from and after the time of Martinmas 1750 Each cart wain or waggon which shall have goods in her passing through these streets either going or comeing Shall be liable in the paytt of a ½ pennie each time he goes or comes thero the said Street to the Customer [collector] . . . and every light Cart in 1 farthing, each Sledge for goeing and comeing one farthing . . . and the Council authorises the Baillies if need be to putt on a gate on the post, or a Crosstree, which ever shall be found most sufficient for effectuating this act.

These 'Causeway Mealls' were put to public roup with the anchorages and shore dues but they were soon dropped. No doubt vociferous 'tail-backs' formed on either side of the Customer at his crosstree.

By the end of the eighteenth century the 1630 stone bridge over the Dreel was no longer adequate for the amount of traffic. It was rebuilt by both burghs in 1795, 'by subscription', just as the harbour was repaired in 1898 — and the burgh's streets and footpaths.

The inconvenience and danger of the turnpike road within the burgh 'had been long felt and complained of as a great evil by the County Gentlemen, by Commercial Travellers and by the inhabitants of the Burgh, as well as those resident in the Neighbourhood', a petition to the new Turnpike Trust declared, and its improvement was contemplated 'with anxious solicitude by everyone connected with the Commercial and agricultural interest of the District'. The road at some points was not more than 13' 3" wide between walls, 'and hence many accidents have occurred'. A big improvement was accomplished between 1825 and 1830 with financial aid from the trustees. At a cost of £450 'a neat footway or pavement' was provided and the main street widened from thirteen to thirty feet and M'Adamized. John

Loudon M'Adam's method of road construction was to put over a firm drained subsoil a twelve-inch thick layer of small stones which the pressure of cart and carriage wheels would bind together. The gravel came from the burgh's foreshore.

There were several other lanes and paths, besides the main street, in the burgh. There was the Path (to the ford), the Loan Dykes, the Tannage road, the Cow Lane, a Becky's path, and a Lombard or Lombart street, all of which have disappeared, and the present Witch Wynd, School Wynd, and Crichton Street. There were also the 'sea paths' for driving sea ware and stones, and the paths to the West Haven, all of which were in constant need of repair and all to be paid for out of the burgh's funds. Wealthier proprietors sometimes helped. Archibald Johnston's offer to re-align the wynd 'by the Bankwell', at the foot of which he owned land, was accepted in 1820. Later in the century Matthew Conolly paid half the cost of repairs to the road in front of *Chesterhill*, and Mrs Smith, proprietrix of the *White House*, paid half the cost of the repair of the Harbour Path, but the proprietors refused to pay half the cost of proposed new paving round the Buckie House corner. A public meeting was therefore held in March 1876 to discuss the adoption of the permissive Police Burgh Act of 1862, known as the Lindsay Act, which would have enabled the Council to impose a rate for projects like this. The *East of Fife Record* was scathing about the response of the burgh's proprietors:

> The inhabitants, or at least the majority of them, at the meeting on Saturday evening, have declined to adopt the Lindsay Act, and have thus indicated their preference for broken Pavements and dirty streets in opposition to a dry and comfortable footpath and a street free from deposits of mud and filth. The Burgh it seems has a permanent income of £122 but from this the whole of the County and local assessments as well as the salaries of officials are paid and when these are deducted all that is left is the small sum of £14 10s with perhaps a few shillings drawn from gravel taken away from the sea beach. There are drains to be repaired . . . the water supply to be kept in order and other miscellaneous but necessary works carried on so that it can be scarcely wonderd at that the burgh is in debt to about £80 and with the prospect of that Sum being increased rather than diminished. The pavement of the principal street has long been in a most disgraceful state and almost unsafe to walk on at night. The mud scraped off the streets is gathered into a series of

heaps close to the footpath which is not very broad . . . and boots are covered with unsavoury mess. Complaints have been loud and frequent.

The Lindsay Act required a two-thirds majority of the Town Council before it could be adopted and that was not now forthcoming. The editor regretted the decision and declared that none of the arguments at the meeting against the Act were of any importance: 'they were rather against any taxation whatever being imposed'. Anstruther Easter, Cellardyke and Pittenweem had adopted the Act, but only twelve hands were raised in favour of it in Anstruther Wester.

It was decided in January 1890 to ask for subscriptions to repair the footpaths. Within a month £34 10s was subscribed and within two, £66 3s 1d. The new paving was in place by June and cost £66 17s. At the end of the month the Town Council unanimously passed a hearty vote of thanks to Stephen Williamson, MP, 'for his liberal contribution towards improving the footpaths of the Burgh, more especially as without this such a very desirable improvement would have been delayed for a considerable period'. (Two years later Williamson proposed to put an iron girder footway on the east side of the bridge to Anstruther Easter. The Town Council agreed to get it done 'on condition that they were to incur no responsibility'.) Another vote of thanks was due to the Misses Jamieson, daughters of the town clerk, who in November 1893 arranged a concert 'in aid of the funds for improving the streets'.

In January 1894 the Council constituted itself into a bazaar committee, with Provost Porter as convener, 'to raise funds to get the debt of the Town paid off'; the aim was to raise £350. One bazaar was held in August 1894 and another in December, the proceeds amounting to £288 11s. 10½d. The Council was soon voting thanks to Stephen Williamson, MP, for a generous offer of £40 to the bazaar specifically for Crichton Street to be M'Adamised and steamrolled and a cement pavement made, and was congratulating itself that Crichton Street had been improved 'without cost to the Bazaar' — or to the Council.

It was as reluctant to impose rates for essential services as the ratepayers were to pay. The Scottish Education Department asked in May 1896 for contributions from the burghs for, in particular, secondary education. The Council replied that the

C

burgh regretted that it could not make any contribution, not only because of the Waid Academy but also because the inhabitants 'are so heavily taxed more especially in consequence of the construction of sewers'. The Council thought that any grants they could make should go to the reduction of local taxation.

So in August 1902 another bazaar and a series of concerts were arranged 'to assist the rates', in particular to pay for repair to the main road. The Council had already appealed to the St Andrews District Committee of the County Council for assistance but the committee had replied that owing to the heavy fish traffic (there were record herring catches in the years around the turn of the century) it would not agree to maintain the roads within the burgh for less than £60 a year and £6 for supervision. An appeal was made to the railway company and the harbour board as the ratepayers 'were not quite in a position themselves to keep up the roads in proper repair'. A meeting was held in September but the ratepayers voted against any increase of assessments meantime. The inhabitants of Anstruther Wester could be generous, as they showed in the early years of the war, but for as long as they could avoid it, they preferred public inconvenience to regular taxation.

The ancient burgh's independence came to an end in 1929 when following the Local Government (Scotland) Act of that year it had perforce to join Anstruther Easter and Kilrenny. Amalgamation had been suggested several times in the past but Anstruther Wester stoutly resisted the idea.

Reports came to the ears of the Town Council in January 1834 that there was to be a union of the three contiguous burghs 'whereby the Town of West Anstruther will be deprived of the Management of its own funds'. The chief magistrate and the town clerk were sent at once to Edinburgh with a list of objections to the proposal. The letter sizzles with indignation. It explained that Anstruther Wester had 25 to 30 acres of arable land worth from 2 to £3,000, together with extensive common for pasturing their 'Bestial', plus a floating capital of £200, and the burgh was 'entirely free of debt', but Kilrenny had only 2½ acres of land and was scarcely free from debt, and as for Anstruther Easter, it had a fluctuating revenue and was in 'pecuniary obligations of from 6 to £800', and it had no land whatsoever. The lands belonging to Anstruther Wester, the letter went on, were specially secured to the baillies and Council by James VI in 1587 and had been preserved almost unimpaired ever since. 'It would be in direct opposition to every established principle of equity' were those lands now to be appropriated for the benefit of any other community. It could not be alleged that there had been abuse in the management of the burgh revenue 'seeing that the present state of its property and funds proves the reverse'. The rights of private individuals, the letter warned, might not be considered safe, 'and an universal division of property might be speedily looked for'. The town of Anstruther Easter had at one time possessed lands which were now worth several thousand pounds, but these were a number of years ago wholly alienated 'and at present belong to a private individual and surely if that Burgh could not preserve or take care of its own property or funds while it had them it has no good claim to a share of what now legally belongs to the Inhabitants of Anstruther Wester'.

The letter explained that as Anstruther Easter had no land the expense of upholding the church, school and manse fell entirely upon the inhabitants. The church was greatly in want of internal renovation, the manse was very old and might soon require to be rebuilt and the schoolmaster's house was at present totally uninhabitable and would likewise have to be rebuilt:

> To accomplish these necessary purposes the inhabitants of Anstruther Easter must be heavily assessed in a short time, and it would surely be the height of injustice to make the inhabitants of Anstruther Wester bear any part in the consequence if the proposed union were carried into effect . . . The proposed union was altogether inexpedient in respect the pursuits, habits and feelings of the Inhabitants of these Burghs are very different from each other the influential portion of the Anstruther Wester community being chiefly agricultural while those of East Anstruther are commercial and connected with shipping and Kilrenny almost entirely a fishing town. The population of Anstruther Wester is about 400, of Anstruther Easter 1,000 and of Kilrenny 1,400 and their interests and pursuits being so very much at variance there exists very little chance indeed of them acting in concert for the general good, but on the contrary there is a strong probability that their union would only produce endless jealousies, heartburnings and division.
>
> The inhabitants of Anstruther Wester are unanimously against the union.

The question was raised again from time to time, receiving little general approval, but it was more seriously considered in 1914.

With the outbreak of war it was dropped, to be taken up again in 1921 and again in 1923, when a conference of the three burghs was proposed. Anstruther Wester refused to have anything to do with it even though the pooling of resources for an 18-hole golf course was to have been considered. The 1929 Act of Parliament put an end to the shilly-shallying, and an end to an era inaugurated by the grant of a Royal Charter over three hundred years before. The Town Council met for the last time on November 25th 1929 under the chairmanship of Provost Robert Brodie, blacksmith and golf cleek manufacturer, who had served on the Council for forty-six years and had been provost for the previous eight. Another era came to an end in 1975 when the united burgh itself was absorbed into the North East Fife District Council, part of a reorganisation of local government that called forth the indignation of the historian Gordon Donaldson who wrote that by the new Act 'history and tradition were coolly disregarded'.

6

The Politics of the Town Council

Early in 1715 the Kirk Session appointed a day of thanksgiving for the accession of the Protestant George of Hanover but for several weeks at the end of the year no services were held 'in regard . . . our Minister was obliged to withdraw dureing the prevailing power of a monstrous Rebellion'. A year later Baillie Patrick Mitchell was rebuked by the session:

> for his sinfull complyance with ye Rebells dureing ye Late execrable rebellion in severall particulars viz. in his being present at ye publick cross of the Burgh the time of proclamation of Their Pretender and drinking his health yr [there] and allowing and witnessing their solemn rejoycings for their pretended victorys and severall other pieces of miscarriage and silly [weak] sinfull complyance wt notorious Desygne of overturning our present very happy Establishment. The aggravations circumstances Heynous Nature and Dreadful tendency of this his sin and how directly Contrary ys [this] his carriage hes been to his Ingagents and character both as a Magistrate and ane Elder was sufficiently demonstrated and layed before him.

John Lyall, former baillie, appeared before the session in 1717 and confessed that he also had been guilty of 'severall steps of sinfull complyance . . . in time of the late Rebellione' particularly in drinking the healths of 'Pretender Marr and severall other rebells at the Cross', ordering the boats over the water with the rebels and making arrangements for the payment of taxes to Marr. He professed his sorrow and promised to walk more regularly in time coming.

On March 6th 1744 the Town Council unanimously resolved to address King George II 'in Detestation of the designe of an Invasion And condemns attempts of a popish Pretender that way'. Prince Charles Edward had just arrived in Paris from Rome and the following year, with a commission as Regent in the name of his father, James VIII and III, he landed in Moidart. Before long his forces were demanding taxes and in spite of its protestation the Town Council made its required contribution. The receipt (for six pounds sterling), 'Given at our Palace of Holyroodhouse the nineteenth day of October 1745', survives among the burgh's papers.

In view of the local attitude to the Stewarts the Council's next protest comes as no surprise. In an attempt to increase recruitment for the army a Relief Act was passed in 1778 which would enable Roman Catholics to enlist. It was regarded by some as the thin end of the wedge of total emancipation. A Bill was proposed to extend the concession to Scotland which the Council 'did unanimously disapprove'. Their member of parliament was to be instructed to oppose it and their representative-designate to the General Assembly was to oppose 'any measures that might be suggested in the Assembly for encouraging Popery in this Kingdom'.

The Town Council had equally strong feelings about the protectionist Corn Laws. Repeal and free trade were popular causes in Scotland and in 1777 the Council empowered their commissioner to the Convention 'to use its Interest in Opposing the Cornbill presently depending in Parliament from passing into law', which they apprehended 'would be attended with pernicious consequences to the commercial and manufacturing interests of the country'. At least three more petitions on the subject were sent to parliament.

Thirty burgesses, heritors and inhabitants in the spring of 1784 sent a petition to the Council, then meeting to elect a delegate to choose a new member of parliament, stating that they judged it their right and duty 'to inform you that we totally disapprove of the Conduct of the late Member for this District of Burghs'. John Anstruther had joined a faction who had disquieted the peace of their sovereign and endangered the constitution of the country:

> If therefor you have any regard to the united voice of your constituents we desire that you may preferr our countryman Colonel Moncrieff to your late Member and that like the City of London, and others of our own Royal Burghs you may elect no Member but one who shall engage by an Act in your Books in good faith and plain terms to support the King and his virtuous Ministry against Charles Fox and Lord North and their late faction, and that such support should be unequivocally continued so long as his Constituents shall judge it to be deserved.

Col. Moncrieff, a native of Crail, bought Airdrie from Sir John Anstruther of that ilk in 1783. He had enjoyed the patronage of Sir Henry Erskine, and Sir Henry Erskine had been no friend of the Anstruthers.

John Anstruther, MP, must have voted with the unlikely coalition of Charles Fox and Lord North which had brought down Lord Shelburne's ministry in 1783. Lord Shelburne, with the concurrence of the king, had promised moves towards a freer trade and a reformed parliament, both of which appealed to most Scotsmen at the time including West Anstruther's petitioners. Fox's faction aimed to diminish the power of the Crown, and North's faction was against any parliamentary reform. John Anstruther, who in 1798 was made chief justice of Bengal, must have voted in 1783 for Fox's India Bill which would have undermined the king's prerogative.

The petitioners' reference to London was to the city's decision several years earlier to draw up instructions for their four members of parliament and to require from them a pledge that they would carry them out. In his reply to the petition John Anstruther assured the magistrates that his intention, if re-elected, was to be guided by the principles of independence and to be bound to no set of men whatsoever in or out of office. This was not quite what the petitioners had in mind; they were all for a little less independence and a little more deference to the wishes of his constituents.

The petitioners might have been surprised at the Town Council's sentiments in 1834. The Duke of Wellington agreed on November 15th 1834 to William IV's request to form a government. Nine days later the Town Council sent a congratulatory *Address to His Majesty on the State of Public Affairs*. The previous ministry, it stated, 'had tarnished the natural Glory [of the country] by succumbing to Revolutionised France . . . and by their sweeping measures of Reform [in 1832] subverted the Constitution of the Country'. The Council, unusually in matters of this kind, was not unanimous, and the address was carried by five votes to two.

Throughout the nineteenth century the Town Council petitioned parliament on a variety of topics: in 1837 and '39 in favour of Rowland Hill's plan for a cheap and uniform rate of postage 'by the purchase of a stamped cover'; in 1838 against the abolition of the Convention of Royal Burghs and in 1884 for a Secretary of State for Scotch affairs; in 1864 against the transportation of convicts to Australia, and in 1877 for a Bill, which did not become law until 1907, for legalising marriage with a deceased wife's sister; in 1886 and 1892, in response to a circular from Mrs Kirkland in Edinburgh, in favour of a Bill for extending the franchise to women, for which women had to wait until after the First World War.

Loyalty to the Crown never wavered. A 'loyal and dutiful address' was despatched in August 1822 on the occasion of George IV's expected visit and a month later the Council unanimously voted five guineas from the burgh's funds 'towards the erection of an Equestrian Statue of H.M. in Edinburgh commemorative of his auspicious visit to his ancient kingdom of Scotland'. The steeple bell was rung during Thursday June 28th 1838 for the coronation of Queen Victoria, and the inhabitants were 'respectfully requested to decorate doors and windows with branches of trees and flowers in honour of the occasion'. There seemed to be a certain lack of enthusiasm for the marriage of the Prince of Wales and Princess Alexandra of Denmark in February 1863: two of the magistrates were to procure 'a flag or flags for the occasion', but a sum of money was voted for tea, sugar and bread for the poor in the burgh and a pie for each child at school. On the death of Queen Victoria in January 1901 a special meeting of the Town Council was convened and a letter of condolence composed. The following day the proclamation of the accession of Edward VII was read by the provost with the local Volunteers drawn up as a guard of honour 'near where the Market Cross formerly stood'.

Loyalty to the Liberal Party was strong, too. When the Town Council was asked to contribute to a memorial to the late Mr Gladstone in 1898 Provost Porter replied that the magistrates were themselves going through a trying time in raising money [for the repair of the harbour] 'although he did not suppose that there was a Council in the Kingdom that was more loyal to Mr Gladstone than theirs'.

Members of parliament for the district were elected by the Town Council 'in like manner as they were formerly in use to do when they choosed a Commissioner for the Parliament of Scotland'. After notice from the sheriff the Town Councils of Anstruther Easter and Wester, Kilrenny, Crail and Pittenweem would each choose a delegate to meet at the burgh whose turn it was to preside, and there the delegates would choose from among themselves a representative for the ensuing parliament. It was therefore important to politically-interested persons that they should have influence on Town Councils. The Anstruther family represented the parliamentary district almost continuously from the end of the sixteenth century until the nineteenth, and up until 1852 there were two, sometimes three, Anstruthers and an in-law, friend or factor on West Anstruther's Council. They were usually elected in their absence and rarely attended Council meetings apart from those called to choose a delegate, and it was often only on that day that they accepted their seat on the Council and took their oaths. Most of the time the system was un-questioned.

Three times in the eighteenth century, however, the Anstruther monopoly was challenged. Amid accusations of kidnapping and corruption two delegates were chosen in 1741, Sir Philip Anstruther of Balcaskie with ten votes and John Wilson, mer-chant in Edinburgh and burgess of Anstruther Wester, with nine. It was objected that those who had voted for Sir Philip had refused to take the oath against bribery 'recently devised to prevent corrupt and illegal practices in the Election of Members of Parliament' and had thus disqualified their votes. John Cunningham, town clerk, 'to avoid trouble', accepted the com-mission of those who had taken the oath and those who had not.

A similar tussle occurred in Kilrenny, where again Cunningham accepted both commissions, and seven delegates, not the usual five, met in West Anstruther's tolbooth. Four delegates, after taking the statutory oaths, voted for Pittenweem's delegate, John Stewart, brother of the Earl of Murray. The three Anstruthers voted for Maj. Gen. Philip Anstruther of Airdrie under protest at the irregular proceedings but Cunningham insisted that he had full freedom to use the privileges of a returning officer 'by Law and practice', and John Stewart, or Stuart as he signed the minute, was considered elected. At the next Council election the vote was put to alter or continue. The Council voted to alter and five members were voted off: Robert Lyall, the leader of the protest, and four of his supporters. Of the five new members three, significantly, were tenant farmers: Robert Bisset in Miln-town, brother of Alexander Bisset in Milntown who was already on the Council and an adherent of the Anstruther party, and Robert Robb and John Brown.

The protesters were determined to prevent the re-election of General Philip Anstruther as he was the only one of forty-five Scottish MPs to support the government when it proposed humiliating penalties on Edinburgh after the Porteous affair, in which an Edinburgh mob lynched Captain Porteous for hanging a condemned smuggler. At the same time the five protesters were, by the standards of the burgh, wealthy and independent men. Robert Lyall was portioner [part-inheritor] of his father's and grandfather's considerable property, James Robertson was a shipmaster, George Colvin a coupar, and John Thomson and George Robb tailors. George Robb represented the Kirk Session and the burgh at the General Assembly on at least four occasions and was commissioner to the Convention of Royal Burghs on two. It is possible that these men, influential and independent in their own sphere, resented their lack of effective political power and the political monopoly of the land-owning Anstruthers. In this connection it is noticeable that of the five councillors who voted for Sir Philip Anstruther as delegate, four certainly and the fifth probably, were agricultural tenants. The Anstruthers were considerable landowners in the district: in the late eighteenth century Sir John Anstruther alone owned a third part of the parish.

The new Town Council continued with few changes for several years, Sir Philip Anstruther attending on most election days. In June 1747 when another parliamentary election was imminent he was unanimously elected delegate, and at the meeting of delegates General Anstruther of Airdrie was re-elected member of parliament as if no protest had ever been made, but the Anstruthers were shortly to be challenged again.

After a little skirmishing at a Council meeting in April 1754 the anti-Anstruther party, led by Baillie Robert Hunter, officer of customs at the port of Anstruther, by a majority of eight votes to four elected as their delegate Sir Harry Erskine, who had purposely come to Anstruther to unseat General Anstruther of Airdrie. The delegates meeting at Kilrenny in May elected Sir Harry as their member of parliament and he continued to represent the district until 1765. As before, the election of a delegate had repercussions on the Council election. It was resolved to alter and Sir Philip Anstruther and four of his adherents were voted out. Sir Harry Erskine continued to be elected a Councillor each year until the year of his death, and like the Anstruthers he only attended for Council and delegate elections.

Sir Harry or Henry Erskine, a gentleman of a rubicund complexion, was the second son of John Erskine, third baronet of Alva and Cambuskenneth in Clackmannanshire. He succeeded to the title in 1747 on the death of his elder brother in the battle of Laffeldt in Flanders. He himself was wounded in north-west France in 1746 and fought under his uncle in Flanders in 1747. A member of parliament for the Ayr Burghs from 1749 until 1754 he was a very fashionable figure in the world of politics. He was one of the few Scots to be honoured by Lord Bute when in 1760 Bute restored him to the rank of Major General which he had lost in 1756 for opposing in parliament the employment of Hanoverian and Hessian troops in Britain. He married in April 1761 Janet Wedderburn, sister of Alexander Wedderburn, 'a man learned in the law'. (There is a portrait of the Erskines' three children by Nathaniel Dance in Fyvie Castle, Aberdeenshire. The elder son was member of parliament for the Dysart Burghs until he became Lord Rosslyn in 1805 as heir to his uncle Wedderburn.)

Three years before this election Sir Harry Erskine had sought a parliamentary inquiry into courts martial at Minorca during the time that General Philip Anstruther was Lieut. Governor there. Sir Harry complained that he had been arrested at Minorca by General Anstruther and confined for three weeks without any charge, and that the court martial was improperly conducted by Anstruther, who, finding the court unwilling to convict, adjourned it, leaving Erskine still under arrest, eventually to be released without being told the sentence of the court. In a later debate in the House of Commons Erskine complained of the 'exorbitant power' of Generals at courts martial and abused Anstruther, who in his turn accused Erskine of being in a conspiracy against him at the time when all the Scots members of parliament opposed him in the Porteous affair. The inquiry came to nothing but the personal rivalry and antagonism remained, hence Sir Harry's arrival in Anstruther Wester. He resigned his seat in parliament in May 1765 on his appointment as secretary of the Most Ancient and Noble Order of the Thistle but died in August at York on his way back to London.

In 1754 Robert Hunter led the party which opposed the re-election of General Anstruther but in 1766, now surveyor of customs, he switched his allegiance to the Anstruther party.

Baillie William Thomson, also of the customs, followed suit. In that age of patronage preferment for government officials was probably more certain under an established political family than under a newcomer like Robert Alexander. He was a merchant in Edinburgh (and probably a descendant of a wealthy sixteenth century family in Anstruther Easter), and was made a burgess and freeman in December and admitted the same month, irregularly, as a town councillor, provoking protest from Robert Hunter. When the Council met in January 1766 only Hunter and Thomson voted for the Anstruther delegate, Robert Fall, merchant in Dunbar and brother-in-law of Sir John Anstruther.

In a disputed election Pittenweem Town Council also voted overwhelmingly for Robert Alexander. The Rev. Walter Wood wrote that 'many scandalous stories are yet [in the 1860s] afloat in the neighbourhood concerning the means used by both parties to gain their ends . . . We have been told that Alexander was ruined by the expense of these contests: and certainly, after that time, the Anstruthers were never able to hold their heads so high as they had done before'. The delegates voted for Sir John and the family continued to represent the burghs until the early years of the nineteenth century under the old system of election, and once again in the later nineteenth century under the new.

The legality of the 1765 Town Council election was challenged. It had been called for September 25th by the chief magistrate, Robert Hunter, but in his absence the meeting was convened a week early. Robert Hunter, supported by Baillie William Thomson, protested that several Council members had accepted bribes and corrupt gifts and that some of them had been kept under confinement from their own families 'in secret and remote places for several days past, In order to Influence them In giving their votes at the ensuing annual Election'.

One councillor reported that Philip Anstruther, writer in Edinburgh, had solicited his vote for Sir John and had offered money which Councillor William Innes had refused saying that 'he would not be biased by any gentleman that way'. Philip Anstruther then gave Anne Waddell, Innes's wife, eight guineas, 'for the purpose of influencing his vote'; Alexander Fall of London gave her six guineas, which William Innes delivered to the Council. Robert Bisset refused money from Philip Anstruther, and his wife, Christina Hay, was subsequently given money in gold and bank notes which Bisset delivered to the Council 'as he would not be bribed by any man'. The money amounted to '32½ guineas in gold, 3 small pieces of dutch gold, a Five Pound Glasgow note and 9 twenty shilling notes'. The following April the notary public to whom the money had been consigned handed it to the Town Council who gave 14 guineas to Innes and Bisset. The larger sum was resealed and delivered to the town clerk 'to be kept till further orders'. Perhaps it helped pay the legal expenses of the appeal to the Court of Session to decide the validity or otherwise of the Council election of 1765.

The decision of the court, confirmed by the House of Lords, was that the election (and that of Pittenweem) was invalid 'on account of Bribery and undue influence'. An Order in Council in June 1767 authorised a new election, this time by a wider poll: a temporary return to the ancient right of all qualified burgesses to elect the burgh council. The sheriff deputies of Fife, Perth and Midlothian called a meeting for July 15th and two lists of fifteen names were submitted and objections considered. The result of the scrutiny was that when sustained objections had been deducted, by a majority of three votes the pro-Alexander Council of 1765 was defeated. The 1768 election brought Sir John Anstruther and his factor, and the following year his brother-in-law, back on to the Council and the family continued to be represented on the Town Council until 1852 when James Anstruther declined re-election, his right to stand having been twice challenged.

The electoral protest in Anstruther Wester in 1818 after the death of Sir John Carmichael Anstruther, MP, sounds more like a theatrical farce than a serious political contest. One day in June on his way from the Milnton to the meeting called to elect a delegate, Councillor Bisset, an adherent of the Anstruther interest, was prevailed on by Joseph Gordon, WS, agent for the opposing candidate, to go to the house of Councillor Charles Gray in the High Street where he was detained with several other councillors. Councillor Col. Robert Anstruther reported the incident to the Town Council and suggested that a magistrate should go and require the councillors to attend their duty in Council. Only three members of Council had so far turned up. Accordingly Baillie Dishington, with a notary public from Pittenweem, two masons, and the Anstruther candidate, Advocate James Maconochie, went to the house of Charles Gray to persuade the recalcitrant councillors to attend the meeting. Baillie

Dishington reported that upon going up the front stair he was met by Joseph Gordon, WS, who positively refused him and his companions entry because the said Alexander Bisset 'was sick and in bed'. Other councillors were in the house but they refused to open their doors to the baillie. Eventually Stephen Williamson, surgeon in Anstruther Easter, on being questioned as to the state of Bisset's health, reported that 'his nerves were a little disordered', but he would soon be well enough to attend the meeting. Dishington was also informed that immediately after the bell for convening the Council had been rung two other councillors had driven off in William Millar's chaise from his house across the road.

It was evident to the Council that the six councillors and the agent had all been 'art and part' of a conspiracy to prevent the day's business of choosing a delegate, but their game of hide and seek achieved nothing as the depleted Council elected the Anstruther candidate, Alexander Maconochie, Lord Advocate of Scotland, who was to preserve the family influence during the time of the Anstruther heir's minority. In September none of the conspirators attended the Council election and all were unanimously voted out. A few years later the district very nearly lost even this unsatisfactory system of representation.

It was reported in 1830 that the East District of Fife was to be disfranchised. A petition to parliament was immediately prepared in which the Town Council expressed its 'mingled feelings of astonishment and mortification' at the proposed deprivation. It had been represented that the district was composed of 'five poor villages without Trade, Property or Population', but reference to unquestionable authorities would show that no less than £50,000 worth of grain and £17,000 of potatoes, 'the growth of the District', were shipped yearly, 'not to mention from 11,000 to 12,000 barrels of Cod and Herrings' which were caught and cured and sent to London and Liverpool. The district was by no means 'small and insignificant':

> Why should five burghs with 6,000 people and one Representative be suppressed while one burgh in the sister kingdom with only 4,000 be retained and allowed to send two members without any satisfactory reasons . . . Neither have any satisfactory reasons been assigned why this District alone in all Scotland should be singled out and made liable to Political disability while others far less important proposed at least to continue.

The burghs had broken no law, the petition continued, and had been convicted of no crime, but had a thriving, industrious, peaceable and loyal population. The Act would be in violation of its chartered rights and 'in breach of the solemn Treaty of Union and in disturbance of the settled order of Parliamentary Representation of Scotland'. The five burghs were not disfranchised and the old system of election was swept away in the Reform Bill of 1832.

7

The Old Burgh

Originally a booth or covered stall set up in a public place for the collection of taxes, the Tolbooth became the seat of local government where in addition to collecting taxes the Town Council held its meetings and burgh courts, its school and jail. The Church Tower, probably the oldest surviving building in the burgh, may once have served as Anstruther Wester's Tolbooth: it had a jail until the early nineteenth century, and the first parish school met on the ground floor. The Rev. James Forrester wrote in the *Statistical Account* that the old Town House was washed away in the exceptional storms of the late seventeenth century; it could have been at risk from the sea only if it had stood at the harbour end of the High Street beyond the *White House*. It was usual, however, for the Tolbooth to be near the market cross and Anstruther Wester's cross was in the main street east of the path to the ford.

The Council's meeting place was found inadequate by 1794 and a new Town Hall was built adjoining the Church Tower. The present stone stair may once have been an outside stair and the wing of the ante room, now the kitchen, added later. On the southern wall of the Council Chamber is a panel of the burgh's arms of three salmon of which the Marquis of Bute wrote in 1897 in *The Arms of the Royal Burghs and Parliamentary Burghs of Scotland*:

> There are two supporters. That on the dexter is a female figure symbolising Justice, but not blindfolded; she holds a drawn sword in her right hand and a pair of scales in her left. If coloured the tunic should be white, and the mantle purple to symbolize the imperial majesty of law. The supporter on the sinister is a young fisherman in his ordinary dress. His right hand rests upon the shield and in his left he holds a fish spear in the form of a trident.

Above the burgh arms is the Anstruther family's crest, 'an armed arm erect, holding a battle-axe proper', which was added to the burgh's arms in 1769 when Sir John Anstruther bought the Lordship of Pittenweem.

The Town Hall was used by the inhabitants for social and intellectual pursuits. In January 1855, the *Pittenweem Register* reported, a ball was held in the Town House on the last day of the year 'attended by a numerous, happy and well-regulated company'. The Anstruther and Pittenweem Mutual Improvement Society was founded that year by some young men of the neighbourhood; it aimed to give its members 'knowledge and fortitude for speaking in public' and met in the hall once a fortnight. Later in the year there was such a good drave 'that there were not rooms and lofts large enough in Cellardyke to contain all the wedding parties' and at least one Dyker brought his party to the Wester Town Hall. Popular readings were held in the hall and regular meetings of societies like the Good Templars and the Anstruther Thistle Lodge of Oddfellows. Robert Sime, letter carrier, booked the hall in 1875 for a dancing class on Saturday evenings weekly.

A correspondent to the local paper in August 1914 commented on the cleanliness of the narrow wynds and the interest of the old buildings and the new, and the stench from the Dreel Burn, but how, he asked, could the civic fathers deal with such cognate subjects as sanitation and amalgamation sitting round a table in a room scarcely twenty feet in length [the ante room?] and facing the street with the rumbling and screeching of motor cars and cycles like the 'mailed fist's armies' through Belgium. 'The sooner amalgamation the better if it provided a healthier and quieter place to meet.'

The year after amalgamation the Town Hall was taken over by the public assistance officer, but after the Second World War it reverted to use as a social meeting place. It was draughty and in need of decoration when in 1981 the Anstruther Improvements Association signed with the North East Fife District Council a five-year lease (since renewed) for the hall. The Association was formed in 1950 with the object of promoting general improvements within the former burghs of Anstruther Easter and Wester. Not the least of its enterprising ventures has been the renovation of the Wester Town Hall.

The heritors rented the ground floor of the hall for the parish school until 1827. Part was then rented as a shop and the remainder as accommodation for the town officer, the police constable, a lock-up and again the town officer. In 1965 the entire floor was acquired from Anstruther Town Council by the congregation of St Adrian's Church as kitchen premises for their new church hall (the former Parish Church) in exchange for church property in Tolbooth Wynd in Anstruther Easter.

There was no feeling in the Wester burgh in the 1870s and '80s, as there was in Anstruther Easter and Cellardyke, that the business of the burgh could only get bigger and better. Because of its relative poverty and apparent stagnation its charming eighteenth-century Town Hall was spared demolition and rebuilding. Now administered by the Improvements Association, it is in constant use.

The burgh grew up on the raised beach round the haven, the shore and the ford. That house aligned to the path to the ford is probably the oldest surviving house in the burgh and was probably built as a laird's town house. It belonged in the eighteenth century to Robert Hamilton of Kilbrachmont who took part in the '45 and marched with the Jacobite forces as far as Preston, but 'being reported to the Government as disordered in his judgment little notice was taken of his escapade'. He died in West Anstruther in 1769. Additions were made at the back of the house early in the eighteenth century, but by 1792 it was reported to be in a 'ruinous situation and the slates falling therefrom frequently to the great danger of the Inhabitants their Children and Strangers passing on the public road'. The owners of the house were unknown but it was occupied at the time by Charles Gray who refused to repair it though somebody did as it was the scene of that farcical political protest in the summer of 1818.

Charles Gray was an officer of a Revenue cutter. His first wife was Elizabeth Burn, sister of Major General Andrew Burn, both grandchildren of the Rev. Andrew Burn, minister at Anstruther Wester from 1702 until his death in October 1760. His second wife (he had three) was Margaret Raiker of a long-established West Anstruther family. His sons all followed careers in the Royal Marines through the influence of his brother-in-law the major general, who in his turn had benefited from the patronage of Sir Harry Erskine. Gray's eldest son, Major George Gray, had an only son Charles who was born in Anstruther, educated at the burgh school and Edinburgh Academy, and was for a while a clerk with Matthew Conolly and John Smith (who married his eldest sister). With a considerable patrimony from his father he emigrated to South Australia where he became a prosperous sheep farmer and as 'Charles Gray of Nareeb Nareeb' was a generous benefactor of his native town.

Two sons of Charles Gray, senior, died as young men in the Mediterranean, another on active service in India and another died in Chatham while a young lieutenant. Charles, the first son of Margaret Raiker, was born in the old house in March 1782 and began his career as a weaver. At the age of 23 years he obtained a commission in the Royal Marines and spent the next thirty-six years on active service, most of them afloat, retiring in 1841 with the rank of captain. His years of service life were combined with a dedication to poetry. Lieut. Charles Gray published a volume of *Poems and Songs* in 1811 and a second volume three years later, and in 1841 a volume of *Lays and Lyrics*. He was one of the most enthusiastic members of William Tennant's *Musomanik Society of Anstruther*, a sociable club devoted to versifying. He was described as a 'neat little duodecimo of a man with a well set up figure, a military air and a weatherbeaten but smiling face'. Dr Charles Rogers wrote that Charles Gray sang his own songs at Dunino Manse 'and related his naval experiences with a good-natured egotism'. He moved to Edinburgh in 1841 'where he cultivated the society of lovers of Scottish song' and died there in April 1851 and was buried in the Dean cemetery. When the railway came to Anstruther Wester in 1863 the birthplace of the poet became the *Railway Tavern*, and after the demise of the railway a hundred years later, the *Dreel Tavern*.

To the west of the tavern by the ford is a house with two date-stones. In the top right-hand corner of the south front a triangular stone is set in the wall with the date 1640 and the initials A.K. for Alexander Keir. He was a wealthy merchant, owning several acres of arable land in the parish, a stentmaster in 1638, an elder of the Kirk in 1642, and almost certainly a baillie. His bevelled table-tombstone stands by the south wall of the Wester Church. It shows that he died in 1667, and his initials and the word MERCHANDE are just legible. Alexander Keir's wife was Beatrix Bissie or Bisset. Their son Andrew, town treasurer in 1663, had a daughter Merrin who married the wealthy merchant Robert Lyall, owner of 'severall tenements and ackers of land in and about Anstruther Wester', and in Pittenweem, Carnbee, Pitairthy and Kingsbarns. He and the Laird of Wester Grangemuir were by several pounds the highest taxpayers in 1695.

The second datestone is in the architrave of the door and bears the initials H B L and the date (1)702. The third storey with the

Keir datestone and the new dignified door-piece were probably added in that year. The initials are for Harie or Henry Beattie and his wife Beatrix Lyall, only daughter and eldest child of Robert Lyall and Merrin Keir and great-granddaughter of Alexander Keir, the builder of the original house. Beatrix Lyall and Henry Beattie, shipmaster and merchant and proprietor of several acres of land in the parish, had nine children between 1687 and 1705, seven sons and two daughters. The two grandfathers, Henry Beattie, senior, and Robert Lyall, both Elders, were usually witnesses at the babies' baptisms and on four occasions Captain William Anstruther, shipmaster in Anstruther Easter, was a witness. On two occasions Henry Beattie 'was absent at sea at the time of the baptism'. There were seven children in the family in 1702 — 'marriage lintels' or datestones give the date of the first house built, or rebuilt, by a married couple.

In 1713 Henry bought from Robert Beattie, shipmaster, possibly his son who was then aged twenty-four years, 'a just and equal half of the good ship named the *Unity of Anstruther Wester*, which had been bought and fitted out at Gothenburg under the name *Eumphrau Hendrika* by an Edinburgh merchant. The other 'just and equal half with the other equal half of her whole sails, masts, oars, tows, cables, anchors, float boats, ornaments and apparalleling as she presently lyes in the harbour of Anstruther Wester', he sold to Sir John Anstruther. Two previous voyages of Robert Beattie, 'master under God of the good ship *Unity of Anstruther*' were to Stockholm, Bremen and 'Norroway'. His death was recorded in the parish register in December 1717 and already in that year affairs seem to have gone badly wrong for Henry Beattie, shipmaster and late baillie, and his son, Henry Beattie, mariner, then about twenty-five years of age.

Seafaring was a hazardous business in those days. Early in 1701 Henry Beattie, senior, collected at the church £16 Scots for Andrew Simpson, skipper in Dysart and his company, 'slaves in Algiers'. The Beatties probably lost a ship and all its merchandise: in July 1717 Henry Beattie sold to two baillies 'ane copper cauldron weighing 3 stone 13 pounds 12 ounces . . . amounting to £3 15s scots which he gives in parte payment of a greater some which he owes to ye session'. Six months previously he had been required by the minister to pay a sum of £24 11s Scots and he owed a widow in Elie £38 7s 6d Scots, probably for merchandise. Five years later the minister of the Kirk put £7 16s Scots into the church box 'from pewter plates bought by him at the Roup of Henry Beattie's household furniture' in part payment of 'Henry Beattie younger his bill to the session'. Rents due to the shipmaster were uplifted to pay off the debts owed by himself and his son. There was £30 Scots as one year's rent of a house 'belonging to Henrie Beattie near the West Port'; £50 Scots due from a merchant of the town as rent 'for ane house and cellars of a pairt of another tenement' belonging to Beattie; a widow owed him eight shillings of bear as the rent for two acres of his land 'with 8 hens or ffourtie eight shillings as the rent thereof for the year'; and another landlabourer owed Beattie '18 Bolls Bear and 16 Hens or six shillings for Ilk Hens', as the rent of four acres of land near the burgh.

Both father and son received generous poor relief from Wood's Mortification, administered by the Kirk Session. Henry Beattie, senior, had also a Sea Box pension, out of which in 1727 he repaid £8 that he had borrowed from the Kirk Box; the following year he was made a pensioner of the Kirk. It seems that in 1723 in spite of their misfortunes Henry Beattie, elder and younger, were members of the Town Council. Henry Beattie died before 1731 and nothing further is recorded of his son.

East of the house by the ford stands a late seventeenth century house of three storeys known as the *Buckie Hoose*. Robert Louis Stevenson (1850-1894) visited the 'triple town' as he called it, as a young boy and again in 1868 when his father was engineer of the Union Harbour. He remembered in later life the 'celebrated Shell House [that] stood outpost on the west', with snatches of verse and elaborate patterns in pebbles, 'artfully contrasted and conjoined', on the outer walls as high as the roof and he liked to think of the eccentric designer 'standing back upon the bridge, when all was finished, drinking in the general effect'. Stevenson in his memory seems to have fused two houses into one. The house still retaining vestiges of shell patterns right up to the roof is at the Easter end of the bridge from where it can easily be admired, but it was the *Buckie House*, not so visible from the bridge, which had the snatches of verse. On the door on a 'bulls-eye advertisement' as Gourlay described it, were the words:

Here is the famous grotto room,
The like's not seen in any toon;
Those that do it wish to see,
It's only threepence asked as fee.

The 'grotto room' was lined with shells and contained a shell-covered coffin in which Alexander Batchelor, slater and joiner, would lie for a further fee of one penny, and in which he was probably buried when he died in April 1866.

At a Council meeting in November 1930, the tercentenary year of the building of the bridge, the advisability of spanning the Dreel higher up to relieve the traffic round the *Buckie House* corner was considered. Plans for a new structure were completed the following year but had to be abandoned because of the economic slump. Six years later a new scheme was proposed costing £16,000, but war was already on the horizon and again the plans were shelved. A road improvement scheme was devised after the war necessitating the demolition of the decorative but decaying house but the late Capt. Russell, RN, of Gillingshill, and T. A. Henderson, the town clerk, thought that it was worthy of preservation and that its removal would only increase the speed of traffic and make the street more dangerous. The Anstruther Town Council bought the house and sold it to the National Trust for Scotland who restored it and the smaller eighteenth-century house next door. Both houses were bought in 1971 and the ground floor of the smaller house became the *Buckie House Gallery* in which the late Derek Thirkell exhibited and sold his own and other artists' work until his early death in 1984.

These were all substantial houses. The simplicity of ordinary houses in the burgh can be gauged from the number left to become ruinous by departing owners. An Act of Parliament of Charles II in Edinburgh 1663 'anent ruinous houses in Royall Burghs' empowered magistrates to sell by public roup any deserted and ruinous house after the owners had been warned, at the Parish Church and Market Cross of Anstruther Wester and at the Cross at Edinburgh 'and peer and Shore of Leith' [for those living abroad], 'to caus build and repair in an Decent way within year and day' the ruinous house belonging to them. In July 1710 Letters were raised against William Lugton, mariner in Holland, son of the deceased William Lugton and Grizel Darsie, daughter or granddaughter of William Darsie, shipmaster. As the old walls, timber and stones on the north side of the High Street near the cross were not claimed, the magistrates sold them at public roup in December 1712, after it had been valued by two reputable inhabitants. A new house was to be 'builded within year and day'.

A 'ruinous house and old walls with the yaird at the back which belonged to Mr Robert Dury, Minister at Anstruther Wester' was disposed of in April 1715. Robert Durie (1555-1616), son of John Durie, a minister at Edinburgh, was one of two of the Rev. James Melville's 'speciall daylie frinds and companiones' when Melville was professor of Hebrew and Oriental languages at St Andrews University (1580-1586). In May 1583 James Melville married Elizabeth Durie, his friend's sister.

It was with this friend that James Melville endured that 'maist wearisome sair day' on his way home from Berwick in September 1586 with his infant son Ephraim and an English nurse. They took the ferry from North Berwick, a large coal-boat 'wherein ther was bot a auld man and twa young boyes, we haiffing twa horses, a boy [and] the nurise'. A light breeze carried them a third of the way across the Firth 'then it fell doun dead calme'. First the nurse, then the baby, and after three hours Melville himself, 'becam dead seik'. As the old man was 'dammist and machles' [benumbed and feeble] Robert Durie had to manage the heavy boat, with oars that were neither 'meit nor handes'. At last at sunset, carried by a haar from the east, they arrived 'within the Aylie [Elie harbour] quhilk was strange to our consideration, na wind blawing'.

In 1588, two years after his arrival in the parish of Anstruther Wester, Melville granted Robert Durie sole charge of the parish which Melville disjoined from the four under his care. Durie accompanied as their minister the five or six hundred 'waiged men' on the 1598 attempt to colonise Lewis. He was one of the Synod of Fife's 'maist grave, godlie, and discreit breithring' but he attended an illegal General Assembly in Aberdeen in 1605 and was tried for treason and banished the following year. He became minister of the Scots Kirk at Leyden where he died in 1616. His ruinous house, subsequently belonging to the Rev. John Dury, probably his son, stood to the south of the High Street.

Ruinous houses were rebuilt in the eighteenth century as two-storey houses with an outside stair, which made construction easier and saved space inside. David Melville, schoolmaster, left the burgh sometime before 1710 and his ruinous house 'with the burn on the north' was sold under the 1663 Act and rebuilt by Thomas Oliphant, wright, in 1724:

[it] now stands floored . . . the storry above the Cellars divided in rooms with plastered partions Bound Doors sash windows with

shutters and oyr [other] windows presses and other conveniences glass smith and mason work with new chimneys and furnishing the same as it stands Thomas Oliphant wright estimate:— Timber, mason and smith and Glazier work included £309 2s 4d [scotts] ffor mason work £18 scotts.

A long list of expenditure follows including 'item two sash windows is £20; item to fourty 8 Lozars of Glass at four shillings six pennys per Lozen is £10 16s'. 'Carradge of stones and sand' was 'one pd sixteen sh scotts'.

Three more ruinous houses were rouped in the next two years. It is difficult to place two of them — one was the property of the minister and the Kirk Session — but it is plain that they were among a jumble of houses; there was little of the present day regularity about the burgh. The third house can be identified.

Letters were raised in July 1710 against 'James Lundie, baxter in Pittenweem and Robert Bruce elder and younger, weavers in Anstruther Wester, heirs of the deceased William Lundie elder and William Lundie younger late Baillie in Anstruther Wester'. This William Lundie, also baxter, was one of the highest tax-payers in the 1695 Tax Roll at £2 16s Scots. The ruinous house with the yaird, oven and bake house, was bought at public roup in February 1718 by Alexander Lundie, baxter burgess, son of James Lundie, baxter burgess of Pittenweem, for £69 Scots. The 'common street' lay to the north and the minister's manse on the west. The house, 'single-storey; harl and pantile; dormered and gabled attic; moulded doorpiece dated 1718' is No. 3, Esplanade. The initials on the fine doorpiece are J L and S W: James [Alexander in the Court Book] Lundie and his wife Sophia Walker. Two years after buying the house Lundie was obliged to declare:

> I being imprisoned Incarcerat [for debt] within the tolbooth of Edinburgh at the instance of Agnes Scott . . . and that thereby I am incapacitat of manadgeing my necessary affairs and business which may be in hazard of Ruin unless the same be speedily taken care of and I having entire confidence in Sophia Walker my beloved spouse for manadgeing of my affairs . . . appoint her my sole and only ffactrix to procure a Disposition to me for the Magistrates to the tenement which belonged to my predecessors.

Commissioners from Crail and Pittenweem reported to the Convention in 1717 that there were many ruinous houses on the

A 1930s photograph of Waid Academy, founded in 1886.

streets and in all parts of the town 'and many houses not in-habited And as to the Inhabitants they are very mean and little or no trafique [trade] used by them'. The rebuilding of old houses in the burgh, however, provides evidence of a growing prosperity, even if in some cases it was of a fleeting nature.

One of Anstruther Wester's most attractive houses is another eighteenth-century restoration of a much earlier house. Sir Harry Erskine in December 1760 bought from William Darsie, son of the deceased William Darsie, coupar burgess, 'that dwelling house fronting the Harbour of Anstruther Wester'. It was already an old house and may have been the home of the wealthy William Darsie, merchant and sea captain of a hundred and fifty years earlier.

Sir Harry Erskine replaced this partial ruin with the *White House* with its crowstepped end-gables and the Dutch-type centre gable, interior Dutch tiles, Memel panelling and Adam fireplace. The house was sold by his son and was subsequently bought by a shipmaster and by a master in the Royal Navy. John Smith, writer, owned the house, and George Peebles, tailor, whose daughter put the house to sale by public roup in January 1909, describing it as a desirable property, 'a seaside house for artists with ample room in the garden for a studio'. After a second roup it was bought by Henry Watson, solicitor in Anstruther Easter, who in the next few years bought the adjacent properties which, apart from one subsequently sold, now make up the present house. The 'cellars' of the two houses facing the sea had been let for storage, one for many years to John Thomson Darsie, fish-curer, of 11 Esplanade.

The house was bought by Louisa Murray, cousin-by-marriage of Henry Watson and daughter of William Murray, who in his twenties went with his brother David to set up a drapery business in Australia. She was a fine water colourist, an expert swimmer, and, in the tradition of those energetic Victorian women who were not constrained by convention and cumbrous attire, she climbed some of Switzerland's highest peaks and was one of the first to take up ski-ing. Louisa Murray died in 1962 in her ninety-fourth year and the *White House* was bought by the National Trust for Scotland, who in 1965 sold it, with a Deed of Conditions for the preservation of the historic house, to a restoring purchaser. Dr Ian Mackintosh, one of the pioneers in Fife in the micro-electronics industry.

Almost opposite the *White House* is a two-storeyed, harled, pantiled and crowstepped building with an inset carved panel. With its small windows, thick walls and floor below the level of the street, it is evidently a seventeenth-century house. In Gourlay's day it still had an external 'antique stair'. The carved panel of a wheatsheaf might indicate that it was once an inn, for which it was conveniently situated at the busy junction of High Street and harbour. (An innkeeper, George Luke, lived there at the beginning of the nineteenth century.) It was the home of Baillie William Thomson, a member of a family of maltmen and brewers who served as councillors and baillies, his father Peter still serving as chief magistrate at the time of his death in 1760. It was probably in this house that the Town Council had to meet in 1741 'when a prisoner was in the Tolbooth where they usually sit'.

William Thomson, eldest son of the chief magistrate, began his career as a mariner but by 1766 he had joined the customs service in which he served for twenty-seven years as landwaiter and surveyor of customs at the port of Anstruther. In 1750 he was elected town councillor and baillie and was chief magistrate of Anstruther Wester for thirty-nine years. At his death in 1794 he left the considerable sum of £1,000 sterling; as a revenue officer in the heyday of smuggling he would have had a share of the value of all seizures of smuggled goods in which he had taken part, so he must have been a successful officer — and a careful investor.

He left £100 to the town for poor householders, the interest of which was distributed each December. Another £100 was left for the schoolmaster in addition to his usual salary; from January 1902 the endowment was paid to Waid Academy. After the decease of two legatees, his brother-in-law, John Reid, ship-master, and his nephew, Peter Davidson, schoolmaster in Dundee, the interest of £700 and the rent of his acres were to endow a bursar at the United College of St Andrews. The Town Council was bound to prefer a native of the parish of Anstruther Wester and the name of Thomson was to be preferred, and failing any of that name the name of Reid. In a list of bursars between 1837 and 1898 seven were from Anstruther Wester, two from Anstruther Easter, and nine from outwith the parish. Only one student was a Thomson and he lived in Dundee. One of the first bursars was John Goodsir, the anatomist, and the other bursar from Anstruther Easter was Andrew Gourlay, son of the book-binder in Tolbooth Wynd and brother of George the local historian, presumably the myopic Mr Gourlay who set up a school in West Forth Street.

The bursars from Anstruther Wester were Archibald Goldie (Goldies were merchants, brewers and blacksmiths in the town since at least 1748); John Budge, son of James Budge, a wright employing two men; William Wood, son of William Wood, gardener; Thomas Wilson, son of Andrew Wilson, joiner and later baillie and chief magistrate, and Henry Chalmers Cargill and Thomas Sherret Cargill, sons of John Cargill, fisheries superinten-dent for the firm of Joseph Johnston and Sons. Both brothers attended Waid Academy, where they distinguished themselves in athletics. Henry was ordained in 1905 but resigned his charge and status in 1921, a year after becoming provost of Brechin. Thomas was ordained to Old Machar in Aberdeenshire in 1903 and assisted in 1915 at the marriage at Brechin of his sister, Christian Gordon Cargill, to the Rev. James Paterson who was ordained to the charge of Anstruther Wester in 1908.

The remaining £100 was left to the 'Good Town of Anstruther Wester . . . to be employed for the Utility of the said Burgh', on condition that his grave stone and that of his sister Barbary

Thomson should be kept in constant repair, the letters cut and renewed from time to time so that they 'always remain legiable', and the stone painted over 'with lint seed oil and white paint every fifth year'. The fine lettering is still clearly 'legiable'.

8
The New Burgh

Anstruther Wester began to assume its present appearance at the beginning of the nineteenth century when the main street was widened. Several houses were removed and others rebuilt to a more regular plan.

Fernbank in the High Street was originally four separate tenements, the grandest of them 'an Great Lodgeing' with a 'Dove Coat' in the yaird. It belonged in 1643 to John Borthwick of Bightie, of a family who from the mid-fifteenth century to the late seventeenth owned the nearby estates of Balhouffie, Lingo and Easter Grangemuir. Among the old tombstones in the Wester churchyard listed by George Gourlay was one commemorating the death in 1599 of the wife of Peter Borthwick of Lingo and Grangemuir, and another in 1627 of Catherine Borthwick, wife of Mr John Darsie. The *Great Lodgeing* was probably the family's town house. A Robert Borthwick inherited it in 1650 and in 1710 his grandson, 'one of the present Baillies of Pittenweem', sold it to George Duncan for 1,150 merks. In 1752 Lilias Shipard, widow of George Duncan of Newhall in Kingsbarns, gave title to the house to her son-in-law, George Dishington (sometimes Dischingtoun), wright in Kingsbarns.

He was almost certainly a descendant of William Dishington of Ardross whose mother Elizabeth was the sister of Robert Bruce. Among the title deeds of *Fernbank* are sasines dated 1530, 1548 and 1647 infefting in various properties several Dishington heirs, among them the grandson of Margaret Dishington or Hamilton, who was the great-great-grandmother of Robert Hamilton of Kilbrachmont, owner of the house by the ford. George Dishington bought his sister-in-law's half-share of the house in 1750 and within the next four years bought from Andrew Lundie of the family of baxters, two old properties 'all now built on and erected in one tenement', and from Robert Lyall an old property on the south 'commonly called the fore chamber' — that cottage at the foot of Crichton Street which in 1969 was rescued from complete ruin by the East Neuk Preservation Society and was beautifully renovated by a purchaser. Dishington then bought a seventeenth century property to the north which belonged to the family of the late Hendrie Lamonts, father and son, merchants and baillies of Anstruther Wester.

To the west of the Lamont property was a common vennell 'leading down to the fore chamber and piece of waste ground, called the Lone', presumably that passageway between the two parts of the present *Fernbank*. The properties that Dishington bought lay to the east of the Lone and there seems to have been no regularity about their disposition. The *Great Lodgeing* was on the High Street to the west of the vennell. Dishington was succeeded on his death in 1784 by his eldest son, George, also wright, who was probably responsible for the erection of the new houses. When the third George Dishington and his wife Ann Rodger inherited the property in 1842 it was described as 'now consisting of two tenements of land or Dwelling Houses of three storeys, fronting the street'. This George was the opponent of the Union Harbour Bill. When in financial difficulties he sold the two dwelling houses to his son-in-law, Captain John Keay, and continued to live in an apartment in the house until his death in 1885. A daughter or granddaughter as a little girl used to collect buckies for Alexander Batchelor of the *Buckie Hoose* and in return he put two rows of seashells across the front of *Fernbank* for her.

On the south edge of the churchyard stood a single-storey house described as 'those Cellars . . . lately occupied by the Minister of the Parish' — until 1703 when the heritors built a new manse across the road for the Rev. Andrew Burn. The old house was let for storage until 1836 when the heritors sold 'the Minister's Cellars' to John Lyall, merchant in Anstruther Wester, for £12 sterling. It was sold again in 1867 for £120 as a dwelling house of two storeys, now known as *Dolphin Cottage*. Across the street are the only two remaining outside stairs in the burgh. All the others in the High Street were removed in the latter half of the nineteenth century when the footpaths were relaid.

Some cottages between the *Buckie House* and the bridge were removed for the road widening and here in 1881 Alexander Watson of Pittenweem built the tenement block *Elizabeth Place*. There were soon problems of 'stagnant water at the north wall facing the Burn', of *fulzie* or sewerage having to be removed from the Dreel and of floodings of newly-installed latrines. In 1904 water and sinks were recommended but the tenants confounded

Elizabeth Place on the right. The last working corn mill on the Dreel was converted into flats in 1976.

the Council's best intentions: twenty-eight of them petitioned against the introduction of water because the houses were unsuitable and the expense would ultimately be borne by themselves. The Council insisted 'as very few houses are without water nowadays'. *Elizabeth Place* was thus defective in many ways from the start. By the 1960s there was talk of pulling down the 'substandard flats' but T. A. Henderson moved to retain the houses and they were bought by the Anstruther Town Council for £500. With a grant from the Scottish Development Department of £29,500, the lowest tender, the restoration was finished in 1968.

The Charter of 1587 described Anstruther Wester as having been recently greatly augmented 'and its bounds extended'. It is possible that the West Port once stood at the junction of the High Street and the path to the ford. The extended bounds of the Charter may have been from this Port to the West Port at the junction of the High Street, Crichton Street and the Loan from the Milnton. On the south side of these extended bounds there seem to have been gardens and only one substantial house, Crichton House, until the 1890s. It belonged for many years to the postmaster and owner of the *Royal Hotel* in Anstruther Easter, William Donaldson, who kept horses and carriages there for hire.

He renovated the house for his daughter in 1899. It was known as the 'house with stairs' which were on the Crichton Street side of the house and were removed at the next restoration in the 1920s.

For some years the three burghs had only one doctor, but in 1926, a year after graduating in medicine at Edinburgh University, a young doctor was persuaded by a chance meeting with a friend of his father to come and set up a second practice in the town, which he did with great success. Matthew Armour was born in Orkney, where his father and grandfather were ministers. He and his parents bought and restored Donaldson's house and converted it into both home and surgery. He was a popular and talented man: a regular exhibitor of the Royal Society of Water Colourists, an international authority on the breeding of budgerigars on which he wrote an authoritative work, a keen and skilled yachtsman, and he even took to the air in his homemade Flying Flea. He died in 1956 at the age of 56. 'No one admired and appreciated the sterling qualities of the fishing community more than he did', the *East Fife Observer* wrote in an obituary of 'this distinguished citizen'.

Another popular and talented general practitioner came to assist Dr Armour on a temporary basis in 1947 and remained in the practice until his retirement in 1977. Dr Alec Wattison, who died at Crichton House (the surgery is still on the ground floor) in March 1987 at the age of 74, was an active member of the Red Cross and honorary station medical adviser for the Anstruther lifeboat for twenty-five years and latterly chairman of the Anstruther R.N.L.I. He was a philatelist, geologist, botanist, lepidopterist, hill walker, keen golfer, great handyman in the surgery, and a superb photographer whose slide shows always attracted large audiences.

Several houses were built in the main street during the nineteenth century but the last to be built within the ancient burgh was No. 29 in 1973 on the south side of the street in a gap site between much older houses. Long before this, however, builders of new houses had moved beyond the bounds of the Auld Toon.

The 1832 map of the new parliamentary boundary shows a scatter of houses along the shore road between the old burgh and the West Haven, among them the recently erected school and schoolhouse at the east end and at the west end a dwelling house and farm steading built some years earlier by Archibald Johnston, younger, of Pittowie, on a tenement of land formerly belonging to the heirs of Robert Lyall. To the east of Johnston's property was *Chesterhill House*, built by Matthew Forster Conolly and his wife Catherine Murray in 1820, two years after their marriage. (The bay windows were added in 1894.) Nine years later he acquired and farmed the Chesterhill lands between the shore road and the road to Pittenweem. He was born in 1789 in Crail where his father ran the Golf Hotel and in 1786 was one of the eleven founding members of the Crail Golfing Society. Matthew was educated at the burgh school, where at the age of seven he met his future wife, the second daughter of the chief magistrate of Crail, and then at Kilrenny to acquire from the 'adept' John Orphat the 'court hand' in which Chancery documents were written. At the age of fifteen he was apprenticed to the town clerk of Pittenweem and four years later went to Edinburgh to an accountant who had by chance seen his handwriting and engaged him 'on account of its neatness and distinction'. His friend Thomas Landale said in a biographical sketch that Conolly's books *Eminent Men of Fife* and *Fifeana*, were written (in his seventies) 'in the most beautiful style of calligraphy'. A magnificent signature by Conolly in the burgh minutes was written when he was 79 years of age. Conolly was unanimously elected town clerk of Anstruther Easter in 1811 and after qualifying as a notary public in Edinburgh was elected town clerk of Anstruther Wester in 1812. According to Landale he never did business in taverns or alehouses as his predecessors often did, and he never advocated litigation in a court of law if it could be avoided.

Many young men finished their education in a writer's office. John Rodger Darsie, son of George Darsie, tanner and chief magistrate of Anstruther Easter, served an apprenticeship with Matthew Conolly in the 1830s before going into business in Liverpool, as did Stephen Williamson in the 1840s. Among Conolly's law apprentices was his future partner John Smith from Kilrenny, and David Cook from Pittenweem, the first of three generations of local solicitors. Lewis Russell, founder of the *East of Fife Record*, was apprenticed to David Cook in 1879, William Bonthron, fishcurer and auctioneer, in 1885, and W. W. Carstairs, businessman in Cellardyke, in 1903.

Conolly died at *Chesterhill* on December 11th 1877 in his 89th year, the oldest serving town clerk in Scotland and the last surviving Knight of the Beggar's Benison. His son-in-law, an Episcopalian like himself, gave a silver gilt communion flagon to

D

the West Anstruther Kirk in his memory. The Town Council minuted their appreciation of his great natural shrewdness, steady attention to business as long as his health permitted, his deep interest in burgh affairs, the kindness of his manner and the great trouble he took to the last in arranging and keeping up several useful charities. The *East of Fife Record* wrote that in disposition he was quiet and inoffensive, and all his actions were characterised 'by an eager desire to avoid giving the least offence to any one'.

In common with so many of that period he suffered grievous losses. His eldest daughter died of diphtheria at the age of four, his wife died at the early age of forty-five (though her mother lived to be 101) and his promising elder son Matthew died at the age of twenty-one. Daniel Conolly, the youngest child, was born in 1832, graduated at St Andrews University in 1848 and began his career as a cashier in the National Bank of Scotland in Anstruther Easter. In 1855 he was a banker in Elie but must have returned to Anstruther as from about 1860 his father's firm was known as Messrs Conollys and Jamieson. On the occasion of his marriage in February 1861 to Rachel Wilson he was described as 'late of the Hudson's Bay Company'. Latterly he lived in part of the Chesterhill farmhouse which had a dairy on the ground floor for many years and was beautifully restored as *Keel Rows* by Mr T. A. Murray in 1977.

The 1832 map shows only four buildings on the Pittenweem road beyond the old burgh, among them the blacksmiths' premises on the Smiddy Acre, one of which was still in use in the 1870s. On the south side of the road was Robert Brodie's smithy which remained a blacksmith's workshop until about 1930 when T. Clarke converted it into the present garage.

The new manse, built (not without problems) by the heritors in 1837 on two acres of land belonging to the Kirk Session, was the first large stone house to be built on the Pittenweem road. Fourteen years later the *Pittenweem Register* commented that it was curious that between Leven and Crail there was only one ticket to be seen 'with the cheering announcement written on it *Ground to Feu*' although there were many spots for building, including the road that connected Anstruther to Pittenweem 'which, if equalled, could not be surpassed anywhere'. A few months previously the little news-sheet had published the population return for the town of West Anstruther: number of

Dr Armour (left) and his brother-in-law Jimmie Brown in the 'Flying Flea' which they built in 1936. G. M. Cowie wrote that he never saw it fly 'but it did at least hop along the field'.

families 92; houses 55; males 167; females 198; total population 365, and added that the only improvement in West Anstruther which had come to its knowledge was the erection 'of a very neat range of miniature houses' in the garden of Alexander Batchelor 'for the accommodation of birds'. Large stone houses were shortly to follow.

The first was the present *Bass View* on the north side of the road built in 1856 by Robert Malcolm, wright in Kilrenny, on 'land called the Butts', that is land where archery was once practised. In March 1863 the house was bought at public roup by Andrew Graham from Anstruther Easter, hairdresser, stationer and eventually tanner, at the high price of £632, 'the best sold property that had ever been offered for sale'. It was bought from Graham in 1894 by Captain John Peattie. Little is known about him apart from the details of his career given by Captain Lubbock in *The Last of the Windjammers*. He was one of the 'passage makers' among the captains of the Shire Line windjammers and from 1885 to 1893 was in command of the *Sutherlandshire*, 'undoubtedly one of the fastest ships in the Shire Line'. He came from St Andrews and was a member of the West Anstruther School Board in 1911.

In 1862 the following advertisement was published by Messrs Conollys and Jamieson:

TO BE FEUED.

Part of the lands of CHESTERHILL, extending to 8 or 10 acres, lying not far from the projected Terminus of the East of Fife Railway, at Anstruther Wester, will be feued for Building Purposes, if suitable offers are made.

The first feu, to the east of the manse, was taken by David Stevenson Reid, factor of the Sea Box Society since 1856. His house *Clifton Villa* was completed in 1865 and was followed by *Mansfield* on the west in 1880 and *Chesterpark* on the east, in 1888. Two stone houses beyond Bankwell Road, not on Chesterhill feus, followed later, *Beaumont Lodge* for a widow from Elie in 1898, and *Orillia*, with its beautiful internal woodwork, in 1915 for Robert Boyter, cabinetmaker, and his wife Margaret Dishington. He bought the wood, and found the name, in Canada where he lived for several years. Before the restoration of Melville's Manse in Anstruther Easter in 1977 it was the manse for the minister of St Adrian's Church.

Captain James Thomson built the first of the double villas on the south side of the Pittenweem road in 1881, at the corner of Bankwell Road, and others were erected further to the east on Conolly's feus between 1896 and 1905. A stone villa for the stationmaster was built at the West Port by the North British Railway Company in 1903.

Only two other stone houses were built on the north side of the road. *High Cross*, the westmost house, was built by David Cook in the year 1870-71 and was named for the nearby high cross which once stood on the highest point of the road between Pittenweem and Anstruther. He lived in the house until 1874 but from the researches of the present owner, Mr Jack Robinson, it seems certain that David Cook built the house for his friend, Captain John Smith.

The son of Ann Young and John Smith, master of the Greenland ship called the *Baffin of Leith*, John Smith was born in 1824 in a house in East Green, now the *Tea Clipper* tea room. At an early age he went to sea with his father but began his professional career at the age of fourteen as boy on the *Jessie of Anstruther*. He obtained his master's certificate in January 1853 and three years later was admitted a member of the Anstruther Sea Box Society as master of the ship *Duke of Wellington* of Glasgow 'engaged in the Foreign Trade'. He made his reputation in Captain Rodger's tea clippers, making some of the fastest times between Foo Chou and London on ships like the *Min* and the *Lahloo*. After the loss of the *Lahloo* in the Sandalwood Straits in the East Indies in 1872, Captain Smith took command of the iron ship the *Maju* of which he was part owner. Dundee was to be his home port so he returned with his family to his native town with the intention, it seems, of occupying *High Cross*. A small room at the top of the house with an unobstructed view of the harbour was made to resemble a ship's cabin; lined with wood, it once had a bunk bed, a ship's stove, mahogany shelves and brass fittings.

The *Maju* left Dundee on her maiden voyage in October 1874 with a cargo of coals for Rangoon. Five days out she was caught in the great gale of Wednesday 21st October and foundered off Barvas on the west coast of Lewis with the loss of her captain and entire crew. Captain Lubbock wrote in *The China Clippers* that Smith was one of those tea-ship commanders 'whose endurance equalled their energy, whose daring was tempered by a good judgement, whose business capabilities were on a par with their seamanship, and whose nerves were of cast-iron'. He was one of those daring skippers 'who carried sail and was not afraid of a reef-studded passage'.

After the death of Captain Smith *High Cross* was bought by James Tosh, merchant and provost of Pittenweem, and it remained in his possession and that of his daughters, Martha Tosh or Oswald and Jessie Tosh, daughter-in-law of Captain Keay, until 1920. Often during these years the three houses, *High Cross*, *Clifton Villa*, and *Chesterpark* were owned or occupied or both by one or other member of the Tosh family. (A Miss Tosh was the first person in Anstruther to own a bicycle.) After the Second World War the house, then *Lyndean*, was bought by skipper Robert Gardner from Cellardyke, a descendant perhaps of the West Anstruther fisherman Martt Gairdner, as both names, Martin and Robert, have been used for generations in the Gardner fisher family.

Westerlea, formerly *Eversley*, between *Bass View* and *High Cross*, was built in 1904 by the Marrs, drapers and clothiers in Anstruther Easter.

The first new house in Shore Road was built in 1862 by James Henderson, salmon fisher, a two-storey tenement (number 24), which the following year accommodated his family and three other tenants. Next door Robert Ireland, farmer, built another for himself and four other tenants. *Lochiel Cottage* was built in about 1883 and in July 1895 a coastguard station for the officers who had been in rented accommodation in the High Street since 1874 was built for the Admiralty. It ceased to be a coastguard station about ninety years later. The substantial stone cottage opposite the school was built in 1864 and *Rosevale* next door in 1877 for J. A. Miller, the shipbuilder. The double villas at the west end of Shore Road were built between 1903 and 1907.

Between the Pittenweem and Shore Roads was a sawmill and below Brodie's smithy a coalyard, and in Bankwell Road below the manse was a market garden established by John Fraser Scott in the mid-eighties. The rest of the Chesterhill lands remained as pasture for a few more years and two dairies on the south side of Shore Road preserved the rural image until the Second World War.

A petition signed by nineteen residents was presented to the town's managers in 1864 requesting repairs and improvements to the Bankwell Road which were necessary 'on account of the increase of the Inhabitants, and of the new houses lately built, and in course of erection in the neighbourhood'. There was a good deal of traffic now upon the road, 'bread carts, fish carts, gigs and other vehicles; but it can scarcely be used in winter in its present impassable state'. The houses in course of erection were *Seabank*, begun in 1864 for a Mrs Mathieson, possibly the widow of Capt. Mathieson who was lost at sea early in 1863; the year before he was admitted a master and manager of the Sea Box Society, 'after five years' residence and in full command at present of the ship *Celestial Empire*'. The house was bought in 1879 by Alexander Paul Russell, son of Lewis Russell who in 1856 founded the *East of Fife Record* at his business of bookseller, stationer and printer at 25 Shore Street, Anstruther Easter.

The other two stone villas in the road were built in 1879-80, *Seafield* for Mrs Georgina Crawford or Key, widow of John Key of the brewery in Cunzie Street, and *Beachview* by Provost Andrew Wilson, joiner. It is now the home of Captain Robert Reekie who

Captain Robert Reekie of the Stag Line, for fourteen years the Line's Senior Master.

was born into a fishing family in St Monans in 1906. He began his career at the fishing and prepared himself for his Skipper Fishing Examination, which he passed in 1929, and took his examinations in foreign-going steamships, gaining his master's ticket in 1940, and a pilot's licence for the Great Lakes of North America in 1962. For thirty-one years he was in command of Stag Line vessels, including convoy duty during the war years, and was for fourteen years the line's senior master.

Thus, with the exception of *Chesterhill Cottage*, the manse and *Bass View*, and Conolly's house by the shore, all the stone villas in Anstruther Wester beyond the limits of the old burgh were built in the years between 1860 and 1914. None of them, apart from those built for Robert Ireland and Andrew Wilson, were built for West Anstruther families, but for incomers, several of them businessmen from the Easter burgh, and some were built as a source of income. The stone cottage at the east end of Shore Road was owned throughout this period, but not occupied, by the family of the original builder in Leven. The attraction of the area was probably not so much the absence of taxation, as Andrew Graham claimed at the meeting to discuss the Lindsay Act in

1876, but the healthy, spacious situation away from the narrow streets of the old burghs.

While the Chesterhill feus were being taken up, Alexander Watson built on the Smiddy Acre in 1874 that once notorious tenement of houses, *Watson Place*. Like his tenement by the bridge, named after his wife, it was for many years and for the same reasons a source of concern to the Town Council. The twenty-two houses gradually deteriorated and by the time of their centenary it was clear that they would have to be brought up to a 'tolerable standard'. It was acquired by a Dundee development company in the 1970s and seventeen new houses were planned. Work was begun in February 1981 but for various reasons was still unfinished two and a half years later. There were threatened compulsory purchase orders, appeals to the Secretary of State for Scotland, and public inquiries. Local dissatisfaction was intense but one great improvement was accomplished in 1985: the building was cleaned and a handsome honey-coloured stone revealed. Meantime the routine breaking of windows never ceased. Finally in the spring of 1987 *Watson Place* was finished, not six months as promised but six years after the work was begun, and a fine tenement of houses now graces the Pittenweem road.

One interesting property remains to be described. On the west bank of a spring or stream at the foot of the Bankwell Road once stood a malt barn, kiln and coble, and several cottages. In 1827 James Millar, shipowner, sold a yard there 'where there were formerly erected a number of small houses, now pulled down', and two cottages, one demolished, rebuilt, and again demolished, and the other owned until 1819 by William Millar, senior, ship-master. Between this little malt steading hamlet and the West Haven was the Dove Cot Yard in the western corner of which stood the dove cot, a rectangular stone building of slightly larger dimensions than the surviving contemporary dove cot in the garden of Melville's Manse. It was built in the seventeenth century and the hamlet must have been as old. The East Neuk Preservation Society began to raise funds for its restoration in 1969, 'doocots being part and parcel of our Fife landscape', but the building was found to be too dilapidated.

The old properties were bought in 1819 and 1827 by Captain James Black, RN, and by May 1828 'a large Dwelling House and offices' were erected on the site 'with gardens belonging to the same and all surrounded with a high wall'. James Black, born in

Anstruther Easter in 1775 in a house on the shore, attended the burgh school and was generally known as 'daring Jimmie'. He entered the Royal Navy at an early age, reaching the rank of lieutenant in 1799, and was wounded in the battle of Trafalgar on the *Mars*. Until a few years ago the ship's figurehead stood in a corner of the garden overlooking the sea. A subsequent *Mars* became a training ship for boys, a kind of reform school, and was anchored in the Tay off Wormit. In East Fife a familiar parental warning to recalcitrant children was that they would be sent to the *Mars* if they did not behave.

James Black was commissioned commander in 1810 and in 1813 as Captain of *HMS Weasel* was engaged in several running battles with the French fleet. He and his crew were commended for their gallantry, perseverance and steadiness, and later again he was commended 'for his zeal and his unwearied endeavours to forward the public service'. In 1815 Capt. Black was nominated a Companion of the Order of the Bath, and was decorated by the Austrian government, being created a Knight of the Imperial Order of Maria Theresa: his successful campaign against the French was fought in the Adriatic in what were then Austrian waters. He was admitted a burgess and freeman of Anstruther Wester in 1825 and died in December 1835 on his return to Anstruther in a smack from London to Leith. The writer of the Goodsir MS recollected his 'white hat surmounting a yellow mottled face, his blue coat and nankeen continuations'.

In his will Captain Black left his new house *Marsfield* to his elder brother, Rear Admiral William Black. He was born in Anstruther Easter in 1770 and like James was a pupil at the burgh school. He saw active service in the Royal Navy during the French revolutionary wars, took part in the expedition to Copenhagen in 1807 and two years later, as Captain Black, was in command of a sloop patrolling the coasts of South America. Altogether he served twenty-two years at sea and was appointed rear admiral on his retirement in 1846. He died at Ormsby in Norfolk in 1852, leaving £1,000 to the minister and Kirk Session of Anstruther Easter, the interest to be 'applied in relieving the wants of the poor', and a further £400 was to pay for the education of poor children in the parish. There is a memorial to his memory in St Adrian's Church. *Marsfield* was inherited in 1853 by the admiral's 'nearest and lawful heir', James Watterston of the family of shipmasters. The house was bought in about 1865 by William Thomson Jamieson, solicitor, bank agent and town clerk of Anstruther Wester. Agnes Jamieson, his last surviving daughter, sold the house in 1920 to Louisa Murray of the *White House* and she gave the property to the trustees of the Murray Library with the suggestion that it might be used for a golf house.

9
The Burgh to the Present Day

At the roup of the Common Good in 1759 a John Robertson, golf ball maker, was a cautioner. Neither his trade nor the game were mentioned again until July 1889 when at a meeting in the Wester Town Hall a golf course was proposed. Within a month five holes were cut at the west end of the Billowness for the short-lived East Fife Golf Club: 'a very pretty little course, delightfully sheltered, though limited'. On April 8th 1891 the Anstruther Golf Club was formally opened there by William Jamieson of *Marsfield* driving off with a handsome new cleek made by Mr Anderson at his factory in St Andrews Road. Upwards of sixty members were present.

To encourage the development of golf 'as an attraction to visitors and a boon to the public in general' the Town Council signed a lease with the Club in January 1896 for its use of the Billowness and the Commonty lands for thirty-five years at a yearly rent of £8. Additional land was, and still is, rented at the east end from the Sea Box Society, the Trades Poor Box Friendly Societies of Anstruther Easter, and some land from the Kirk Session traditionally, and suitably, called the Greens.

The Club endured various 'financial and other vicissitudes' and almost 'faded into obscurity', but in the early 1900s membership rose to nearly 200 and the course was 'not what might be termed first class but it was of a very sporting nature'. The Council took over and extended the course in the summer of 1914; the new holes were: 1. Hynd, 220 yards; 2. Old Tom, 360 yards; 3. Johnny Dow, 190 yards; 4. Fluke, 265 yards; 5. Cunighar, 170 yards; 6. Chain Road, 248 yards; 7. High Cross, 236 yards; 8. Bass View, 160 yards; 9. Marsfield, 220 yards. It was a 'decided improvement' on the old course. In 1919 the course was given back to the Club with donations of £45 from both Easter and Wester Town Councils. 'Fore!' the *Observer* called in July of that year, 'the grass in the field adjoining the Billowness Golf Course was cut last week and as many as 74 golf balls were found'.

The Club negotiated unsuccessfully for several years for land for an 18-hole course until 1934 when H. H. Edie of Cornceres at the other end of the town proved willing to sell land for the purpose. The professional golfer James Braid, no less, examined the site and thought that it would make a first-class course. In view of a substantial increase in rates, however, the Council decided to defer the project 'until a more favourable time'. Louisa Murray's offer of *Marsfield* as a clubhouse was accepted in 1923 and in 1945 the Club bought the house, the garden ground and the dove cot yard, now the car park, for £500. (The private part of the house was sold in 1953.) A burden in the deed of gift prohibiting alcohol and gambling on the premises was circumvented, legitimately, when a restaurant and bar extension were added in the spring of 1984.

The local interest in golf stimulated a new industry in the burgh. A golf-cleek factory was set up in 1913 by Robert Brodie, blacksmith, on the site of Matthew Conolly's two old cottages at the foot of Crichton Street. The foundation stone was laid on the last day of 1912 by the Rev. G. S. Anderson of Kilrenny, who said that anything done to promote honest labour should be encouraged 'as there was a very serious want of industry in the district'. Seventeen years later the factory was gutted by fire but David Ramsay of Kilrenny and Alex Birrell of Cellardyke, partners of Anstruther Golf Irons Ltd, were working there in 1964. Both were country blacksmiths 'who had turned their backs on the declining horse shoe trade to meet the insatiable demands of golfers through-out Britain' — and in America and Australia. It was one of the few establishments left 'where it was possible to watch golf irons being forged by hand', but only for about another ten years.

The burgh's main occupations in the past, apart from domestic service, were the local trades of cordiner [shoemaker], tailor, glover, baxter, flesher, maltmaker, brewer, wright, mason, plasterer, slater — and in 1750 a 'thicker of houses' — blacksmith and tinsmith. In 1752 James ffleeming, shoemaker, with the Council's permission, set down Tann pits on his property within the town. Fifty years later, along the Pittenweem Road near the Session's land, John Rodger, burgess, set up a 'Roperie' which was removed when the new manse was built, and later Alexander Burd, ropemaker, rented a piece of the town's common at the Milton Muir for a ropewalk. Pigot's Directory of 1837 mentioned a 'pretty extensive cart and plough industry', which was probably

John Brattesani's East Pier Bathing Station, opened on June 16th, 1928. The chimneys on the right belong to the gasworks in East Green.

on that plot in Crichton Street described as a sawmill and joiner's yard, and as late as the 1880s there was a coachbuilder in the burgh, but all had gone by 1912. Several industries had been thought of in the past, the Rev. Mr Anderson said in 1912, and nothing had come of them, but the game of golf would encourage the only industry the town had, that of 'visiting'.

Elie was already a popular summer resort by the 1850s, but further to the eastward, the *Pittenweem Register* remarked in 1851, was an unknown country to Edinburgh folk who, 'if they were made aware of the fact that comfortable and cheap lodgings could be had, would surely come and see what sort of place the extreme east coast of Fife is'. When folk did begin to come to the unknown country they came as often from Glasgow as from Edinburgh, and in the 1980s they still come, and many who were brought here as children in the summer now bring their own.

With Matthew Conolly's advertisement for the Chesterhill feus in 1862 was another headed 'SUMMER FURNISHED LODGINGS IN FIFESHIRE'. One of the attractions of his marine villa was that 'SEA-BATHING may be had at the Foot of the Garden'. Several inhabitants petitioned the Town Council in the summer of 1864 to remove boulders and large stones at different parts of the shore 'so as to improve and increase the facilities for bathing'. The Council and the Session each contributed towards the clearing of the West Hynd and the construction of a bulwark. Further improvements followed and the local paper reported in the summer of 1914 that the Hynd 'did look class and up to date' with its five new bathing boxes: 'Anstruther has suddenly sprung into fame as a watering-place.'

A Billowness Improvement Committee was appointed by the Council in 1922 to plan and raise funds for a pond to the west of Johnnie Doo's pulpit. It was opened in August 1927 at a cost of £400 and was nearly doubled in size in 1935. The money was raised by the inevitable bazaars and by a weekly crossword puzzle in the *East Fife Observer*, something new in those days. Another great fund-raiser was the school of dancing run by 'Tom Arlyn and Dainty Dot', a Mr and Mrs Drinkwater from Lancashire who up to and after the Second World War organised local concerts for all kinds of charity. Between 1950 and 1964 the newly-formed Anstruther Improvements Association raised £2,000 for the upkeep of the pool and its equipment, bathing huts and duck boards, a chute, and even an 'ocean wave', but in that latter year a violent storm destroyed the outer wall and the once popular bathing pond was reluctantly abandoned. A new sea wall and promenade was built at the Hynd in 1933, and it is still a popular beach on sunny summer days, for those who come with their windbreaks.

The 'EAST OF FIFE RAILWAY', Conolly advertised in 1862, was about to reach Anstruther. As early as 1841 the Town Council gave £3 to a preliminary survey of a railway line through Fife but not until August 1861 was a line to Anstruther Wester begun. The Leven and East of Fife Railway's single track with passing loops was opened on September 1st 1863. Work on the extension had started fourteen months before, the local paper complained, no great engineering had been required and work had not been held up by bad weather, but for some reason the greatest railway contractor in the country [Sir Thomas Bouch] had been unable to complete a short line of little more than six miles. 'If this be the celerity and "railway speed" the public have in prospect for their accommodation', the paper continued, 'the old slow-coach state of matters would be almost preferable'. There were over eighty passengers for the first train in the morning, the great majority of whom were half dealsmen on their way home from the fishing.

Anstruther railway station, looking west, built in 1887 and closed in September 1965. It is now the site of an industrial estate.

The ride was very comfortable, the paper reported, and the scenery delightful, apart from the dull stretch of the Lundin Links.

Plans for the new Union Harbour were then being considered and it was suggested that the west breakwater should be converted to a pier to connect the harbour and the station and cut out cartage. The railway company sent an engineer in February 1868 to make a survey and another in 1911 when a new deepwater harbour scheme was proposed. The engineer explained that:

> In order to ensure easy gradients and curves for express fish trains . . . a short branch railway should be constructed, leaving the present main line about Milton Muir farm, pass under the Pittenweem-Anstruther road near *High Cross* and thence debouch on the shore at *Marsfield House*, and extend along the same towards old West Anstruther Pier . . . From the House suitable siding accommodation could be laid down as indicated . . . which if required, could be carried along Shore Street as far as the present Middle Pier.

That was one failed plan that nobody can now regret.

It was proposed in August 1880 to link Anstruther Wester with St Andrews. A bridge was built broad enough to carry the line and a road over the Dreel, and Anstruther Wester's original terminus became a new goods station. Passenger traffic was opened as far as Boarhills on Saturday September 2nd 1883. In 1904 there were five hundred visitors at Anstruther station, more than three hundred of them from Glasgow, and a coast express was inaugurated from Glasgow to Crail in 1910. The coast railway's great drawback was that all the stations were on the edge of or beyond the burghs. Bus services which came right into the burghs provided a more convenient service after the First World War, and with the decline of the fishing and the increase in the number of private cars after the Second, the number of passengers steadily declined. The last passenger train left Anstruther on September 9th 1965 to a 'memorable send-off' and the booking-office ran out of tickets. Provost James Braid of St Monans thought it would be suicidal for a coastline of holiday resorts 'and a development area crying out for industry' to be deprived of a railway service, but he did not think it would be the last passenger train. With little waste of time, however, the rails were lifted and the track that could have become a coastal way for walkers and cyclists rapidly disappeared back into the farming landscape.

At the beginning of July 1914 the local newspaper was congratulating Anstruther on its fame as a watering-place; at the end of the month the portents for the country 'were of a most gloomy description'. The Firth was closed to all traffic and reservists and Territorials were immediately mobilised, almost the full local strength reporting at once for duty, and within ten days they had left for the front. Before the end of the month West Anstruther with a population of only 500 contributed £50 from its Common Good to the War Fund and subscribed within two days 'no less than the sum of £52 4s 8d'. There were lighting and travelling restrictions and at times despondency, but the burghs busied themselves with parties to clean and pack sphagnum moss for use in surgical bandages, whist drives, bazaars and concerts to raise money for comforts, for Belgian refugees and then for the armed forces. Within a year or two there were food shortages, then rationing and eventually ration cards, and by the end of the war 'the Queue system' had become part of life. And throughout the four years of fighting came the dreaded telegrams from the War Office.

The annual Armistice Day Parade passes Waid Academy on the way to the cemetery.

One of the first was to Mrs Tosh of *Mansfield*, widow of James Tosh of Thirdpart. Her only son, William, emigrated to Australia before the war to take up sheep-farming but joined up as soon as war was declared and was killed in action at the Dardanelles in September 1915. A month later Thomas Pringle in Pittenweem Road learned of the death of his son, William Fortune Pringle, aged 22, killed in action in France. A year later Stephen Drummond, joiner in Shore Road and a former chief magistrate, received the news of the death of his son, Tom Drummond, killed in action in France. He was 20 years of age, 'well-known in the district and a promising young fellow'.

Church bells were rung, flags hung out and a thanksgiving service arranged in Anstruther Easter Town Hall at the news of the Armistice on November 11th 1918. About a dozen meetings were then held to discuss a War Memorial but the public was apathetic in the whole matter, the *Observer* thought: 'Anstruther people do not turn out for public meetings'. The two Anstruthers finally agreed to the erection of a joint memorial on the Billowness and Sunday 22nd November 1921 was appointed for the unveiling and dedication.

'A finer day [for the ceremony] could not have been desired'. After a service at the Easter Town Hall the ex-servicemen under Lieut. Col. T. D. Murray, all the local associations, and representatives of the three Town Councils and parish churches, marched across to the Billowness, where an estimated 2,000 people from all parts of East Fife were gathered. The memorial, in the form of a Scottish baronial tower, was designed by the architect C. F. Anderson in St Andrews and built by James P. Thomson of St Monans. The three panels were carved by John Y. Thomson, sculptor in Leven, and the total cost was about £500. There are twenty-four names on the Anstruther Wester panel, all but one of whom served in the army, twelve of them in the Black Watch. The Anstruther Easter panel contains the name of one woman, Elizabeth Johnstone, and twenty-four men of whom four served in the Royal Navy. Wreaths were placed around the foot of the memorial and Major Maxwell, town clerk of Anstruther Easter, read out the names of the dead, and Sir Ralph Anstruther gave the address.

Saturday July 19th 1919 was set aside by Royal Proclamation as a public holiday for the celebration of peace. All inhabitants were asked to decorate their houses, and flags were flown from the church steeple and Waid Academy's tower. Drifters in the harbour flew their flags at half-mast in tribute to the men who had not returned, but later in the day all flags were fully hoisted. The celebrations were held in Waid Academy Park and a fancy dress parade undertook a circumambulation of the three burghs from the railway bridge to Tolbooth Wynd in Cellardyke and back to the Waid Park. Every child was given a new 1918 penny and the day ended with a magnificent beacon on Kellie Law. There were to have been fireworks and a bonfire at 11 p.m. at the Billowness but the fireworks failed to arrive on time because of a railway strike, and spectators arriving at the advertised time missed the bonfire as it had been set ablaze early 'by some over-impatient youths'.

'A fit country for heroes to live in' was the promise of Lloyd George's campaign in the General Election of 1918. Housing for working men was notoriously inadequate in industrial cities and in the small town of Anstruther it was not unusual for an entire family to occupy one room. The houses of wealthier burgesses too must have been seriously overcrowded. Few of West Anstruther's houses were large but they accommodated above the 'cellars' not

Seventeenth-century crowstepped gables and pantiled roofs. The tower on the Billowness golf course in the distance is the War Memorial erected by Anstruther Easter and Wester in 1921.

only the baxter, the brewer or the wright and his wife and several children, but also a servant and an apprentice or two.

The Addison Housing Act of 1919 obliged local authorities to build houses for working men, the government reimbursing them for all expenditure exceeding their income from a penny rate. The local Council was against the scheme. According to Provost Porter the working people of the burgh did not require new houses: what they had in mind were houses that could be let in summer. Persuaded by the town clerk, however, the Council acquired land and agreed to borrow £13,500 for a housing scheme in Bankwell Road, and the houses were ready in 1923. The Shore Road scheme was completed in 1928 but because of increasing financial difficulties government subsidies were gradually withdrawn and ceased altogether in 1930. Other schemes followed after the Second World War: the Milton on former town lands in the 1960s; the Gardner by Shore Road in 1974; Dreelside on the site of the old goods station and in 1985 the small scheme further to the west named, appropriately, Muirfield. Privately built bungalows along the Pittenweem Road were followed in the '60s by the houses of St Adrian's Place, and all the gap sites in the burgh's new suburb were thus variously filled.

A new business, with permission from the Dean of Guild Court, was opened in 1927. Thomas Gardner of the Cellardyke fishing family started a bus service between Newport and Leven with his father in 1924. Their first buses were open vehicles along one side of which were small doors, one to each row of seats. Their new bus station was built on Trades Poor Box land between *High Cross* and Thomas Gardner's own house, *Westerlea*, which is still the home of his widow, former councillor Mrs Agnes Gardner.

Mrs Gardner, the daughter of a Blairgowrie town councillor, served a five-year apprenticeship in the town clerk's office there before coming to Anstruther in 1940 for further professional experience. It was at the Council table that Agnes Conacher met the widower councillor Tom Gardner and three years later they were married. Mrs Gardner was elected to the Anstruther Town Council in 1956 and two years later to the County Council, on which she served for sixteen years. In 1975 she was awarded the M.B.E. She continued to represent the locality on the North East Fife District Council until 1988, always as an Independent candidate. Housing was her main interest and she helped promote the restoration of *Watson Place* and the *Harbourlea* sheltered housing scheme in East Green (and chose the name). Tom Gardner died in 1973 and when the housing estate behind Shore Road was finished in the spring of 1974 it was named Gardner Avenue in his memory. His motor service amalgamated in 1931 with the General Motor Carrying Company which was bought a few years later by W. Alexander & Son Ltd. The bus station closed down in the late '70s and is now the Region's depot for gritting lorries.

Another new business was set up in the burgh in 1934 on the site of John Forrester's sawmill and joinery yard in Crichton Street: the *Regal* cinema, built for Sidney Fuller, later of *Rosevale*. It was formally opened on July 19th by Provost W. W. Carstairs. The whole erection from start to finish was indeed 'regal', the *Observer* enthused; with 100,000 bricks it had taken ten weeks to build 'from bare earth to completion'. It was designed and built by Cowiesons Ltd, St Rollox, Glasgow, 'and was the last word in comfort, beauty of design and colouring'. There were two projectors, and the sound apparatus was by the world-famous Bauer Ltd, London. When the building was being demolished the

One of Tom Gardner's buses in Shore Street in the 1920s. To the left of the Market Cross is Stephen Williamson's Memorial Fountain erected in 1905.

last manager, Lindsay Berwick, who had attended the opening as a child from Arncroach, salvaged one of the projectors and it is now in a Stuttgart museum. The first programme was *Footlight Parade* starring James Cagney. After the war a local consortium ran the cinema until 1972 when filmgoing succumbed to television. The cinema was demolished in 1978 and on the site, now named Regal Court, five two-storey houses were built.

In 1947 a young man arrived in Anstruther with an ambition to open an hotel. 'Eddie' Clarke was born and brought up in Kirkcaldy and after serving three and a half years of his five-year apprenticeship as a joiner, he was called up as a member of the Territorial Army at the beginning of the war and was trained in the Catering and Quartermaster Corps. He served in North Africa in the Royal Corps of Signals, 51st Highland Division, and was awarded the Military Medal. He left the army as a sergeant with a determination to run a business of his own (a youthful ambition had been to become a professional cyclist), but first he completed his apprenticeship. He eventually bought a shop in Shore Street, Anstruther Easter, and took the lease of the shop next door when the lease expired in 1952. Having done all the joinery work himself, he re-opened it as a cafe which became the rendezvous of teenagers after a dizzy evening at the *Empire* cinema in Cunzie Street.

Eddie Clarke introduces his daughter, Eleanor, to the Queen at the Craw's Nest Hotel in July 1982. Also in the picture, with the Duke of Edinburgh, are his wife Gladys and his eldest daughter, Elsie Stewart.

The manse in Pittenweem Road, 'on a large scale in every respect', was put up for sale in 1961 and proved difficult to sell but the site and the size of the house and garden were ideal for Eddie Clarke's purpose and he bought it in 1963. He took the name of his hotel from the story of Charles II's visit to Anstruther early in 1651 when he was entertained 'att the Laird of Enster's house all night', and is reputed to have said, to the Laird's embarrassment, what a splendid meal he had gotten in a craw's nest. The hotel sign was designed by the late James Selbie, principal teacher of art at the Waid.

Members and their wives of Anstruther Rotary Club, of which Eddie Clarke was a founder member, were entertained at the opening ceremony of the *Craw's Nest Hotel* on Sunday May 19th 1965, and members and their wives of the Town Council on which he served as a councillor for six years. There was only one criticism, the local paper wrote: 'that the hotel was in Anstruther thus depriving the residents of an excuse for a holiday in it'. An extension was opened in 1970 (the roof of the manse can still be seen above it) and on the hotel's twentieth anniversary an extension in the grounds was opened, increasing the number of rooms to thirty-one, but sadly, Eddie Clarke had died in the January of the previous year at the age of 63. He endowed a prize in catering at the Glenrothes and Buckhaven Technical College and had himself won many awards for his hotel, but undoubtedly the high point of his career as a hotelier was in July 1982 when Mr and Mrs Clarke and their seven daughters and sons-in-law, who all take a part in running the hotel, entertained to lunch the Queen and Prince Philip during a royal visit to Fife.

The arrival of the railway in 1863 provided the impetus for the burgh's new tourist industry, and the opening of the *Craw's Nest Hotel* a hundred years later confirmed its success. Anstruther Wester now has a garage and grocery store, a hairdresser, and a peripatetic ice-cream van, but 'visiting' remains its only industry and golf its main recreation.

10

The Parish Church

In 1177 twenty-eight parish churches were recorded in the deanery of Fife and in the list of stipends that of Eynstrothir was 10 merks, Kilrathenie 26 merks and Abercrombie 6 merks. (Pittenweem was in the parish of Eynstrothir until it was erected into a separate parish in 1588.) The consecration of Eynstrothir's church to Nicholas, a saint of the Roman Church, on June 28th 1243 was probably a *re*-consecration. De Bernham, Bishop of St Andrews since 1238, was known for his 'abnormal activity' in consecrating churches on completion of their endowments and in 1243 he consecrated fourteen churches, among them 'Karal, Kilretheny and Eynstrother'. All that is known of its early years is that a Friar Haldane ministered in the church in the mid-fifteenth century; that in June 1503 James IV landed at Anstruther to say 'ane trentale of messes of Sanct Nicholas'; and that in June 1559 John Knox marched with a 'rascal multitude' and preached his 'idolatrous sermon' there and altars and images were pulled down.

The church was of the usual Roman pattern of sanctuary, choir and nave, but about this time the building or part of it was rebuilt, the sanctuary at the east end probably being removed to conform to a Protestant form of service. The choir survived for some years; there is a reference in 1628 to 'twa Kirk doors of ye quoir', and in the *First Statistical Account* the Rev. James Forrester wrote that the church appeared to be a very ancient building 'from the remains of a large choir'. By Forrester's time only the nave of the old pre-Reformation church must have remained. In February 1628 David Maisterton was to fill in the windows of the Kirk 'in glass and wyre in tyme heirefter' and the Kirk Session in 1751 arranged to have placed 'some panes of glass about the Kirk to keep out the swallows which abuse the church'. In 1775 Mr Dickson was paid £2 5s 'for glazing the Kirk windows'.

The original side aisles, the 'Kirk Ayles', separated from the nave by a row of pillars, required mending in the spring of 1756 and in October of that year it was reported that there was to be no

Anstruther Wester's pre-Reformation church (much altered over the years). On the left of the sixteenth-century tower is the Wester town hall built in 1794.

sermon, 'the wind having unroofed part of the Church'. The session clerk was to write to the heritors that the nave roof 'was intirlie rotten', that the windows in the 'high stories' [in the wall between the roof of the aisles and the roof of the nave] must be repaired and the south gallery made new. The heritors, who were responsible for the maintenance of the church, the manse and the school, were to meet with all convenient speed to discuss what was 'most fit to be done'.

By 1760 nothing had been done and a meeting of heritors and tradesmen was called in January to discuss the 'ruinous fabric of the Church'. Sir John Anstruther explained that no repairs had been made 'on account of the bad weather', and made a rather astonishing proposal to the presbytery for a scheme which suggests that the building was indeed so ruinous that it was hardly worth restoring as a parish church. He proposed to unite the two parishes of Anstruther Easter and Wester into one and make the Wester church into a collegiate church. The suggestion caused consternation in the burgh. George Robb, elder and town councillor, appealed to Sir Harry Erskine, their Member of Parliament 'and one of their number'. The Session appointed Thomas Oliphant and George Robb to procure as many heritors in the parish as possible to present a petition to the presbytery of St Andrews 'not to concur with Sir John in joyning the paroches', but in September the minutes record that 'nothing further was done on account there were so few members present'. The proposal was dropped and the church was 'new-roofed in 1761'.

There were several falls of plaster in the church in 1845 and the Session deemed it inadvisable 'and highly dangerous to have worship in the church, in case of anything occurring during Divine Service to cause a panic which may be followed by serious and probably fatal results'. By the following year the church had been 'entirely modernised' and reduced in size for the third time, to its present dimensions. Matthew Conolly's son-in-law, Dr Gordon, wrote a few years later that several then alive 'would remember the rows of fine arches left standing in this church, which is now a tasteless erection within and without'.

A General Assembly Hymnal was introduced in 1875, a choir formed within a few years, and in 1883 a fund started for an harmonium, to which there were no objections from the congregation though there were in many churches, and in January 1884 the ancient institution of precentor was abolished. One of the earliest was George Waid, to whom in 1630 the Session 'promest the somme of twentie marks yearlie for uptaking of ye psalm'. The schoolmaster was usually both precentor and session clerk. The first two 'harmoniumists', appointed in 1884 and '86, were women, the first in either the parish or the burgh to be appointed to an official, though minor, public position.

The Kirk Session of minister, deacons and elders (chosen from among the congregation and often the same men who served on the Town Council) managed the affairs of the church and parish. Their duties included visiting, the management of the finances and, what seems to have taken up a lot of their time, the moral discipline of the parishioners.

The commonest offence was 'evill conversation' or 'scandalous correspondence' [fornication]. In the seventeenth century the guilty woman, who could hardly deny the offence, was 'ordainit' to be put in the pillory 'and to stand therein from eight hours in the morning to twa hours efternone', and on Sunday to stand at the Kirk door in sackcloth 'bair futtit and bair legit'. Public repentance before the congregation on three consecutive Sundays superseded the warding and the sackcloth, and the few who refused to appear for public rebuke usually gave in as their children would not receive baptism until repentance had been made.

Punishment for the men varied. In 1628 an offender was 'ordainit to make his repentance in manner following viz. to stand at the Kirk door on Sonday in sac cloth and put himself on ye stool [of repentance] and crave god and ye congregation pardon and to pay ten lib' [pounds]. Inhabitants of some social standing, however, were spared the public humiliation. Euphane Williamson in 1628 'grantit that she was with bairne to Mr John Dairsie' (the 'Mr' denoting until the nineteenth century a man of property and status) and was ordained to go 'to ward [the pillory and then the church for public rebuke] on mononday nixt' and she was to abstain from 'the said mr Johne his house and companie in tyme theirefter'. His punishment was to make his repentance 'according to ye order and payit 6 lib'. There was no mention of sackcloth. William Dairsie, shipmaster, also guilty of scandalous carriage, was ordained to enter in the ward 'and continow therein day and night for ye sight of eight days' and to pay Janet Fogow's 'penance soume', but the Session then dispensed with William Dairsie 'anent his going to ye waird' and referred the amount of his penalty 'to his own Discretioun'. A few years later Norman Fairfull, another wealthy merchant of West Anstruther, did not appear in church to admit his guilt and his appearance was not insisted on, but two months later he sent to the Session through a neighbour 10 marks to be given to the poor. Until the mid-eighteenth century fines for fornication must have provided a steady income to the Session; and others stood to gain.

An Act of Charles II's first parliament decreed that 'every Inferior person is fineable for fornication in the sum of £10 Scots' one half to be disposed upon pious uses in the paroch where the offenders live or the offence has been committed and the other half to be divided into two equal parts one half to the Informer and prosecutor and out of the other half to satisfie the person who shall be imployed for bringing the person accused to Justice and the remainder to be disposed of to pious uses as the Judge shall think fit'. In March 1719 the town treasurer and procurator fiscal brought a case against a local servant girl who had been guilty with a soldier of a regiment of foot stationed in the burgh. She was instructed to pay the procurator the sum of £10 Scots 'and to remain in prison until the sum was paid'.

Servant girls were particularly susceptible to the sin of fornication either with fellow servants, with whom they unavoidably closely cohabited, or with their employers or his sons. The last case of 'scandalous correspondence' was brought to the notice of the Session in 1900. One reason that the Session was so concerned with the sins of the flesh was that illegitimate children might become a burden on the church's Poor Box, which was not solely for the poor but also covered day-to-day ecclesiastical expenses.

From about the middle of the eighteenth century a certain independence becomes evident among the parishioners in their making what came to be called 'Irregular Marriages'. The first recorded was in 1745 when Robert Rob, weaver and town treasurer, son of the first Baillie Alexander Rob and later to be chief magistrate himself, was married to the daughter of the late chirurgeon in Elie by the minister of the Episcopal church there. The couple were 'seriously exhorted suitably to their offence to acknowledge their sin in making such ane unbecoming and disorderly step'. They had to go through another marriage service in their own parish church and make their vows 'according to the sound and orthodox princll [principle] of this present established and Constitute Church'. It was equally reprehensible to marry elsewhere even in the Constitute Church. In 1776 it was decreed that all those guilty of 'irregular marriage' were to pay 10s to the poor.

In the evangelical atmosphere of the nineteenth century many guilty of fornication, including a few men, confessed their sin voluntarily to the Session, though a few others towards the end of the century betook themselves to North America rather than confess. The more common offence among the parishioners at this time, however, was 'ante-nuptial fornication' which was admitted by several otherwise respectable inhabitants. The couples were 'gravely rebuked and admonished', but no longer it seems before the congregation.

There were other offences for which the parishioners were called to account. Margaret Caddell was accused in 1628 of harbouring beggars 'and suffering them to ly togidder on the floor'. She denied it but was put on probation. This problem of vagrancy seems to have become particularly serious at the beginning of the eighteenth century. 'Servants and others that are presently come to reside in the Parish' were frequently reminded to bring in 'against the next session day' their certificates from the minister of their former parish: without a certificate they were liable to be considered vagabonds. The early years of the eighteenth century were difficult enough for the people of Anstruther Wester without the addition of other impoverished persons.

Witchcraft is never mentioned in the parish records although several women of the burgh were condemned and executed during the worst years of the persecutions, between 1590 and 1680, as appears in the records of St Andrews and the Synod of Fife:

> 17 July 1588: quhilk day comperit Agnes Melvill elder dochter to umquhill [the late] Andro Melvill elder sumtyme redar at the Kirk of Anstrothir . . . being delatit as ane suspect of witchcraft.

A few years later Agnes was referred to as a 'condamnit witch' which implies that she was executed. In 1613 Agnes Anstruther was indicted on suspicion of witchcraft and the following year she and Isobel Jhonestone were to be proceeded against. Several ministers were appointed in 1643 by the presbytery of St Andrews to go to Anstruther Wester to give their advice 'if the dilations against Isobell Dairsie' were sufficient for apprehending and trying her, and again two months later they were to go 'Friday nixt to give their advice how she salbe used in meate, drinke, sleepe, bed and the lyke'. In January of 1644 the ministers were to 'goe to Anster the morne, and attend the execution of Isbell Dairsie'. In May 1666 the trial was commissioned of Margaret Guthrie in Carnbee, 'prisoner in the tolbuith of Anstruther Wester suspected guilty of witchcraft', yet not a word appears in the parish records about either the trials or the fates of these unfortunate women.

Oddly, in these years of religious hysteria, one case is reported which sounds like an opportunity for the witch-hunters, but no referral was made to the presbytery. The minister and elders were convened on July 19th 1642 'for taking tryell anent the life and behaviour of Isabell Traill'. They all declared they knew her to be 'ane wicked and evil liver and a blasphemer of god's name and ane striker of their neighbours'. Finding that the said Isabell had already been sent out of the parish for the 'miscarriages in her lyff and conversation', the minister and elders did conclude that if the said Isabell be found hereafter troubling any person 'she shall *ipso facto* be banishit ye toun and parish perpetuallie and for ever'. A restrained punishment in the circumstances. Two years later Isabell Traill was still in the parish being reprimanded for 'fornications and absences on Sabbath and fighting and scalding'; the following year she was given 14s 6d from the Poor Box.

As the local witch-hunt was approaching its climax in Pittenweem, Anstruther Wester's parishioners seem to have been only too willing to run to the Session with tales of their neighbours' backslidings. David Toddie was cited in February 1700 to appear the next session day 'for making use of charms'; he had been seen casting up the ground in the twilight but declared that he was using no charms but was looking for a Lyme Stone that was thought to be there. Christian Lessels was charged in October 1716 and 'Interrogate upon threatening mallifice to her neighbours and using charming for ye recovery of ane child yt was sick'. A women was summoned in 1721 for consulting a dumb man with some of her clothes for divining whether her baby was to be a girl or a boy.

In the absence of a police force the Kirk Session shared with the magistrates responsibility for keeping the peace. Cases brought before them show that better-off inhabitants were as uninhibited in their behaviour as the poorer. Grissel Balfour, of a landed family and the wife of the wealthy shipmaster William Darsie, was involved in a female brawl in 1603 and complained to the Session that Janet Waid had called her Queen of Hell and Janet Waid gave in her complaint that Grissel had called her harlot.

Robert Bail was summoned and rebuked in January 1710 for refusing to restrain his children from making disturbances in the church in time of divine worship, 'as also for his withdrawing from the Church when admonished by the minister'. Three boys were summoned to the Session eighteen months later 'for playing and making anoize in the Church in time of divine worship', and the following year five boys were summoned, including David Melvil, the son of the schoolmaster, for breach of sabbath by throwing stones and earth into 'Patrick Tailzer his house', 'and other scandalous miscarriages'.

'Breaching of the Sabbath' was itself a serious offence. David Jamesone was accused in 1628 of 'not keeping of the Kirk' on the sabbath day. He explained that he 'keepit the Kirk and preatching' every sabbath in Pittenweem, but this was not good enough and he had to promise 'to keep his own parish church heirefter'. A woman was threatened with excommunication for not attending church, and baptism was refused to the children of parents who failed to attend church regularly. Profaning the sabbath by drinking and selling ale was a frequent offence among both men and women. One woman summoned for 'trubling the Town upon Sunday . . . and for drinking ye tyme of ye communion' was ordered to be put in the pillory the morne 'from 8 hours to twa efternone and give she be found heirefter not to kiep ye kirk on Sunday or to make any trubbell in ye town ordains to be banishit'.

Drunkenness in the burgh was as prevalent as fornication. Most cases seem to have been dealt with by the burgh court, but offenders had often to appear before the Session for exhortation to reform. Two men were summoned in January 1719 to acknowledge their fault in imposing upon a third to drink to excess. A fourth, David Anderson, gave no satisfying answer and evidenced no sign of his sin 'but on ye contrairy carry'd insolently before the Session by saying that James Ross had much need of a good dram In regard he had got a very cold day ye day befor being his marrige day'.

That same year an elder and leading inhabitant of the burgh was found guilty of swearing, brawling and fighting for which he was fined by the magistrates. The offender, William Dairsie, couper burgess, also withheld his charity collection for the poor 'this two or three months'. He was summoned by the Session but failed to appear. A month later the minister informed the Session that he had spoken with William Dairsie, *in private*, and had tried to obtain his submission to discipline 'but found no satisfactione from him but upon the contrair he gave more offence'. Dairsie was brought before the burgh court for calling a baillie 'a damned rascale . . . and several other opprobious indecent unmannerly and unbecoming expressions not worthy to be rehearsed' and was sentenced to prison 'but the prison being full with a prisoner' he was fined £50 Scots. Finally towards the end of September 1720 he appeared before the Session, acknowledged his sin and promised to reform. The Session then put it to the vote whether he should be publicly or privately rebuked; the vote was carried for a private rebuke before the Session, but William Oliphant dissented because he thought that his 'severall offences and scandalous carriages were so very serious and offensive' that he truly deserved a public rebuke. The schoolmaster agreed, but there was no public rebuke, presumably on the principle that public censure of prominent citizens would subvert the stability of society.

Another of the burgh's foremost inhabitants, Baillie Robert Lyall, with three friends, was summoned in 1736 for 'untimeous and excessive drinking . . . fighting, and playing at cards on Tuesday night last till 3 o'clock in the morning'. (Earlier that year Baillie Lyall was refused baptism of his child because he had withheld his collections for the poor 'these twelve months past', had neglected to put his children to school and was guilty of 'habituall and untimeous drinking'. He was rebuked in private.) Eight days later Thomas Edison 'after some sullen struggle' promised to amend and reform in time coming, as did Baillie Robert Lyall and the others, but as the session clerk sadly observed, 'their promise would be like Samson's green withies'.

The Rev. James Forrester wrote in the 1790s that there were three alehouses in the parish 'which do not seem to have any bad effect on the morals of the people', but in 1837 a petition was sent to the Town Council from the Session and a number of inhabitants 'complaining of great irregularities in consequence of the excessive use of ardent spirits'. Even the officials of the church were not guiltless; in 1848 the precentor, John Goldie, was seriously admonished for very unseemly and unbecoming conduct in drinking and rioting on the Lord's day. A few years before, the town beadle, who was also the town officer, was dismissed as he had frequently been complained of for drunkenness and misbehaviour, and was not re-appointed gravedigger 'on account of his intoxication at the last funerals'.

The duties of the church officer were to oil the clock, ring the bell, wash the communion linen, clean the church, light the stove and keep the churchyard in order. He had also to dig graves for which the varying charges make a poignant list: graves for 'stillborn babes . . . for youths up to 14 years old . . . for children up to 9 years old including Infants'. The Mortcloth Box's 'little mortcloths' were in constant use. The mortcloth was used to drape the deal coffin as it was borne to the grave, and charges for the use of the cloth varied according to whether the Best Cloth was used (£2 10s Scots in 1723), or the Worst Cloth, which was cheaper, the Best Little Mort Cloth or the Worst Little Mort Cloth (13s 4d). By the end of the century no distinction was made between the Best and the Worst, only between one for an adult, 3s 6d sterling, and one for a child, 2s sterling.

The churchyard was probably more extensive at one time than it is today. Murray Jack, architect in St Andrews, suggests that in medieval times the church would have stood in the centre of its graveyard, which might have extended into the ground now occupied by *Elizabeth Place*. In the 1960s when several members of the church were reflooring the apartment under the Town Hall they found half a dozen skeletons under the flagstones.

A number of iron-barred cages, 'cumbrous metal boxes', were to be seen in the churchyard in the mid-nineteenth century. The sea-coast churchyards of East Fife were reputed to be the haunt of 'resurrectionists' from Edinburgh who exhumed bodies for scientific purposes, so Anstruther Easter formed a Mortsafe Society in 1830 'for the security of the Bodies of their friends and relations when interred'. The Society's padlocked cages were rented to paid-up members and left in position for about six weeks. The minutes of an Anstruther Wester Society do not survive but the Town Council allowed two guineas 'to assist the Society in this Parish in procuring mort safes for the protection of the dead' and Anstruther Easter applied to the Wester burgh in 1842 for the loan of a safe. The cages ceased to be used after about 1850. One or two remaining in the Wester churchyard were removed, with knee-deep weeds and nettles, in 1885. The ancient churchyard, with those of Anstruther Easter and Kilrenny, was closed for burials in 1936.

Income from seat and mortcloth rents, feu duties and land rents, marriage dues, fines and weekly sabbath collections went into the Poor Box, the church's general fund, from which sums of money were lent at interest: £30 Scots to David Waid in 1603; £1,000 Scots to the Burgh Council of Anstruther Wester in 1691; 300 merks to the Laird of Montquhannie younger in 1703, for the repayment of which the Session had to use 'all legall diligence against him' in 1706 to get it back; and £20 to Captain William Adamson in 1806. Land was bought 'out of the Box', as in 1732 when an acre at the West Haven was bought for 300 merks from Henry Lamonth, two acres from Robert Robb in 1774, and in 1874 half an acre to the west of Pittenweem which was partly bought with a legacy from the late Rev. Hew Scot 'for behoof of the poor belonging to the Established Church who were not on the roll of paupers'. Wood's Mortification was also put out on loan. This was a sum of money of 500 merks Scotch bequeathed in 1693 by Henry Wood, residenter in Cellardyke, for relief of the poor in

Anstruther Wester, with similar sums to Anstruther Easter, Kilrenny and Montrose, because 'it had pleased the Lord to deal bountifully and liberally with him and he was desirous to honour the Lord with his substance by communicating a part thereof'.

The Sunday collections were put into the Poor Box unless they were for specific objects of charity, like a collection in 1721 for 'one in Largo taken slave by Algerines'; others in 1747 and 1748 for Highland schools; in 1750 for a church and school in Silesia; and in 1839 for education in the Highlands and Islands. In September 1805 there was a special collection, intimated from the pulpit the previous week, 'for behoof of widows and Fatherless children of the late unfortunate sufferers in Cellardyke'. But always a few shillings were reserved from the Sunday collection 'for the Poor at the door'.

The first poor rate was imposed in the parish in 1741 in obedience to an act that each parish should stent for its own poor. The heritors imposed a tax of £25, half to be paid by the heritors and half by householders and inhabitants. Six persons were taxed at Grangemuir, eleven at Milntoun, and thirty-one in the burgh. Following the election of 1741 Sir Philip Anstruther, as was customary, gave £5 3s Scots to the Poor Box, the proprietors of East and West Grangemuir gave £11 15s and £8 18s Scots respectively, and William Anstruther gave £12 11s Scots. Sir Harry Erskine gave two guineas for the poor after his election in 1754 and another guinea at the election of 1765. In 1777 Sir John Anstruther made a present of 'half a bole of Flax seed to Poor People the Session thought needful' (and the Session agreed to pay the rent of the ground in which the flax seed was grown). General Campbell of Monzie, MP, gave £15 for the poor of the parish in 1802 and later in the century there were donations from the MPs Edward Ellice and Stephen Williamson. Poor money was usually distributed directly to the poor, except in 1830 when Mary Chalmers 'in great want' applied for assistance. The Session 'considering both the situation and habits of Mary Chalmers deem it prudent to afford her provisions instead of money'.

The Poor Box was in the care of the church treasurer and was opened when required in the presence of the Kirk Session. In April 1703:

> The Minister and Elders opened the Box and found
> of silver money .... lib 138.13.08 (Scots)

of copper 013.06.00
of Bullion 2 ounces drop
sold for 008.08.00

The Kirk Session seems always to have remained solvent and to
have been both judicious and compassionate in the distribution of
its funds.

It showed great concern in 1800 that the widow and six children
of John Wilson, 'mariner of this parish lately lost on his passage
back from Gottenburg', were thereby reduced to distress and
poverty. The Session gave them a weekly allowance of 2s and
paid the quarterly fees of his two children still at school. It was
church policy, largely inspired by John Knox, that every child
should go to school. In 1575 the Kirk Session of Anstruther
Wester thought it meet that all the youth in the town should be
caused to come to the school 'and sic as are puir shall be furnished
upon the common expences'.

A beacon of coals in an iron chauffer was kept alight on the
church tower, the first light for shipping on the Fife coast, until
the erection of an exact copy of the tower on the Isle of May in
1636. The steeple and 'bell-house' were added later. In 1742 it was
reported to the Session that the bell was 'in hazard of breaking
when it rings by the insufficiency of the house it hangs in'. A new
bell was installed by the heritors in 1789 (by Watt of Edinburgh),
and according to Dr Ogg it was regarded as the finest bell in the
East Neuk. The burgh's managers and the heritors resolved in
November 1856 to replace the dilapidated and dangerous steeple
with a new one with turrets at each corner to a design by Mr
Milne, architect in St Andrews. 'From the well-established
character of the architect', the Record reported, 'it is confidently
expected that when completed the tower will be both substantial
and ornamental'. Fortunately perhaps the managers found that
the town could not afford the renovation and it was decided to
'alter the shape of the present spire and cover the same with
slates'.

Before retiring in 1868 the managers replaced the old clock in
the tower with one made by James Ritchie & Son, clockmakers
in Edinburgh, at a cost of £90. A hundred years later the clock had
ceased to function. The late Dr Greig of the Anstruther Improvements Association initiated a plan to repair it and secured the co-
operation of, and contributions from, the Congregational Board,

the Anstruther Town Council, the East Neuk Preservation Society and the National Trust for Scotland. The restoration was by the original firm of James Ritchie & Son. At the time of its installation the clock was 'quite modern . . . the first Denison Gravity Escapement public clock in Scotland'. It was decided for financial and historical reasons to keep the original mechanism rather than electrify the clock, and members of the Improvements Association have kept it wound since its re-installation and dedication by the Rev. J. N. Hutchison of St Adrian's Church in 1970.

The tower no longer housed the school after the 1696 Act of Parliament bound heritors to provide a schoolhouse and salary for the schoolmaster. The Session house to the east of the kirk-yard was taken in tack for a school in 1718, but after the building of the new Town Hall the heritors rented the ground floor for the purpose. The Rev. James Forrester wrote that the schoolmaster's salary was £8 6s 8d a year with 10 merks a year from the Session for teaching poor children. The fees at that time were:

English	14d a quarter
Writing	1s 6d
Latin	2s 6d
Navigation	£1 1s

The schoolmaster, Forrester continued, was esteemed the best teacher of navigation on the coast, 'his chief attention being directed to that branch' (the last minister of the parish, the Rev. James Paterson, prevented by defective eyesight from making a career in the Royal Navy, taught navigation at Waid Academy for many years), 'and all the young people in the Parish, without a single exception, are thought to read English, and the principles of the Christian religion'.

The ground floor of the Town Hall was found by 1827 to be 'very deficient in accommodation' for a school and in 1829 the schoolmaster, 'from age and infirmity', was unable to discharge his duties in an efficient manner and in consequence the school had 'fallen off, the children being obliged to go to neighbouring parishes'. Matthew Conolly's 'West Port park on the south of the Turnpike road' was eventually decided on for a new school, schoolhouse and playground, to plans drawn by William Lees, the schools inspector, and at the beginning of 1830 the work was begun. The total cost was £400 15s 3d. James Finlay Walker of East Anstruther was appointed the new schoolmaster at a salary 'equal to the average price of two chalders of oatmeal', with the £4 from Thomson's Mortification, and school fees at the following rates:

for English reading: .... 2s 6d a quarter
Writing: 3s
Arithmetic: 3s 6d
English Grammar: 4s
Latin junior class: 5s
Latin senior: 6s
Geography: 6s
Practical Mathematics including Mensuration, Land Surveying and plain Trigonometry: 10s 6d
Navigation by dead reckoning and double altitudes: £1 11s 6d
Lunar observations with ditto: £2 2s

Thus both the agricultural and nautical traditions of the burgh were to be catered for. In 1857 the Town Council showed itself to be up-to-date by voting a sum of £2 to the schoolmaster 'to be expended on assisting to purchase chemicals and chemical apparatus'. 'There is an excellent parish school in Anstruther Wester', a guide book declared three years later.

The old school was demolished in 1959, to the regret of many of the older inhabitants, and a modern building erected on the site at a cost of £20,177. After the Education Act of 1872 the Kirk Session was no longer responsible for the appointment of the school-master and soon it was to be relieved of its last traditional parish function, the administration of poor relief.

In June 1895 the new Parish Council, established the previous year by the Local Government (Scotland) Act, required informa-tion from the Session about the sources of its funds for the poor of the parish, which the Session supplied. Two months later the Parish Council requested the Session to hand over to it its land feus. The Session was not pleased, but four years later 'after legal advice and prolonged litigation and to save further litigation' it agreed to convey to the Parish Council those Trusts, granted 'for behoof of the poor by the Testators', of the Tofthill (just over four acres) in the parish of Pittenweem, and the New Dykes (about two and two-thirds acres) on the south side of Pittenweem Road near the High Cross.

Anstruther Wester surrendered its civic independence in 1929, and it was announced in 1961 on April the 23rd that:

> On this day the parishes of Anstruther Wester and Anstruther Easter were united at a service held in Anstruther Easter by the Rev. Wilfred Hulbert, Moderator of the Presbytery of St Andrews, under the name of Anstruther St Adrian's.

The ancient but much renovated building is no longer the heart of the burgh's life, but as the church hall it serves a useful purpose as an agreeable centre for recitals and exhibitions, and the still necessary activity of fund-raising.

Part II

East Anstruther

11
The Harbour

Anstruther 'be eist the burne' was granted by David I to a Norman knight, William de Candela, in the early twelfth century. Sir Ralph Anstruther, in a talk to the Anstruther Improvements Association in 1985, related how a Norman, William Ironarm of Hauteville in Coutance, enrolled in the forces of the Prince of Salerno in 1035 to repel an invasion of southern Italy by the Moors, and how seven years later he was joined by two of his half-brothers, one of whom was William the Younger. As Count of Apulia William Ironarm distributed to his brothers various commands, one of which was the defence in northern Apulia of a place called Candela, under whose walls all travellers and invading armies between Rome, Brindisi and the Levant had to pass. Twenty years later Duke William of Normandy recalled Norman knights from southern Italy to take part in the conquest and pacification of England and many of them eventually moved north to seek their fortunes in Scotland. As Sir Ralph said, it seems reasonable to assume that the command of Candela was given in the mid-eleventh century to William the Younger, and that the William de Candela who arrived in Fife some seventy years later was his grandson. By 1130 this William de Candela, Lord of Anstruther, was living in his castle at the mouth of the Dreel. His grandson, Henry, following the custom of the Normans in Scotland, took in 1225 the name of the barony which he had been granted.

The lands of the barony and the Elie estate were sold by the Anstruthers in 1853 to William Baird, the eldest of the Baird brothers, ironmasters of Gartsherrie, Lanarkshire, who played a vital part in the industrial development of Scotland in the nineteenth century.

The Barony of Anstruther consisted of the hamlet at the mouth of the Dreel 'and not many acres of land', so the value of the king's gift was probably as much in the hamlet and its fishing as in the acres of land. It was created a burgh in 1541 with the right to build a harbour, and thirty years later when it was erected into

The Shore in the 1870s, before the closure of the old harbour mouth. The leading light stands above the old shipyard.

a Burgh of Barony John Anstruther of Anstruther was authorised by James VI to build a harbour 'with safe anchorage for small and great ships', that is for both fishing and trading vessels. This early harbour would have been a pier erected for the protection of the anchorage along the foreshore. (Anstruther Easter adopted an anchor for its coat of arms.) The harbour was later described as being 'weill and substantiouslie biggit'.

It was probably this pier, the basis of the present middle pier, which figured in a 'heavie accident' on the Rev. James Melville's arrival in Anstruther in the early summer of 1587. English pirates were 'hanting in this firth and vther pairtts betuix Zarmouth, Orknay and Schyteland', and taking the local men's goods 'in the narrow seas on their way to Flanders'. Melville recorded in his *Diary* how a local 'creare' or single-masted barque was pillaged by an English pirate 'and a verie guid honest man of Anstruther slean thairin'. Whereupon the men of Anstruther rigged their own fast sailing boat, and with two large ships commissioned by the Convention of Royal Burghs went off to chase the pirates, to the great grief and anxiety of the minister. The pirates were caught off the coast of Suffolk and the men returned with the pirate ship and half a dozen pirates, 'whairof twa war hangit on our pier-end'. The others were dealt with in St Andrews and the whole affair was accomplished 'with na hurt at all to aine of our folks, who ever sin syne hes bein frie from Einlis pirates'.

The following summer early one morning a shipfull of Spaniards 'maist miserable and pitifull . . . arryvit within our herbrie'. The ship would have anchored in the bay and the Spaniards probably landed on Anstruther Easter's sandy shore in the ship's small boats. The captains were entertained most 'humeanlie' by John Anstruther and the men were allowed to come ashore, and on the advice of James Melville, were given 'kale, pottage and fish', although he was well aware of the reputation of the Spaniards for their 'prideful and crewall' ways with non-Catholics. The remarkable feature of this episode was that Anstruther was one of the few places that treated the starving men with any kind of Christian charity. In the Highlands, Ireland, England and Wales they were slaughtered as soon as they stepped ashore.

A list of anchorage dues that the burgh was permitted to collect in 1610 gives some idea of the size of ships coming into Anstruther Easter:

of every ship of 60 tons and over	23s 4d ilk ship,
of 40 tons	19s 8d,
ilk barque and crear of 12 lasts and over	13s 4d,
ilk bot with ane topmast that be clos [decked]	6s 8d,
and ilk oppin bot	3s 4d.

The money collected over the next seven years was to be 'imployit by the burgh on the reparation of thair harbour'. Two years later the Convention gave Anstruther permission to impose a tax of 6s 8d 'to be takin of everie dreave boatt cumming within their harbarie ilk season of the fisching to indure the space of sevin years allennerlie [only] and to be imployit upon the reparatione and bigging of thair wast [west] pier and harberie'. Thus at the beginning of the seventeenth century Anstruther Easter had two piers enclosing the foreshore.

The records of the Sound Toll between the years 1574-1582 and 1618-1627 show several vessels sailing each year from Anstruther Easter to Danzig and Königsberg in the eastern Baltic and

Harbour and Shore Street in 1885. A 300-yard stretch of concrete to enclose the dilapidated quayside was built in 1887.

occasionally to Lübeck in Germany. Among the shipmasters were Alexander Black and William Black (he was a commissioner to the Convention in 1597, 1601 and 1603 and just over sixty years later other Alexander and William Blacks were commissioners for the burgh); David Brunset [Burnside], and David Alexander, who like William Black owned tenements along the present Shore Street; Andrew Strang; and a George 'Wacht', possibly Waid. Two masters named Law or Low appear in the lists sailing to Danzig, Andrew in 1574 and '76 and Robert from 1619 to 1628 also calling at Stockholm and Malmo. In the 1630s an Albrecht Law or Low was one of the Scottish merchants resident at Danzig and a Thomas Law of Anstruther, a lacemaker, obtained civic rights in the city in 1634. It is possible they were all members of the same Anstruther Easter family.

As the result of invasion and civil war the burgh was seriously in debt in 1656 'forby the publick [burdens] and the maintenance of our harbour exceedis our common gude 222lb 6s 8d':

We hadd within this few zeires [years] of shippes 19 now we have only (three of them small and worth little) four, we hadd of barks five now we have but one, of late we hadd off boates going to ye

Orknay fishand and busching fifteen . . . Since and we was a burgh we had sundrie vessells sumtymes a guid many that went to the Isles fishing, this zier we have not one. Many wholl families have removed themselves from us to our neighbour burghs becaus of our gryt and unsupportable burdens . . .

One of the burdens was the quartering in the burgh of a company of foot and half a troop of horse 'where they have remayned above this four monthes, and as yet remaynes still, soe that furnishing coalls and candlelight to the guard and in souldiers quarters the wholl cess which was appoynted to be collected and applyed to the reparatione of the harbore . . . is exhausted'. Anstruther's harbour, if repaired, was one of the 'safest and steadable harbours on all the coast side'.

An Act of Parliament in 1661 gave some protection to the burgh by a declaration that Crail, Kilrenny, Anstruther Easter and Pittenweem 'shall be favoured above strangers in fishing in the Orkneys', and the Convention agreed that the burgh should have 'an ease in the alteration of the tax roll'. For the next few years its annual tax was reduced to three, two then one shilling (in 1649 it had been 16s), and in 1698 it was granted the sum of 500 merks 'for the present repairatione of ther pier, town house, shambles and harbour'. By 1691 Anstruther Easter was in such a bad way that Mr James Halson 'being the only persone present of thrie new elected ballies Refused to accept of his office of Balliarie In regaired The Towne is Soe burdened with Debts'. The Council minutes continue:

> *Nota.* It is to be remembered That from the forsaid Sexteinth day of September 1691 to the twenty Sexth day of September 1694 Ther was noe Magistratts in office within the said Burgh for In regaird The Toune was soe grievously burdened with debt Those who were elected would not accept of thair offices.

Between the years 1667 and 1689 the customs records show twelve trading vessels belonging to the burgh: the *Christian*, the *Charles*, the *Johne*, the *Marie*, the *Providence*, the *Hope*, the *Isobel*, the *Philip* and the *Phoenix*, the *Saint Georg* and the *Barberie*, all 'of Enster' or 'Eanstruther'. Their masters included George and John Gourlay, Thomas Dishintoune, Robert Gardner, William Eanstruther who was also a shipowner, William Anderson, Thomas Halson, Robert Wood, Thomas Kellock, John Toddie and

The *Radiation*, the largest fishing boat built in Anstruther, at Aitken's yard, in 1957.

Alexander Stevinson (who in 1695, 1700 and 1701 was a commissioner for Kilrenny). The outward traffic was to Newcastle, London, St Malo and Bordeaux, Holland, 'Norroway, Gottenberrie and Dantsick', with herring and white fish, salt, malt and barley, goat skins, linen yarn and ticking, and coals from Dysart and Wemyss. A surprising export from about 1680, considering the difficult times, was 'victual', mostly to Norway and occasionally to Holland. Dr Charles Rogers wrote of a meal mob from Anstruther Easter seizing corn at Stravithie in 1720 as no agricultural produce was available at the town's market. Farmers were getting better prices in foreign markets.

The *Christian of Anstruther*, Thomas Kellock, master, made what was a routine round trip in 1689, leaving 'Eanstruther' for the Sound in March with a cargo of herring and white fish and returning in August from Stockholm with 12 tons of iron, 2 lasts of tar, 160 fir deals, and 400 pounds of rough hemp. In July 1689 Alexander Stevinson, master, imported from Rotterdam in the

Barbarie of Eanstruther for David Leslie, merchant in Crail and Anstruther:

> Ane box containing Books va[lue] 120 lbs Scotts,
> 2 boxes containing 70 pd candy,
> Ane Matt containing 50 pd steel hemp,
> 12 pound brass pans va 8 lbs [Scotts]
> 6 round chears [chairs],
> Ane old looking-glass va: fouor lbs Scotts.

In September the *Barbarie*, John Toddie, master, brought into Anstruther for David Leslie: old iron, several reams of brown paper, 'unbound books valued at 166 lbs Scotts' and a box of unbound Bibles, raisins, white thread, a barrel of 'cappers' [capers], a pock of madder [vegetable dye], alum [used in dyeing], a barrel of fustickwood [yellow dye], 20 iron pots, a box of old pictures worth £26 scots, lintseed, a box containing glasses valued at £80 scots, a hamper of lemons valued at £6 scots, and 100 barrels of onions. In May of the following year John Toddie brought from Rotterdam among other goods for Leslie 'four iron pots, ane old table, lemons and ten pounds wrott [worked] silke'.

John Gourlay, master of the *Phoenix of Eanstruther*, brought from Danzig in June 1690 lint, iron and rough hemp for himself; a similar cargo for Robert Wood, shipmaster; rough hemp and window glass for James Nairn in Elie; and 90 lbs of 'amber oyll' for an Edward Marjoribanks; and at Rotterdam picked up barrels of 20,000 needles, brass buttons and 3,000 thimbles, almonds, cinnamon, nutmegs, mace, cloves, linseed oil, pepper, raisins, French barley, 150 lbs of whalebone, 200 musket locks, and 12 gallons of hock.

William Halson, shipmaster and shipbuilder, sailed through the Sound from Anstruther to Danzig in ballast in 1784, to Königsberg again in ballast in 1785, and in 1792 he made two voyages, leaving Berwick for Memel in April in ballast, returning to Grangemouth with barley, and sailing in September from Rouen, where he had probably taken herring, to St Petersburg, returning to Leith with flax, tallow and laths. He made similar journeys in 1793, '94 and '95, going out with herring and returning with rye, linseed, flax and tow.

There was one other cargo important to Anstruther although it was never carried in Anstruther vessels: 'pann tyles'. They may have been brought as ships' ballast in earlier years, but 25,500

Boats' biscuits for family and friends at the departure of the herring fleet for the Great Yarmouth winter fishing, c. 1930.

pantiles were brought into East Neuk ports from September 1689 to September 1690 in lots of from six hundred to six thousand tiles, customs duty being charged at the rate of £1 4s Scots on every thousand. (Fifty years later Henry Short of Anstruther was carrying a cargo of 42,500 Easedale slates.)

Daniel Defoe wrote of his visit to Scotland in 1706 that as one must expect a great deal of antiquity in the country of Fife, so one must expect to find all those 'antient pieces [burghs] mourning their own decay and drooping an sinking in ashes'. But by this time both Anstruthers seem to have been picking up again after the disasters of the seventeenth century. The herring had returned and Anstruther Easter, a former Creek of the Custom House of Kirkcaldy, was promoted to a Port of the Custom House in 1710, a position which it retained until it was reduced to a sub-port in 1827. As in the Wester burgh shipmasters throughout the eighteenth century were assessed for the highest tax.

Almost every winter parts of the harbour were 'shaikin lous' in winter storms. The general insecurity of the structure is frequently illustrated. In February 1708 John Low, town treasurer, was instructed by the Town Council:

> to cause carrie out of the harbour, the haill stones and rubbish that is therein with all expedition, and further to buy what trees and timber may be needful for the peer for securing the stones upon the same In regaird the old trees are all broken and the stones falling off the peer daily.

And that was not the only problem. Since before the burgh had a charter the townspeople exercised the right of 'winning stones from within the sea mark, and clay from the Loan, for the building, beeling and repairing of houses built and to be built', but they carried their right a little far. In the summer of this same year the Council was forced 'yet again':

> to Enact, Statute and Ordain That noe Inhabitant within this burgh nor noe other person whatsomever Shall at any time hereafter take or cause to take Any Stones off the new Peer Under payne of Ten pounds Scotts to be paid by each contraveener . . . and the same to be Intimat to the Inhabitants by touck of Drum . . .

The baillies visited the back of the pier in 1713 and found the back side of the pier 'under its ordinaire defects'. Two years later the 'visiteers' of the harbour appointed by the Town Council reported that they found the pier back and middle 'severall places of it decayed and decaying and louse and to need reparation and that very speedily'. They appointed several men 'skilled to this end' to oversee and call out the inhabitants and burgesses to the work, with a fine of six shillings Scots 'for every deficient person so warned'. The treasurer was to provide money for what tools might be necessary 'yet wanting' and to pay the principal workmen. That was in May and the work was not finished in August, so the Council recommended that the work should be continued 'after the dreave', presumably because most of the workmen apart from the stonemasons were fishermen.

The following incident illustrates the flimsy nature of the piers. John Aitchison's ship the *Elizabeth of Pittenweem* with a load of salt belonging to Thomas Matthy of Prestonpans 'in a fair gale wind' ran upon the round head of the pier which was 'shattered and bulged' and would in all probability fall if not taken down and repaired. The matter was settled in a most civilised fashion. The

Steam drifters at Anstruther in the early '30s. In the background, fish boxes are stacked high in front of the light-coloured house. On the skyline is Chalmers Memorial Church, and to the right the lifeboat shed, with the top of the gasholder in East Green just discernible behind it.

baillies and Matthy each appointed masons to examine the damage and agree on an estimate which Thomas Matthy declared himself willing to pay. Changed days! When the derelict *Ben Gulvean* damaged the wall of the outer harbour in 1978 the ratepayers had to foot the bill.

A few years earlier two 'mylne stones' were settled in the harbour with Iron chains and rings so that 'in all tyme comeing Each big vessell or small vessell that shall make use yrof shall pay to the Customer of this burgh alsmuch as they doe in Ely after we have got notice therof'. A hundred years later rings were still being used for mooring in the harbour — and the same storm damage, inspections and repairs continued, with the added difficulty that from 1811 for several years the town treasurer refused to produce the town's funds to pay for the necessary work.

Like the east pier the west pier would have been the usual

rubble-filled drystone bulwark along a natural reef. Colonel Anstruther, MP, successfully petitioned Parliament in 1726 for a grant for its improvement and in 1731 work was begun on the re-building of the west pier but it proceeded very slowly. Eventually in 1749 to cover the cost Parliament granted Anstruther the right to levy a duty of 2d Scots 'on everie Scotch pint of ale or beer that shall be either brewed, bought in or sold within the town for the term of twenty-five years'. This spurred on the work and in 1753 the pier which extended 'nearly as far as that on the East' was finished, providing, with the east pier, a basin which was 'commodious and safe', and in which the tonnage of shipping nearly doubled before the end of the century, from 80 tons to 1,400 tons. In 1755 the grant was renewed for a further twenty-five years.

By the mid-eighteenth century, then, the harbour had (comparatively) firm east and west piers and there only remained parts of the foreshore to be strengthened. It was reported to the Council in 1757 that the sea was daily encroaching upon the beach and ground to the eastward of the harbour:

> and was so far advanced as to render the gateway from the Shore east to Andrew Waid's houses almost unpassable and if remeid be not provided the sea will probably beat in (as in a Tempest a few years ago it lately threatened) on the east side of the Harbour and destroy the same and the works lately made.

The Council therefore went in a body and inspected the encroachments and agreed that a 'proper sea fence, Dyke or Bulwark shall be erected this summer season to strengthen that part of the Harbour betwixt Andrew Waid's Yard Dyke to Baillie Waddell's Warehouse South Gavel [gable]'. This must be the warehouse that still stands above the outer harbour with its gable-end to the sea, on which is a stone panel of a barque or brigantine and the date 1737. Thomas Waddell was a shipmaster and merchant, a baillie of Anstruther Easter, and in 1744 one of the managers of the Anstruther Sea Box Society.

Two dockyards are marked on a late eighteenth-century map of Anstruther, one on the east pier and the other in the angle of the west pier and the shore. (In a list of Shore Dues in 1799 the rate of Plank mail for each ship 'hawled up to be lengthened or repaired' was 5s 6d, and for each ship built the 'Dock mail' was 1d per ton).

The 70-foot *Reaper*, FR 958, an early 20th-century 'Fifie' fully restored by the Scottish Fisheries Museum, Anstruther, by the summer of 1987.

Baillie Robert Waddell, shipbuilder, like Thomas a native of Cellardyke, built several Baltic brigs and many smaller craft, probably on the east dockyard near the warehouse. His detailed account book for the building of the *Ship Euphan of Borowstonness* survives with descendants in Australia. It shows that he built the brigantine at Anstruther for a firm of Bo'ness merchants, which included two Dutchmen, 'Her Keel being Laid Taysday the third Day of Febrewarie one thousand and Seven Hundred and thirty eight years She Launched Thursday the Eight Day of June 1738'. The full cost of the ship and all her apparelling and incidental charges 'in the time of her building at Anstruther and outrigging at Bo'ness and Leith was £406 sterling'. Robert Waddell owned property in Anstruther Easter and was probably a relation of the Rev. Andrew Waddell who was minister of Anstruther Wester from 1761 until his death in 1767 at the age of 32.

The buttress at the Brae by Waddell's warehouse south gable was finished in 1802. The shipbuilder, Alexander Paton, took up the first lease of the timber yard at the Brae for £7 10s and continued to rent it until he moved to Newcastle in 1815. (Eight years before with David Rodger, corn merchant and brewer, he leased the old shipyard by the west pier 'for erecting a saw-pit thereon' — the original Folly, perhaps). Alexander Paton, junior, followed his father as shipbuilder. James Henderson and George Marr were permitted to build boats on the Brae in 1818 and '19 and Messrs Taylor and Robertson to erect a shed for curing fish at the Harbourhead.

There was as yet no pier along the Shore, just a drystone dyke reinforcing the edge of the raised beach. In old title deeds houses along the Shore are described as 'bounded to the south by the sea flood', but between the houses and the dyke there must have been sufficient room for horses and carts — and for a certain amount of business.

Baillie George Willis complained to the Burgh Council in August 1819 that for several years past a number of persons 'as well Burgesses, Inhabitants and Strangers', without any authority from the magistrates or benefit to the town, were occupying 'Piers, streets and vacant ground in curing Herrings and in storing them thereon until a market offered as well as storing salt and empty barrels until a fishing commenced'. 1809 to 1830 were years of government bounties for landing and curing herring, and the folk of Anstruther and district were obviously making the most of them. Baillie Willis proposed that the town should too, by imposing moderate charges on fish and barrels. The congestion in and around Anstruther's busy piers and narrow wynds can well be imagined.

Shipbuilding seems to have lapsed for some years in the nineteenth century but Christopher Pottinger was building ships in the burgh from about 1850 and in the early 1860s built the first fully-decked fishing vessel in Anstruther, 63 tons and 60 feet long, requiring a crew of ten. He removed to Leith in 1871 and was followed by one of the most successful of Anstruther's shipbuilders: William Jarvis, ship carpenter of the Barque *Anglia of Liverpool* and residing in the parish of Kingsbarns at the time of his marriage in November 1864 to Elizabeth Duncan of Anstruther Wester. He launched his first boat in the summer of 1872.

Jarvis was well-known on the east coast of Scotland for the excellence of his work. He built 'Fifies' and trawlers for owners in Aberdeen, Montrose, Bervie and St Andrews as well as in Cellardyke and Anstruther, and in 1884 was commissioned, along with other shipbuilders around the country, to build a number of lightweight craft for the Nile expedition for the relief of General Gordon. Jarvis had his boats ready on time, but the expedition arrived in Egypt too late to save Gordon. In 1885 he built the *David and Alexander*, 'a carvel-built or "Fifie" boat', for an owner in Aberdeen: it was the largest boat in the port at Aberdeen, 'attracting the admiration of the fishing population of Footdee. There were more comforts for the men and the cost without sails and rope was £290'. The sails were made by Messrs Johnston in East Green. He built his first steam liner, the *Maggie Lauder*, in October 1891 for the newly formed Anstruther Steam Fishing Company. The whole harbour was decorated with bunting and shops closed for half an hour for the launching from the middle pier. 'The models and workmanship of the crafts always gave entire satisfaction to the fishermen', the *East of Fife Record* wrote in an obituary on his death at 1, Union Place in February 1909, his experience led frequently to his appointment as a surveyor of damaged vessels, 'and his opinion on matters connected with his business was eagerly sought'. He died in his 74th year and must have retired a few years earlier as in 1904 the yard was leased by John Miller, previously Jarvis's foreman.

Shipbuilding declined in the 1930s but was resumed after the Second World War. The *Argonaut*, launched from Aitken's yard at Harbourhead in 1953, was the 'largest of its kind ever built in Anstruther yards' until 1957 when Smith & Hutton built the *Radiation*, 92 feet long, the largest fishing boat but not the largest boat: during the war minesweepers of over 100 feet in length were built at the yard. The *Radiation* was acquired by the Fisheries Museum in 1985 and is being restored at Tayport to be leased as a pleasure steamer on the west coast. The yard, already owned by a

Dundee firm, closed for good in 1975 and Hutton's shed was removed from Harbourhead about six years later. Fishing boats come to the middle pier for maintenance and servicing by local engineering and joinery firms, and to the low-tide beach at the west pier for careening and painting, but all that is left to show of Anstruther's long tradition of shipbuilding is the slipway, or what remains of it, to the east of the lifeboat shed.

A Cellardyke correspondent suggested in the local paper in 1855 that from the prosperous state of the fishing and the large increase of boats belonging to the place, there was never a more suitable time for the fishermen to provide themselves with a harbour 'which could be taken at all states of the tide, and in all kinds of weather'. The fishermen soon collected £500 and obtained estimates of between £10,000 and £12,000 for a new harbour at 'Craignoon', halfway between Anstruther and Cellardyke harbours to the seaward side of the Sorland Rocks. Anstruther Easter also wanted more harbour improvements, but 'what Anstruther wanted Cellardyke wouldn't have' and each went its own way, getting nowhere.

As the herring fishing industry steadily advanced the Government became concerned in the 1850s about the loss of life and the number of wrecks especially off the east coast of Scotland: a thousand lives and a million and half pounds of property lost each year. A Select Committee was appointed in June 1857 to inquire into the provision of Harbours of Refuge (typically of governments there were for the first six months no members of any nautical profession on the committee) and decided to advance money for the improvement of ten existing harbours. It was soon rumoured that Elie (which was not even a fishing station!) was to get a grant of £30,000 to become a refuge for fishing boats. The appalling thought put an end to the wrangling. On Friday October 11th 1857 a public meeting was held in the old Town Hall of Anstruther Easter: 'The Hall and staircase were densely crowded, and a great number were unable to gain admittance . . . It was one of the most enthusiastic meetings', the local paper reported, 'that we have ever seen'. Resolutions for a 'Union Harbour' were passed: Anstruther Easter would surrender its harbour revenues, Cellardyke fishermen agreed to abandon the Craignoon scheme and contribute the £500 already collected and the managers of Anstruther Wester gave the scheme their hearty approval. The Fishery Board were to be asked to make a new survey, 'the expense thereof to be defrayed by voluntary contribution', and a memorial was to be presented to Parliament.

As an earnest of their unanimity and enthusiasm plans were immediately made to widen the pier as far as the bight as it was 'so narrow and in such bad order that a cart cannot pass, and it is consequently unsuitable for landing the boats' cargoes'. It was also proposed to strengthen and repair the bulwarks at the back of the east pier — a task that the Burgh Council seems to have put in hand many times before. As well as the greatly increased number of fishing boats coming into the harbour, which had trebled in the previous thirty years, Anstruther was already exporting a considerable quantity of grain and potatoes in coasters belonging to the port.

A government grant was secured and work on a new pier to the east of the original pier was begun in the spring of 1866. The engineer was Thomas Stevenson, son of Robert, builder of the Bell Rock and other major lighthouses who in 1829 had proposed a 200-foot extension of the east pier at a cost of £3,000 (but the sum was beyond the resources of the town), and father of Robert Louis, the writer, who came to the burgh in 1868 'as a young man to glean engineering experience from the building of a breakwater'. In those days, he wrote later:

> though I haunted the breakwater by day, and even loved the place for the sake of the sunshine, the thrilling seaside air, the wash of waves on the sea-face, the green glimmer of divers' helmets far below, and the musical clinking of the masons, my one genuine preoccupation lay elsewhere.

In a letter to his parents in July 1868 he was not quite so flattering; he was 'utterly sick of this gray, grim, sea-beaten hole'. He had a cold in his head, which probably accounted for his spleen, and longed to get back among flowers and trees 'and something less meaningless than this bleak fertility'. He lodged with Baillie Brown, cabinetmaker, in *Cunzie House* (or *Kenzie House*, as he wrote it), 'and there, as soon as dinner was despatched, in a chamber scented with a box of mignonette in the window' and a 'factory' of dried rose-leaves, he would proceed in the candle light 'to pour forth literature'. There was only one thing in connection with the harbour that tempted him, and that was diving, 'an experience I burned to taste of'. He had been sent to watch the harbour works as preliminary training for what was at that time thought to be his future profession, but 'when I'm drawing', he wrote, 'I find out something I have not measured, or, having measured, have not noted, or having noted cannot find, so I have to trudge to the pier again ere I can go farther with my noble design'.

The *East of Fife Record* marvelled in the spring of 1867 at the progress that was being made on the new outer pier: '150 yards of strong mason-work 20' to 30' high . . . a large portion of the inner wall and the 'Rowin' stone' ground excavated . . . large stone blocks quarried and brought to the spot . . . one is astonished at the progress . . . The new East Pier will be about a quarter of a mile long and in fine weather will form a promenade which will be unsurpassed on this side of the Forth'. But the building of the new outer pier was beset with difficulties. So much storm damage had to be repaired each year that the original grant of £30,000 was far exceeded and at times the money ran out and the work came to a halt. Blocks of concrete were first used to reinforce the back of the new pier in 1871 and it was not until the following year when concrete was much more extensively used that matters began to improve — although not from the stonemasons' point of view. Seeing themselves put out of a job they referred derisively to the 'putty pier'. Fish were landed for the first time at the new pier in 1874. For the next twelve months the harbour had two entrances, the original mouth facing south west and the 'cut mouth' through the old east pier into the outer basin, but by the end of 1876 the old entrance to the south west was closed and by 1877 the main work was completed, twenty years after the enthusiastic public meeting which inaugurated the plans for a Union Harbour.

One of the greatest demonstrations ever seen, the *Record* reported in March 1880, was witnessed when the safety rail and new lighthouse on the west pier were formally handed over to the harbour commissioners. The gifts were from Miss Hannah Harvie in Cheltenham to mark the centenary of the birth of Thomas Chalmers. She was the daughter of a Glasgow shipowner and had no connection with Anstruther and never visited the burgh but she was interested in the welfare of fishermen. She donated Anstruther's first lifeboat in 1865 which she asked to be named after Admiral Fitzroy who assisted fishermen and sailors with his meteorological forecasting system.

The North Carr lightship in the outer harbour was opened to the public in 1978.

At that meeting in October 1857 John Todd, fishcurer in the East Green, commented that although fishing boats were getting larger and the amount of fishing tackle doubled, the fishermen were not taking any more fish. There were already ominous signs, he said, that the inshore grounds were being over-fished.

James Murray, skipper, pioneered the south fishing to Yarmouth in the autumn of 1863 and by the turn of the century, after a decline in the '90s, record catches of herring were being landed at the Union Harbour — and fish scales were everywhere, even up to the goods station, 'coating the streets and clogging the drains'. (This suggests the derivation of Nether Kilrenny's name of *Silverdykes* corrupted into *Sillerdyke*.) Fish buyers came from Scotland, England, Germany, Russia and the Baltic countries. So successful was the fishing that the harbour commissioners were considering further improvements when war broke out in 1914.

In 1923 a legacy of £5,000 was bequeathed to Anstruther Harbour by John Black late of Liverpool, son of the late Thomas Black, surgeon in Anstruther. During his lifetime John Black made several donations towards the upkeep of the harbour. This welcome news inspired the commissioners to renew their efforts, but as their plans and negotiations for a government grant progressed, so the fishing industry deteriorated. The main improvement planned was the widening of the west pier. Work was begun in 1931 and was completed at a cost of £20,000. The old stones on the outer face of the pier were replaced in the eighteenth-century manner, with the narrow stones set vertically as being less likely to be lifted by wave action than if they were laid horizontally. The pier was opened on January 4th 1933, Provost Carstairs presiding.

True to its old tradition the harbour had one last fling: on August 25th 1937 as the inner basin was being deepened, the west pier burst. By an heroic effort the damage was repaired and the pier finished by the scheduled date, December 21st, and the rubble left outside the new pier was conveniently washed away in a winter storm. The Shore quay was widened again — the first quay, 'a wall 300 yards long from the Folly east to the slip at the top of the Middle Pier' was built in 1887. The jetty planned for the outer basin was built in the inner basin in 1939 and the harbour as it is today was complete. The improvement scheme, carried out by Robert Terras, junior, of East Wemyss, was completed at a cost of £21,500. Fifty years after the reconstruction, repairs were needed at the end of the middle pier at a cost of £88,000 and work was started in 1988 on the reinforcement of the pier facing it across the cut mouth.

The local paper commented in December 1937 that all was set for a prosperous herring fishing but the decline in the industry had not abated. The 1933 herring season at Yarmouth was 'one of the worst in the history of the trade'. The winter herring improved a little in the mid-'30s but tariff barriers, currency restrictions and the build-up of continental herring fleets affected exports. 1938 was a year of gluts, closures of Fife ports, and the dumping of catches back into the sea.

The harbour must have been a delight to the youth of the town. Girls and boys crossed the harbour from drifter to drifter (a few fell into the water), stringing herring on their fingers as they went. There was the biscuit ceremony when everyone went down to see the fleet leave for Yarmouth and all the children were given a ship's biscuit ('Morton's were good but Birrell's were so hard'.) There was the 'Scranning' for loose herring which boys strung together and sold to nearby farm cottages, and there were many small boats in which to acquire nautical skills.

The first steam drifters appeared at Anstruther at the end of the nineteenth century (sail lasted until the 1920s) and at the industry's peak 300 and more used the harbour. In 1931 Anstruther had 120 motor boats and 53 steam drifters. In both World Wars all the drifters were commandeered by the government and in 1945 only three returned. With the loss of the drifters Anstruther ceased to be the hub of the Fife fishing industry. Then the herring disappeared. In the 1950s, however, seine-net fishermen found that the formerly worthless Dublin Bay prawns were a commercial proposition and this led to a small canning factory in Station Road for the export of 'scampi' to Spain (they are now frozen), so in the 1980s Anstruther Harbour, after its centuries-long association with the herring fishing, is left with small boats fishing for lobsters, partans [crabs] and prawns. Large fleets of fishing boats are unlikely to return to the Union Harbour: modern vessels can no longer afford to wait for high tide for their coming and going and skippers find it more economical to take their crews by road to Aberdeen with its deepwater harbour and railhead. The herring shoals are increasing once more, but will the cry of 'Herring in the Haikes' ever echo again in the streets of the ancient burghs?

The Folly, once piled high with herring boxes and now packed from April to October with parked cars, has become more and more a centre for entertainment. There was dancing on the pier at night in the months of July and August in the 1950s, and later pipe bands and sales of work. In the 1980s the annual Lifeboat Gala Committee sets up stalls on the Folly and organises a raft race, with teams from each public house racing from the Castle Street beach to the outer harbour — where John Brattisani erected wooden bathing huts in 1928. Miss Lovatts Amusements rented the middle pier for three months each year from 1956 for ten years, and still a fun fair arrives each July with roundabout and bingo. In 1968 Captain William Anderson bought a former line-fishing boat from an Orkney family, renamed her the *Hilda Ross* after his wife, and for almost twenty years ran summer trips to the Isle of May. (She now sails in Scandinavian waters). The

Revenge and *Sapphire* have taken her place.

In the summer of 1842 the first steamer, the *Stirling Castle*, was bought by James Tod to carry freight between Anstruther and Leith and passengers for both business and pleasure, and the *Xantho*, an iron steamer built on the Clyde for the Anstruther and Leith Shipping Company at a cost of £3,600, arrived at Anstruther Harbour on November 4th 1848. The following year the company paid tribute to John Smith, writer in Anstruther, as the 'foremost contriver' in the company. In 1855 a new paddle steamer, the *Forth*, was launched for the company at Leith at a cost of £1,500. The *Forth*, Captain Allason, sailed from Anstruther three or four times a week, calling off Pittenweem, St Monans and Elie: cabin 3s 6d return, steerage 2s 6d. The *Record* reported in 1868 that the goods traffic was keeping up exceedingly well and the passenger traffic was likely to do the same. A dividend of 6% was paid that year but the Forth Rail Bridge killed the sea traffic to Leith. The shipping trade generally fell off and the Anstruther Custom House closed in 1890.

In the late 1970s the Scottish Fisheries Museum bought the *Reaper*, a 'Fifie' which fished in Shetland waters until 1968, and a 'Zulu', the *Research*, two wooden drifters, almost the last of their kind, built respectively near Fraserburgh in 1901 and at Banff in 1903. The restoration of the 70-foot *Reaper* as a two-masted sailing lugger with a set of sails and many original fittings was completed by the summer of 1987 when she took to the sea again manned by members of the museum's boat club. In the outer harbour sits the North Carr light vessel. Stephen Williamson, MP, campaigned successfully for the first North Carr light vessel which was anchored on the reef in 1889. The present vessel dates from the early '30s and is rather a liability, costing the District Council more in maintenance than she earns from tourists. Cruising yachts berth in the harbour during the summer months; parties of sea anglers hire former fishing boats for day trips; and divers explore the waters of the May; but of herring boats and trading vessels there are none.

One element of Anstruther's maritime tradition survives, the Sea Box Society of Anstruther Easter, founded in the early years of the seventeenth century. All its papers, with all the public registers belonging to Scotland which Oliver Cromwell lodged in the Tower of London, were lost on their return to Scotland in 1660 on account of Lord Clarendon's delay in searching through them:

'they were sent down in winter: and by some easterly gusts the ship was cast away near Berwick'.

The Society's Charter was re-issued in 1784 after an application by among others John Reid, Thomas Ballardie, James Ballantyne and Willian Halson, all shipmasters. No person was entitled to be a member of the Society 'unless he be a shipmaster treading from or residing in the Burgh of Anstruther Easter' but 'any common Mariner, or Sea faring people' belonging to or sailing in ships from Anstruther Easter who contributed to the funds could be 'assumed into the benefits of their charity'. The sea captains and their Factor ran the Society so successfully (one of its earliest investments, which it still retains, was in farming land at Cameron and others were in land in Anstruther Wester) and so many non-native shipmasters settled in Anstruther to take advantage of its provisions that it was stipulated that shipmasters had to live in the town for five years' continuous residence before they could be admitted members of the Society and receive its benefits.

It was not always easy to gain admittance: members had to be admitted in person but often there was no quorum as all the managers and masters were away at sea, and when there *was* a quorum the applicant himself might be at sea. Sons of managers were admitted at half the entry money but they had to pay the full poor money each year. A master's pension was £26 a year until 1858 when it was raised to £28, and supplements were paid in the case of ill health. Widows of masters received £4 10s a quarter.

Captain David Thomson, master of the *Garthpool*, was Boxmaster in his time and was succeeded by Captain Robert Reekie who was Boxmaster for thirty-one years. Now under Captain Shirreff the membership of the ancient Society numbers eight, which though small is higher than it has been for many years.

12

Houses in the Old Burgh

The Smugglers' Inn

The topographical features of ford, raised beaches and small streams shaped the burgh of Anstruther Easter. The High Gait came up from the ford — the bridge was not built until 1630 — and had to cross, at their shallowest or narrowest point, the various streams that drain the immediate hinterland. After crossing the ford, travellers going to St Andrews turned left up the Loan opposite the inn. Travellers going to Crail continued eastward to the lower Cunzie Burn, up the Kirk Wynd to the School Green, which was once a pasture for cattle, and along the edge of the upper raised beach, crossing the stream that runs between *Bellfield House* and the *Hermitage* and another stream that flows down Hadfoot Wynd. (The name comes from the days long before Macadam when pedestrians had to mind their step or 'haud the feet' as they came down the steep banks of the burn.) The highway, marked on the eighteenth-century map as 'the road to Crile', continued along the edge of the upper raised beach to the Caddy's Burn, now flowing under Burnside Terrace, and descended its right bank to the shore, entering the burgh of Kilrenny on stepping stones. All the paths leading from this High Gait to the shore were narrow wynds like the two that survive: Wightman's Wynd and Tolbooth Wynd.

The houses of the old burgh were built on the lower raised beach to the south of this common gait. The high walls or 'back dykes' of gardens extending to the upper beach formed a protecting wall around the town and when necessary the narrow wynds could be easily closed against vagabonds or carriers of the plague. The oldest houses lined the highway from the ford, the narrow wynds, and the shore from Dreel Castle to the Balmerino monastery lands of St Ayles (now the Fisheries Museum).

Four properties on the High Gait make up the present *Smugglers' Inn*. They were divided in the past by a 'common vennel or passage that goes down to the burn', a passage still

The Smugglers Inn. The vennel leading down to the burn is behind the door on the right. In the rear of the picture is the Victorian house and draper's shop built by Provost William Murray.

there but no longer open to the sky. The oldest surviving parts of the inn, to the east of the vennel, form a right angle, one arm of which is aligned to the ford and the other to the Loan which leads to the town's Common Good lands and to St Andrews. The properties were feued in the mid-seventeenth century to Henrie Smyth, burgess and baillie in Anstruther Easter. He was one of the five Council members who in 1662 refused to renounce the Solemn League and Covenant as required by Charles II's first Parliament and was later appointed a member of a committee of six to manage the burgh's affairs 'in respect ye Ballies who were chosen will in no ways accept office', on account of the town's debts. He seems to have improved older houses on the site, retaining the eastmost and selling the westmost.

Gourlay wrote that the *Smugglers' Inn* (the *Commercial Hotel* in his day) was a noted tavern in the days of Queen Anne and that it was the headquarters of the Earl of Strathmore when in 1715 he proclaimed the Pretender at Anstruther Cross 'with pistols and wine'. Gourlay is wrong about Strathmore, who came no further than Kilrenny — it was John, Master of Sinclair, who proclaimed James VIII and III in the East Neuk burghs — but he was right about the wine, as Sinclair insisted that the health of the pretended king should be drunk in every one of the burghs after the proclamation, 'otherwise the ceremonie was null and void'.

The burgh's experience of the Rising of 1715 was not a happy one. Men were called to arms in September 'by touck of drum through the toun' to join the Lord Lieutenant of Fife near Strathmiglo, and the Town Council ordered a guard to be kept 'this night and every night till further orders of fifteen men at least with the armes of the toun'. On October 20th the magistrates wrote to the Lord Provost in Edinburgh that:

> Upon the 12th current Came to this Town between 10 and 1500 foot and horse, hailed down our boats & Compelled all sorts of people to go in the boats. A boat belonging to Elias Le Blanc wherin was Donald Mcgrigor, Andrew Dickson and James Trant fishermen, Robert Rattrey and James Martine weavers, William Edmiston, Coupar, George Moress and Robert Wilson, Land labourers, with Arthur Bruce blacksmith; were taken on board a Man of Warr called the Bell afterwards as we are informed put on board the Royall Ann Galley.

The chief magistrate and baillies looked to Edinburgh for the return of these unfortunate men to their families. The following April the Council, who like their Wester colleagues were no Jacobites, sent an address to George I on the success of his arms and the quelling of the Rebellion.

When the mouth of the Dreel was Anstruther's harbour the vennel provided the quickest and easiest access to the High Gait for travellers arriving by sea. Thus the vennel, the High Gait and the road to St Andrews formed an important junction, a suitable site for an inn. The eighteenth-century map shows a post office or posting house at this point.

Henrie Smyth's great-grandson sold the eastmost house in 1780 to James Mercer, vintner, and in 1791 Mercer bought the property next door. He was a town councillor in 1782 and town treasurer in 1790, and each year from 1793 until 1819, the year of his death, he was re-elected treasurer. He was commissioner to the Convention in 1805, 1809 and 1810, and collector of cess, assessed taxes, income and property tax, but he was hardly the best man to be managing public money. In April 1811 James Mercer was obliged to hand over his inn to the receiver-general in Edinburgh because he was in debt to the government to the extent of £908 6s 4d sterling.

The property was bought by Archibald Johnston, younger of Pittowie, who having improved it sold it five years later to Andrew Robertson, vintner, who named the inn the *Commercial Hotel*. In 1843 he bought the property to the west of the common vennel and built a large hall which extended over the common vennel and created the present pend. The hall was the scene of notable jollifications, one of them in 1848 to celebrate the arrival of the steamer *Xantho*. Upwards of forty gentlemen were present:

> A happier party never met . . . the dinner was sumptuous and did Mr Robertson great credit . . . the liquors were all that could be wished — almost everyone in the room's health was drunk, the songs went round merrily, and every man looked, and no doubt felt, as if care had never formed a wrinkle on his brow. The company enjoyed themselves until a late hour and then separated.

The evening before, a supper and ball in the Town Hall, celebrating the same event, continued until five o'clock in the morning.

This property to the west of the common vennel was inherited in 1651 by Alexander Paton, 'eldest son of David Paton, burgess in Anstruther Easter', both possibly forbears of Alexander Paton the shipbuilder. There was then a house and stable on the site.

To the west of the Paton property was an equally old, if not older, house which belonged in 1651 to Andro Strang, shipmaster in Anstruther, who sailed from Anstruther to Danzig and Stockholm. In 1641 he bought a bell for Anstruther Easter's new Parish Kirk, handsomely decorated with a medallion containing his portrait bust, the arms of the Strang family of Balcaskie, and an inscription: *ANDRO STRANG BOUGT THIS BELL WITH HIS OWNE MONEYES.* Beneath an ornamental band is another inscription which says in Latin that Andro Strang, baillie of Anstruther, 'had me made and presented me as a gift. Master Lurgen Putensen [a Danish bell-founder] made me at Stockholm'.

In 1645 the Town Council was in great straits for the payment of £800 Scots 'to ye present armie on futt within this kingdome, who are to be presentlie heir to plunder given ye same be not payit this week'. It was impossible in the circumstances to collect the sum by taxation so they had to borrow it. Paton, Strang and Captain David Alexander were among the wealthy inhabitants who put £50 each into the town chest and declared that 'giff ye same be cheirfully peyit to them at Candlemas nixt, they will

F

accept fourtie-fyfe punds money for everie fyftie they have advancit'.

The architect Murray Jack assigns this house to the late sixteenth century, and clearly by its alignment to the ford (which accounts for the awkward corner) it predates the bridge of 1630. Although it has been altered over the years the outline of a small Scottish tower house remains. The projecting tower would originally have contained a spiral stone stair, but now houses a linen cupboard. The Strang family owned the 'skeith quarter' of Kilrenny and the lands of Balcaskie until the early years of the seventeenth century, so this was probably their town house. The property was bought at public roup in 1905 by Mrs Stuart of the *Commercial Hotel*. An hotelier from Ayr bought the hotel in 1959, and in the early '60s he bought some old and derelict cottages in the Loan to provide a car park. Mr Campbell Macintyre thought the name *Commercial Hotel* out of date, so with a touch of romance, though not without some justification, he changed the name to the *Smugglers' Inn*.

Smuggling was for many years a thriving business in the East Neuk: a letter from the Convention in July 1744 warned the burghs against the 'pernicious habit of smuggling brandy, tea and other foreign commodities'. The local collector of customs reported in 1807 that smuggling vessels, usually from Flushing in the Netherlands, would come into the Firth with about a thousand ankers [eight-gallon casks] of brandy and gin and would be met by small boats from the fishing towns of Fife and Angus which would convey loads of twenty or more casks to the shore. These were carried by 'Carts, on the Backs of Men and Women and Horses' who conveyed them 'either to the Consumer or to Concealment at no Great Distance from the Shore'. There is no evidence that the inn was involved in smuggling but it does not require much stretch of the imagination to see it as a setting for the running of contraband goods: the sheltered reach of the burn mouth below, the narrow vennel leading up from the burn, cellarage at the inn for concealment, and the common loan out to the countryside to the wealthy and no doubt respectable consumer.

The collector's report continues with a heartfelt complaint that the revenue officer lived in the midst of a people who nine times out of ten were friendly to the smuggler and enemies to the officer; 'with a Great Part of the Men of all Ranks in this Part of the

Castle Street from West Anstruther's pier. The house on the left stands on the site of Dreel Castle.

Country at least, the smuggler is still thought a more Honourable Man than the Officer who Detects him and it requires a certain Degree of Firmness and Contempt for the opinion of the World to bear up against it'. Two local incidents prove his point.

A lugger, chased by a revenue cutter in December 1820, jettisoned over sixty casks of gin which were picked up and some of them opened and sampled by local fishermen about fifteen miles to the east of the Isle of May. One law-abiding fisherman, with some hope of a share of the prize money perhaps, informed the customs officers who immediately went down to Cellardyke and Anstruther harbours to await the arrival of the boats 'but the greater part of the different crews being so much in liquor, it was with considerable difficulty the Officers got the Spirits conveyed to a place of Safety, not only from the Fishermen that were drunk, but also from the women who usually meet waiting the arrival of the Boats'. A number of the crews of the boats that landed at Anstruther were also much in liquor and Peter Murray quarrelled with his crew at sea about delivering up the spirits, 'several of

them being much against his doing so'. Other casks were brought
in to Pittenweem and St Monans, and again the officers received
'great obstrucyion from the Mobs at both these creeks . . . and had
great difficulty in keeping possession of the Spirits'.

The other incident concerned 'Men of Property' who engaged
in the pernicious habit. David Fowler, master of the brigantine
the *Barbara and Mary* of Anstruther, of 87 tons burthen and £500
value, on his way in June 1804 from Norway to Anstruther,
picked up at sea three pipes of foreign brandy [a pipe was a cask
holding about 105 gallons]. Because of 'Baffling Winds' he was
obliged to stand over to the south shore of the Firth and when
discovered by his employers at Anstruther 'they went of to him in
a boat and by their advice and assistance got of Empty ankers and
filled them from the three pipes during the night when they were
all carried ashore, but he neither knows what became of them nor
where they are nor has he received one shilling on their account'.

The investigation of the 'Smuggle' and the search for the
brandy went on for several months. A small quantity of the spirits
was obtained, 'the quality seems good and no way injured by Salt
Water and of full import strength', and twenty casks were
reported to have been delivered to John Rodger, merchant in
Anstruther. The collector clearly wished to exonerate David
Fowler, the master, which was not surprising as David Fowler's
father in Cellardyke had been a customs official until his death in
1796, and Fowler himself 'had never been suspected of being
concerned in Illicit trade until this instance'. It seemed to the
collector that one of the two owners of the brigantine was a
principal in the smuggling, and it was not to be supposed that
David Fowler would have run the spirits 'without the concurrence of one of the Owners who lived so close at hand'. This same
owner's son was an apprentice on board the brigantine, and the
smuggle really began with him when he returned on board with
the empty casks. The collector had to admit to his superiors that
he and his colleagues had not been able to discover what became
of the brandy as both master and owner 'either did not know or
pretended not to know anything of the Matter and without their
assistance it would be impossible to have it out'. And he never did
have it out.

The owners of the brigantine were both 'Men of Considerable
Property'. One of them was William Leslie, farmer at Kingsbarns,
'but residing at seven miles distance from this place it was not

likely that he was acquainted with the transaction until it was finished'. In the collector's humble opinion the culpable owner 'who lived at Cellardyke close to the town of Anstruther', was Stephen Williamson, 'farmer on the Barrony of Balfour': the well-to-do Stephen Williamson, farmer and shipowner, father of Archibald Williamson, the young apprentice involved in the smuggle, and grandfather of Stephen Williamson, the future businessman and member of parliament.

The Bank House

In 1663 Sir Philip Anstruther built a new manor house (on the site of the present Crail Road and the Clydesdale Bank) above and to the east of the ancient crossroads and overlooking the narrow high street with its irregularly-placed stone houses and cottages. Several of these, as old as Henrie Smyth's property, were rebuilt in the eighteenth century 'fronting the street'. When the National Bank of Scotland in May 1832 opened in Anstruther the first bank between Leven and St Andrews, Matthew Conolly, writer and town clerk, was appointed agent and the bank was started in one of these rebuilt houses which Conolly had bought in 1826. His law office was on the ground floor and the bank, reached by an outside stair, on the second. The bank bought Conolly's property in 1856 (he retired from the bank the following year) and built on the site a large bank house faced with dressed stone and a pillared portico. To the east of this the bank bought a two-storey dwelling house, previously two cottages, and in 1883 erected on the site a 'telling room', with living accommodation on the floor above, all faced with dressed stone and with a second portico to match the earlier building.

To build stables the bank bought in 1856 the shambles at the foot of Wightman's Wynd — the stones of Dreel Castle had probably been used for the new Manor Place, but the remaining vaulted ground floor was given to the Town Council by Sir John Anstruther in 1808 when the town's old shambles near the mercat cross was blown away in a storm — and acquired in 1900 a range of old houses on the west side of Wightman's Wynd for a garden. These were demolished and stone lintels of doors and windows can still be seen in the wynd's west wall. The square tower at the foot of the wynd and the wall with a 'dumb-bell' loophole, both dating from the sixteenth century, were part of the house bought in 1749 by Charles Wightman, a wealthy merchant, and reputedly a successful smuggler, after whom the wynd was named. The 'battlements' were constructed by Henry Watson, bank agent, as a reminder of the former castle.

The impressive porticos of the bank and bank house were removed during road improvements before the Second World War. In 1959 the National Bank was vested in the Commercial Bank of Scotland and three years later the 'telling room' was sold to a firm of solicitors and the bank house was sold as a private dwelling house. In 1986 the two bank buildings were rejoined and became the East Neuk Outdoors Activities Centre. The ruinous stables at the foot of the wynd were replaced in 1962 by *Dreel Lodge*. Some large sandstones below the west wall of the lodge are all that remain of the ancient castle that once overlooked the busy haven.

Chalmers' Birthplace

To the northeast of Charles Wightman's house was 'the lodging and house sometime occupied by William Clark thereafter Sir Philip Anstruther and the north yeard thereof'. This is the house now known as Thomas Chalmers' birthplace. William Clark was appointed Anstruther Wester's first Protestant minister in 1560. As the Reformed Church had insufficient funds to appoint a minister to every parish, he had the charge of three others, including the parish of Kilrenny. William Clark 'of maist happy memory for godliness, wisdom, and love of his flock' died in 1583 and was succeeded by the Rev. James Melville. Philip Anstruther (1631-1702) inherited the Barony in 1649 and in 1651 was host at Dreel Castle to Charles II, who presented him with three silver gilt cups to mark the occasion. It was probably while subsequently building the Manor Place that Sir Philip lived in the 'lodgeing' which he then feued to the masters of the Sea Box: John Gourlay, Alexander and William Halson, Thomas Kellock and George Smyth. Their successors sold it in 1707 to Philip Brown, 'one of the present balleys of Anstruther Castle, skipper burgess'.

This was the Philip Brown, skipper, who owned property on the shore of Anstruther Wester. He was one of the wealthiest burgesses of the Easter burgh and with two others was the

The recently restored 16th-century house in which the Paton brothers and Thomas Chalmers were subsequently born. In the 1840s the Post Office was on the right of the main door.

highest subscriber towards an assistant for the Rev. William Woodrope who some time previously had 'in a most dreadfull and extraordinair manner broke his leg' and was no longer able to perform his pastoral duties. Brown was first elected baillie in 1705 and was first baillie in 1715, and it can be seen from the number of missed Council meetings how often he was away at sea. He died sometime before July 1730 when his son, Philip, inherited his fore tenement, now No. 4 Castle Street, and the back tenement, the sixteenth-century 'lodgeing', which Philip Brown, younger, described two years later as having been 'rebuilt by my father', with the 'closs and yaird now converted into a large closs from the north street'. In September 1732 Philip Brown, shipmaster, signed a marriage contract with Jean Nairne and on the same day transferred the back tenement to his sister Helen Brown.

The back tenement was at the foot of the slope from the High Gait and Philip Brown, senior, must have raised the level of the yard to the level of the first floor of the three-storey house, providing access from the High Street as it is today. In the north wall of the original ground floor can be seen stone lintels of former windows. Helen Brown added a postscript to the deed of transfer:

> Whereas Philip Brown my brother has granted me the disposition to
> the house Nevertheless as he has occasion for the use of the Brew
> house and cellar as also the garret of the said house Therefore I
> Helen Brown hereby oblige myself and whosoever shall succeed
> me to the said house to allow my said brother . . . full and free use
> of the said Brew house cellar and garret during all the days of his
> lifetime.

He presumably needed the garret to store his ship's gear and
trade goods, and the brew house cellar to make ale for his crews
when at sea. Helen Brown, born in 1684, was married first to
Philip Paton, merchant in Anstruther. The postscript was written
by her son, Philip Paton, who probably began his career in a
writer's office in the town. He married Agnes Loch, daughter of a
wealthy local merchant, and they continued to live in the back
tenement where their four sons were born, Philip, Charles,
Robert and David.

Philip, the eldest son, born in October 1739, attended the burgh
school and as a young boy sailed to the Mediterranean and the
Baltic in a vessel belonging to his uncle. He could have qualified
for any of the learned professions but chose the Royal Navy
which he entered at the age of fifteen. He was made a captain in
1789, a rear admiral in 1795 and a full admiral ten years later. His
service at sea was during the worst days of press gangs and
mutinies, one of which, on his ship, the *Prince George*, was
successfully suppressed 'by the wise, prudent, officer-like conduct on Captain Paton's part'; he had profound sympathy with
the seamen's grievances. 'In his person he was about the middle
size, in his disposition kind and friendly; in the ships he commanded he maintained strict discipline under the guidance of a
sound judgement and a benevolent temper. He was much loved
by the seamen' — and none of them deserted when he gave leave
to his crews at Portsmouth. He made his home at Fareham and
died there in 1815 at the age of 76. A granddaughter of Philip
Paton, or Patton as he signed his name, married a merchant
captain from Southampton named Jellicoe and was the mother of
Admiral Earl Jellicoe of Battle of Jutland fame.

The second son Charles went to sea in merchant ships and
entered the navy as a midshipman in 1758 at the age of seventeen,
gaining the rank of captain in 1795. During the whole of the
Napoleonic Wars he was superintendent of transport at Ports-

mouth. He also lived at Fareham where he died at the age of 96, 'a highly esteemed and respected officer'.

Robert and David Paton entered the service of the Honourable East India Company but David died at Calcutta in 1778 as an ensign in the infantry. Robert was appointed an assistant surgeon in 1764 at the age of twenty-one but transferred to the infantry and as captain became an ADC to Warren Hastings who was then governor of Bengal, and when Hastings became governor-general of India in 1773 Robert Paton was appointed his military secretary. At the age of 33 Robert Paton retired with the rank of colonel after a short but distinguished career. He returned to Fife and in 1774 bought the estate of Kinaldy but was recalled by the East India Company in 1802 to serve as governor of the island of St Helena. He retired five years later and removed to Hampshire to be near his brothers, dying there in 1812. His granddaughter, Mary Jane Torrens, married Sir Ralph Anstruther of Balcaskie in 1831 and was the great-great-grandmother of the present Sir Ralph. Sons of Robert and Charles Paton served as midshipmen on the *Bellerophon* at the battle of Trafalgar in 1805. Philip Paton, senior, moved to Kirkcaldy as collector of customs there and none of the brothers returned to Anstruther to live.

Thomas Chalmers was born in the back tenement on March 17th 1780 while his father, John Chalmers, built his new 'north house' above the mill. James, father of John, came of a family of small landowners and ministers of the church in Fife and settled in Anstruther as a dyer, shipowner and general merchant, and married Barbara Anderson, a member of a local seafaring family. His prosperous business passed to John, his eldest son, who married Elizabeth Hall, daughter of a wine merchant in Crail, and with his brother-in-law started a thread manufactory in a building below the north house, now the site of a small public garden. Thomas, the fourth son of their fourteen children, attended the burgh school and at the age of twelve the University of St Andrews.

His earliest ambition was to become a professor of mathematics and his eldest brother James commented that in the early days of his ministry Thomas's mathematical studies appeared to occupy more of his time than his religious studies. On the occasion of his first sermon at the age of 19 James wrote that it was the 'opinion of those who pretend to be judges' that he would shine in the pulpit, but yet he was rather awkward in his appearance.

'We, however, were at some pains in adjusting his dress, manners, etc, but he does not seem to pay any great regard to it himself'. He never overcame this awkwardness but his lack of vanity made an impression on the Quaker, Joseph Gurney. 1803 to 1815, while Chalmers was at Kilmany, were the years of the Napoleonic wars and he not only fulminated against Napoleon in the pulpit but joined the Volunteers, holding commissions as chaplain and lieutenant, and he claimed that if nature had fitted him for any one profession above another, it was that of military engineer. After a serious illness at Kilmany he devoted himself more seriously to his ministry and thenceforward was an ardent Evangelical and became famous for his preaching throughout Scotland and abroad.

Every cause that Chalmers adopted he advanced 'with zeal and enthusiasm', but his causes were often controversial and frequently inconsistent. He opposed state relief for the poor; the system of poor relief that he instituted in his Glasgow parish depended ultimately on the poor helping the poor. The scheme received much public attention but many in the church rejected it and its success did not long survive his removal to Edinburgh. He believed that the state should support the church 'as the highest instrument of good to the people' and contribute financially to its upkeep while respecting its complete freedom and independence. The contemporary conflict in the civil courts over the right of the owner of a living to appoint a minister and the right of the congregation to reject the appointee resolved itself into a conflict over this question of the independence of the church. Thomas Chalmers declared that either the church's spiritual independence should be recognised and secured 'or the connection between her and the State be dissolved'. In May 1843, with Dr Welch the Moderator, Chalmers led more than four hundred ministers out of the Established Church to found the Free Church of Scotland of which he was elected first Moderator. His action was not universally applauded but it was principled, and as always he showed himself a masterly organiser. In 1842 when disruption seemed inevitable he provided a plan of financial support for all outgoing ministers, the Sustenation Fund, without which the Free Church would never have survived — as it did until 1929 when it was reunited with the Church of Scotland.

Thomas Chalmers died in his sleep on the night of May 30th 1847. Over a hundred thousand people lined the streets to pay

Dr Thomas Chalmers, evangelical preacher, academic, and leader of the 1843 Disruption of the Church of Scotland.

their respects at his funeral, 'by far the grandest and most impressive that had ever been witnessed in Edinburgh'.

Charles Chalmers, the second youngest of the family, was born in the north house in 1792. He failed to complete his studies at St Andrews University because of ill-health and went into a new publishing business in Glasgow with William Collins, a friend and admirer of his older brother. The business nearly failed and he resigned, moving to Edinburgh to complete his degree. Like Thomas, he was good at mathematics and science. While studying he took some students into his home as boarders and coached them for their examinations. Finding the work congenial, he opened a school for boys in 1828 and five years later moved it to the old Merchiston Tower, and took the name Merchiston Castle School.

The back tenement was bought from Philip Paton in 1792 by George Robb, writer, who lived in the front tenement and whose son Charles was in the Royal Navy. Anstruther Easter provided the navy with a number of men during the wars with France and several masters and officers lived in Castle Street. Charles Robb was made a captain in 1810 but perished at sea five years later. His daughter, Charles Ann Robb, inherited the back tenement and in 1848 she sold it to her aunt Agnes Robb and Agnes's husband the Rev. John Murdoch who was ordained in the Evangelical Union Church in 1830. While he was pastor the Union Church was built in the new Crail Road in 1833. It is now a store for the Gray & Pringle ironmongery business.

The post office was installed in the house during the Murdoch ownership, in the small room to the right of the front door, with Agnes Robb as postmistress ('Letters from all parts arrive every morning at 3.0 and are despatched every evening at 7.0.'). In about 1851 the post office was moved across the High Street to the former business premises of the late John Chalmers, leaving behind the name of Old Post Office Close.

Thenceforward the back tenement was occupied by two tenant families. In 1885 after two public roups it was sold to Robert Fortune, druggist and chemist in Rodger Street and an active member of the Baptist Church. Hay Fleming described the house in 1886 as dingy and dilapidated when it was put up for sale, but already Robert Fortune had repaired the roof and put on a new face of cement, and was planning to renovate the house inside, 'leaving intact the wooden pannelling and box bed' of the room in which Thomas Chalmers was said to have been born. It was put up for sale again in August 1918 after the death of Mrs Fortune when it was occupied by two families, the Swans and the Budds. L. Cpl. Thomas Swan, a regular soldier in the Black Watch, was awarded the DCM for gallantry in November 1914 and was killed in action in December at Festubert — 'Hell's Corner'. L. Cpl. Alexander Budd of the Tank Corps, who had been awarded the DCM for conspicuous gallantry and devotion to duty in April, was recommended in September 1918 for the Military Medal for distinguished services in the action at Amiens in northern France.

Fearing that the house might possibly pass into the hands of someone who might demolish it or reconstruct it, Helen Murray or Pittendrigh of *Adelaide Lodge* bought it 'in order to hand it over to a public body who would hold it as a memorial of a famous and revered native of Anstruther'. The date of the conveyance was November 11th 1918, Armistice Day, so the gift of the back tenement to the community was regarded as both a memorial to Dr Chalmers 'and as a memorial to the coming of peace'. Mrs Pittendrigh handed the house to the trustees of the Murray Library which had been a bequest to the burgh of Anstruther from her brother David Murray.

The house continued to be occupied by two families, both sharing the only water closet at the back of the cellar, next to Philip Brown's right of way to Castle Street, with an ancient gunloop for a window. The female members of the two families approached it with hatpin and candle even in daylight. Coal fires were used for cooking and oil lamps for lighting until 1914 when gas lighting was put in the living room. When the lights of the Free Church went down for the sermon the light in the living room went up and if it remained up for only twenty-five minutes, William Smith's grandmother would say 'the Minister has little to say tonight'.

No funds were available to the trustees in the 1960s when the house was badly in need of repair. A wide appeal was launched in 1966 to preserve as a family home the birthplace of Thomas Chalmers but the response was disappointing and plans for the restoration and a Chalmers Museum on the ground floor had to be abandoned. Eventually in 1979 the trustees came to an agreement with the National Trust for Scotland who, seeing the improvements that Messrs Murray & Wilson, joiners, had made to the old houses in Post Office Close, offered them the back tenement in 1980.

Work started in the close in 1979 with the renovation of the flat above the baker's shop in the High Street and the removal of between 30 and 35 tons of debris from the huge old baker's oven, built in what had originally been a single-storey cottage, entered from Wightman's Wynd, with stone walls two feet thick. A seventeenth-century house in the close which had also belonged to skipper Philip Brown, elder, was then restored. The original entrance to the house was in the wynd at the foot of an internal stone stair. Peter Murray carefully preserved several interesting features and rebuilt the dormer windows to the original traditional design.

Work on the back tenement started in September 1981 after the removal of several hundred pigeons. The original stone stair columns and stairs survive and a great open fireplace with corbelled pillars surmounted by a stone lintel seven feet long was uncovered on the ground floor, the original first floor. Many of the old joists and beams were ships' masts with the tapered ends squared with pieces of timber to take floor boards of various widths, and in the basement a ship's stem had been used as a door lintel.

The box bed in the east room had to be removed but the best pieces of the original pine panelling were put in the former post office room and replaced, appropriately, with balcony panelling from Chalmers' Memorial Church. Two fireplaces and mantels were brought from the minister's vestry in the church and the board room. The stone slates of the abutment were recut, rebored and rehung in the original fashion on tile battens, but with new wooden pegs. Pantiles were reclaimed from an old cottage at Frithfield Farm to eke out the best of the original tiles, and stone window sills in the south wall were replaced with sills from an old cottage being demolished near Pitscottie. It was a magnificent restoration both inside and out and deservedly won a Civic Award.

Robert Alexander's House

High on the south wall of No. 14 Rodger Street a 'dormer head', which gives some indication of the style of the original house, has the initials R A and G A and two coats of arms, for Robert Alexander and Grizel Anstruther, and the date 1631. The couple built their house on what was then the edge of the town. On the north was the laird's arable land and Doocot yaird, in the north-east corner of which, by the Cunzie Burn, stood the laird's teind barn and barnyard; on the west was the Cows Close, now upper Rodger Street, where cattle would have passed on their way to pasture, and on the south was the High Gait. Calvert's Wynd, running from the Cows Close and the High Gait down to the shore, was another narrow wynd like Wightman's Wynd. It was widened in 1827 and the new road (called the 'new road' almost up to the Second World War) was named after the then chief magistrate, David Rodger, corn merchant. Two eighteenth-century cottages, somewhat altered, remain at the foot of the east side of the former wynd.

The 1631 datestone on a house in the High Street with the arms of Robert Alexander and his wife Grizel Anstruther.

Grizel was a daughter of Sir James Anstruther of that Ilk, Heritable Carver of James VI and Master of the Queen's Household, and one of those Fife adventurers who in 1598 undertook to develop the 'maist barbourous Isle of Lewis'. A Robert Alexander who died in 1577 was a maltman in Anstruther, as was his son John, and Robert, grandson of the maltman and builder of the house, was a merchant. Through a cousin's influence at court he, his cousin, and his brother, Captain David Alexander, received permission from Charles I to form a Fishery Society of Great Britain and Ireland, which was granted a Royal Charter in 1632. It was a time when the fishing industry was being generally encouraged: to oust the large fleets of Dutch herring busses fishing Scotland's coastal waters; to build up an export trade; and to act as a training school for mariners in time of war.

David Alexander was a shipmaster and sailed from Anstruther to Königsberg in the summer of 1619 and again in 1622; and a William Alexander made the same voyage in 1620, and '21, and a voyage from London to Stockholm in 1622. In 1643 and 1648 both Robert and Captain David Alexander were commended in Acts of the Scottish parliament for putting the kingdom 'in a posture of defence'.

Baillie Robert Alexander took a prominent part in 1634 in securing the erection of the burgh's own parish church. He was the Town Council's commissioner to the Convention on several occasions and represented the East Neuk burghs in the Scottish parliament. He had an annual rent of bear 'furth of the lands of Innergellie', and inherited from his grandfather Robert two acres of land in Pittenweem. Another Robert Alexander, merchant in Edinburgh, almost certainly a descendant, was the owner of the whaling ship *Rising Sun* which failed at the whaling and transferred to the West Indies trade; he came to Anstruther Wester to contest the election of Sir John Anstruther in 1766.

There is an elaborate tombstone to the Alexander family on the west wall of the churchyard which has on the left pilaster the usual symbols of the transitoriness of life and on the right the tools of the maltster's trade.

After the sale of his High Street house to the National Bank in 1856 Matthew Conolly, town clerk, moved his office to the upper floor of the Alexander house; on the ground floor Andrew Gourlay, bookseller and bookbinder, had his business, having started as a bookbinder in Tolbooth Wynd when he came from Pittenweem in the 1830s. The house has been rebuilt but the low-roofed ground floor is probably original, and it was here in the shop that his eldest son George overheard the stories that he later published.

George Gourlay was born in Pittenweem in January 1832 and died in Anstruther in August 1891. By his death from an inflammation of the lungs at the age of 59, the *East of Fife Record* declared, the locality lost one of the most unique and interesting personalities of the district. 'In his young days he showed unusual aptitude, but a defect in his eyes, from which he suffered all his life, imposed upon him the task of trusting to his memory for information . . . one of the most retentive memories any one could possibly wish.' He submitted his stories to Fife newspapers and was persuaded to collect and publish them. The first of his three volumes, about Cellardyke, was published in Cupar in 1879 and the last in 1888: *Anstruther: or Illustrations of Scottish Burgh Life*, 'his most ambitious and by many considered his best', for which he received several acknowledgements 'including a post card from Mr Gladstone'. He had access, probably in the town clerk's office upstairs, to the early seventeenth-century minutes of the Burgh Council, which have since unfortunately disappeared, so his many excerpts from the records are invaluable.

The three-storey house on the east side of Tolbooth Wynd was the Minister's Manse from the late 17th century until 1715.

The Manse

On the south side of the High Gait behind the eighteenth-century inn, now the *Royal Hotel*, is a small two-storey house with crow-stepped gable to the highway and half of a marriage lintel with the date 1633. Where the level of the street is above the level of the floor of a house, there can be little doubt about the age of the building. Further east, halfway down the Tolbooth Wynd, formerly Andrew Gardner's Causeway, is a derelict three-storey house with a short outside stair. It was built in the mid-seventeenth century by William Hamilton, a wealthy burgess of Anstruther who later bought the estate of Easter Grangemuir, and was inherited by his son, Andrew Hamilton, in 1672. From the time of his arrival as minister of the parish in 1686 it was occupied by the Rev. William Woddrope. (His predecessor from 1677 to 1686, the tragic Rev. Edward Thomson, lived in a stone house in the High Gait below the Manor Place.) In 1705 John

Darsie, couper burgess, baillie and treasurer, proposed to the Town Council that Hamilton's house should be bought by the town 'to be a manse in all tyme comeing' and the Council paid Sir John Anstruther 'six hundreth merks Scots' in part payment of 700 merks, the agreed price of the feu of the house in the wynd. It remained the manse until September 1718 when the Council contracted with Sir John Anstruther to exchange the house in the wynd for the manse built by James Melville, which Sir William Anstruther had bought in 1637. The Council then sold the house in the wynd to John Darsie, couper burgess, and it remained in the possession of his descendants until 1926. All but two of the old houses in the ancient wynd have been empty now for many years.

13
The Malt Barns

Malt, with herring and cod, was a staple commodity of the burgh before the Union of 1707. Barley was grown on the arable lands above the town and each of the streams running down through the town had its malt steading. There were three on the Cunzie Burn in the eighteenth century. Behind the manse in Tolbooth Wynd was the malt barn, kiln and coble 'sometime belonging to Sir William Anstruther of that Ilk' and after him to William and Andrew Hamilton — Sir William Anstruther died in 1647, which dates the barn to the early seventeenth century — and on the north side of the High Gait were malt steadings on both banks of the Burn. Another on the south side of the churchyard, belonging first to William Alexander and then to Captain David Alexander, was demolished by 1720.

In the Back Dykes beyond the School Green on the east side of a small stream there was in 1728 'an Malt Barn, malt grannerie, Corn Barn, Kiln, Coble with the yard and piece of ground'.

Further east on the stream in the 'Hadd-the-feets' Wynd were two malt steadings, one on the west bank belonging in 1727 to William Halson, skipper. The other on the east bank was 'towards the head of the peer' on that tenement, 'commonly called St Ails Chappel', which was granted to the monks of Balmerino by the first William de Candela in the twelfth century. The surviving walls of the ancient chapel probably served as the malt barn. It was owned by four generations of Lumsdaines. William Lumsdaine of the third generation married Helen Duncan in 1708 as his second wife and built on the St Ails land two houses one of which fronted the 'vennel that leads to the harbour'. Both houses are now part of the Scottish Fisheries Museum and the date stone W H-H D 1721 remains over the door in Hadfoot Wynd. Baillie Lumsdaine owned arable land between Melville's Manse and Hadfoot Wynd and another acre 'commonly called the Kilne Acre' — St Ayles Park.

The local malt industry seems to have declined before the end of the eighteenth century. The Darsie family acquired the malt

171

barn behind the former manse in Tolbooth Wynd for their fish-curing premises until the death of Provost Darsie in 1896. The massively timbered barn and the shell of the manse are now a joiner's yard and store.

The malt steading at the foot of Hadfoot Wynd was also a fishcuring yard by the beginning of the nineteenth century and by 1844 it was managed by the young William Halson Anderson who lived in the Lumsdaine house. Both Halson and Anderson forbears were property-owning shipmasters and masters of the Sea Box, and both families acquired during the later eighteenth century, by inheritance and purchase, nearby arable land including the Kiln Acre. Fishcuring and coopering were carried on in the yard until the decline of the fishing and latterly the ancient group of buildings comprised a house and shop and a ship chandler's business. Parts of the old buildings were let for net lofts and the storage of fishermen's gear and the courtyard was used for the barking and drying of nets.

The National Trust bought the decaying property in the early 1960s as part of its Little Houses Scheme, but Baillie Thomas Anderson Murray, slater and builder, with the late Provost Carstairs' collection of McGhie paintings and relics of the fishing industry in mind, suggested that the site was ideal for a museum in which to exhibit them. The proposal was endorsed in the 1965 Council election when T. A. Murray was returned unopposed. The following month the Town Council bought the St Ayles property from the National Trust for £1,800 and in 1968 the Scottish Fisheries Museum Trust Limited was formed. The museum was opened in 1969 by Dr John Grierson, the Scottish film-maker. As a tourist and educational attraction it is a great asset to the burgh.

The malt burn on the north side of the High Street on the west bank of the Cunzie Burn was bought in 1804 by Alexander Tennant, merchant, the father of William Tenant, poet and professor of oriental languages at St Andrews University. Tennant sold it to George Russell, tenant farmer in East Pitkierie and brewer. The *East Fife Observer* announced in August 1919 that alterations were being made to that property 'known as the brewery', though at some period before 1919 it was an aerated mineral water factory. On November 27th 1919 the former malt barn was opened as the *Empire Picture House*, 'the first night's proceeds, amounting to £12, going to the Nursing Association'.

(The first cinema in the town was opened in the Town Hall in 1912). Like the *Regal Cinema* in Anstruther Wester the *Empire* was a popular source of entertainment until the arrival of television in the 1970s. The barn is now a boat shed.

In the mid-eighteenth century the barn on the east bank of the Burn was the property of James Johnston, vintner and town treasurer and founder member of a local whaling company. His heirs sold the premises in 1795 to James Rodger, merchant in Anstruther, and his son David Rodger, junior, brewer, inherited the property in 1817. When it was sold in 1839 after his death it consisted of:

> Brewhouse Malt barn kiln, Granary, cellars and close . . . and the whole machinery and fixtures within the premises comprising the Malt Mill, and steep copper boiler Mash Tun two fermenting Tuns two coolers and a water cistern. And the water which is collected in that field or Park to the north of the Church yard as lately possessed by David Rodger.

The water was brought to the Brewery by conduit. (*Cunzie House* was known at that time as *Conduit House*). The brewery changed hands three times during the next few years until it was bought at public roup in 1858 by the only offerer, James Key, brewer in the Westgate of Crail. It was managed by his son John and then by his son William Key until William's death in June 1920. He lived in the adjoining three-storeyed *Brewery House* which was occupied in the early eighteenth century by James Darsie, maltman, whose three daughters sold it in 1768 to Baillie James Johnston who sold it with the brewery to James Rodger; it was Rodger who heightened the walls of the original single-storey house. The name was changed to *Belmont House* in 1965.

In the seventeenth century the malt steading in the Back Dykes was part of a tenement 'containing several houses, yards and others'. It was acquired in the 1760s by James Black, merchant in Anstruther Easter, and his eldest son, Andrew Black, late merchant and Comptroller of Customs there. They sold it in 1801 to James Rodger, owner of the Cunzie Burn malt barn, and in 1816 his son David Rodger sold it to John Goodsir, surgeon in Anstruther Easter. Malting and brewing had clearly ceased here too.

John Goodsir, one of three surgeon sons of the much respected John Goodsir in Largo, bought the malt steading in 1816, about three years after settling in Anstruther Easter as the town's doctor. By the following year the malt barn had become 'my large dwelling house of three storeys'. He then bought the property to the east consisting of 'Stable and Hay loft Gig house Coal house, Cellars and other outhouses with the garden'. This was the Baxter's Barn of James Melville's time, which, rebuilt as a house and offices and with a garden stretching down to the lane at the foot of the manse, belonged from the latter half of the seventeenth century to a family of small farmers. In the most recent renovation of that part of Goodsir's house a large fireplace with wide stone lintel and stone pilasters was uncovered and carefully repaired. John Goodsir, senior, died in 1848 and was buried in Largo churchyard.

The sons of the surgeon were educated at the Burgh School. In his thirteenth year the eldest son John, born in Anstruther in 1814, attended the University of St Andrews where he had a greater aptitude for Latin than for Greek or mathematics, but his absorbing interest was Natural History. Local fishermen sent up to the 'shy lanky boy' and his brother Henry any oddities that they found in their nets. He began his career with a five-year apprenticeship to a dentist in Edinburgh, but after two years gave it up for medicine and in 1835 returned to Anstruther. During the five years that he practised in the burgh with his father he gave lectures on natural history to Literary and Philosophic Societies in Cupar and St Andrews and built up a small menagerie and a model museum which included fossils from local limestone quarries. A Memoir on Teeth that he gave to the British Association in 1838 made his name known in wider scientific circles and in 1841 he was offered the post of Conservator of the Museum of the Royal College of Surgeons in Edinburgh, and a few years later the Chair of Anatomy at the University, where his classroom became 'the most crowded in the whole University'. The German pathologist Virchow dedicated his book *Cellular Pathology*, published in 1858, to John Goodsir as 'one of the earliest and most acute observers of cell-life'. Unsociable and hardworking he neglected his health and died at Wardie in 1867 at the age of 53: 'he lived only for science and unquestionably died in its service'.

The second Goodsir son was a minister, and the third, Henry, anatomist and naturalist, sailed in 1845 as assistant surgeon with Sir John Franklin's polar expedition which was lost searching for a

This house in the courtyard of the Scottish Fisheries Museum was built for the Abbot of Balmerino in the 16th century.

north west passage. The fourth son (probably the author of the Goodsir MS) graduated in medicine and sailed twice to the Arctic in the search for Franklin's ship, and the fifth son studied medicine in Europe but 'came home to die . . . truly a victim to his zeal in anatomical pursuits'.

John Black of Liverpool, who left bequests of £5,000 to Waid Academy and the Union Harbour, was born in the Goodsir house, the elder son of Thomas Black, surgeon, who came to Anstruther in place of Dr Goodsir. Thomas was born in 1819 in East Wemyss but may have belonged to the Anstruther family of Black. He married a daughter of Archibald Williamson's sister Barbara, and was several times baillie. At his death by drowning at the age of 45 years a monument in Anstruther churchyard was erected to his memory by public subscription. The house was known as *Rosebank* while it belonged to James Cairns, veterinary surgeon, but a Miss Erskine of Cambo bought it in 1937 and named the former malt steading and Baxter's Barn the *Hermitage*.

Only one part of the malt steading on the west bank of the Hadfoot stream survives but its history is part of another story.

14

The Shore

Facing south above a sandy shore, sheltered on the north, and well watered by small streams, the narrow, low raised beach was well suited for the settlement of seafarers. Some built their dwellings facing the sea but others were set gable-end to the sea as a protection against storms and faced each other across a narrow close. Several entries along Shore Street and, at the east end behind rebuilt houses, some pantiled cottages gable-end to the sea remain, but only Walker's Close survives as it might have been three hundred years ago. It retains its flagstone paving and a central drain (now concreted), a cottage with an outside stair and two cottages gable-end to the sea with a token cutaway corner at the north end. The close, which once led up to the 'north gait' on the upper raised beach, is entered through a pend between two seventeenth-century houses and at the back of the pend is a corbelled stair turret, an old Scottish architectural feature that so appealed to Charles Rennie Mackintosh.

A close to the east was laid with concrete in 1916 and an outside stair removed, but the six houses on the east side of the close are much as they were built, close together, and except for the corner cottage which faced north, all gable-end to the sea. The north cottage belonged to several generations of Blacks one of whom, John Black, master of a ship belonging to Captain William Anstruther, sailed for Norway in 1684 with a cargo of malt. The cottages have all been modernised internally but external features indicate their age: thick walls, low rooms, crowstepped gables, pantiled roofs, corbelled upper floors, and on the house behind the *Ship* a decorated skewputt. (The tavern's turret was added in 1899.)

Seventeenth-century shipmasters owned property along the shore, among them John Gourlay who owned two half tenements, now 34 Shore Street. The ground-floor rooms are low-roofed and in recent renovations a large stone fireplace was uncovered in the back tenement. To the east were the tenements of David Burnside, shipmaster, and the Elie sea captain Robert

Nairne, and on the west was property belonging to Captain David Alexander. Beyond Alexander's property the line of houses on the shore turns gradually north westwards as it follows the mouth of the Cunzie Burn. Several of these houses retain old features: in one is a wide fireplace on the first floor, and the rounded wall of a former spiral stone stair, both uncovered during renovation. Other houses were rebuilt or demolished. At the end of the line at the junction of the Burn and the stream from the Back Dykes is a late sixteenth-century building, crowstepped and pantiled, with a corbelled gable, and a corbelled stair turret, one of the three oldest surviving houses in the burgh. The Burn now flows through the Folly wall into the harbour behind the slipway jetty.

The shore between the head of the west pier and Calverts Wynd became the business centre of the burgh where in the seventeenth century a tolbooth, mercat cross, and flesh shambles were erected. Nearby on the lower Cunzie Burn small houses were closely packed in the Back gait, Card's Wynd, which may have been named for the carders of linen fibres, and Shore Lane.

Number 11 Shore Street, one of the remaining seventeenth-century shops along the shore, was the burgh's 'centre of learning' when William Cockburn, bookbinder from Edinburgh, opened a business of bookbinder, bookseller and stationer in 1786. It inspired Archibald Constable from Carnbee to serve an apprenticeship there before establishing his publishing business in Edinburgh. The writer of the Goodsir MS (in the National Library) recalls the bookseller, with his 'yellow wig backed with formal curls . . . a braw dressed man', than whom no man 'during his long period of residence was more respected or better liked . . . He was always talked of and addressed as *Mister* Cockburn', whilst other shopkeepers and tradesmen rarely had a prefix accorded to their name 'save when entitled to Bailie (Beelyey)'.

There was a counter on each side of the shop, racks of canes and walking sticks, and a glass case with among other things 'many coloured sealing waxes and equally variegated wafers'. The writer in 1884 remembered the 'subtile mingled odours of Russia, of Morocco and of Calf', and the goose quills, 'bundles of them, sheaves of them, shelves full of them each bound tightly with red and black cord'. A well selected Circulating Library filled the shelves of the back premises. After the battle of Waterloo, the writer continues:

Scarce a town on the coasts of the Firth that could not boast of its quota of . . . veterans and Anstruther . . . had its full share of them. I can recollect of more than one Admiral and sundry Post-Captains, with not a few straight-backed erect *Militaires*. In their forenoon walks they all gravitated towards the low-ceiled Russia and Morocco smelling shop of Mr Cockburn.

It was from these premises that William Cockburn published the first edition of William Tennant's *Anster Fair*.

In a close towards the eastern end of the shore a house was built in the early seventeenth century by John Lindsay of Newton of Nydie, merchant in Anstruther Easter. He was admitted burgess in 1640, elected baillie in 1642, Commissioner to the Convention of Royal Burghs in 1656 and representative Elder to the Church Assembly. In 1644 during the Civil War he was chosen by the baillies and Council of Anstruther 'capitaine' to drill and organise the inhabitants 'when occasion shall serve'. He died in 1676 and his 'principal back house' passed to his son Alexander Lindsay, skipper in Anstruther, and then to his grandson, John Lindsay of Newton of Nydie, shipmaster and merchant in Crail.

Gourlay recounts how in 1708 three officers, 'the tallest of whom was none other than the Chevalier', landed at Anstruther with muffled oars at dead of night from Admiral Fourbin's ship and made their way by Low's Close to Lindsay's house and the secret room behind the panel. The French vessel that brought the Old Pretender into the Forth in 1708, however, returned to France without ever putting the prince ashore, but as so often there is a grain of truth in the tradition: in 1704 John Lindsay married into a well-known Jacobite family, the Leslies in Crail. He and his wife probably never lived in the principal back house as they built on the north side of Crail High Street a house still known as the Leslie house, bearing on the front a carved stone with their coats of arms and monogram and the date 1710. John Lindsay died in 1714 at the age of 33 and is buried in Crail churchyard where his tombstone states in Latin that he was a merchant of Crail and that he was descended 'not so very remotely' from the noble family of Lindsay.

Two years after her husband's death Helen Leslie transferred the principal back house to her younger brother, David Leslie, merchant burgess of both Crail and Anstruther, who married into another of Crail's Jacobite families. His only surviving daughter sold the principal back house and some adjoining land in 1790 to

George Ayton, relative of the Aytons of Kinaldy and purser in the Royal Navy. Five years previously George Ayton bought from two heiresses of William Lumsdaine a piece of arable land to the north of the back house, 'which was converted by me George Ayton into a garden surrounded by a stone wall'. In 1782 and '83 during the War of American Independence George Ayton was purser of *HMS Rainbow*, and on several occasions his ship carried prisoners of war, both French and American. He may have bought the house and land in Anstruther with his share of prize money. In July 1803 George Ayton, then residing in London, sold the principal back house and garden.

Most of the owners of the back house in Old Post Office Close left the burgh for careers elsewhere but the owners of the principal back house in the close by the shore were all incomers. The new owner in 1803 was John Clarkson then residing in Pittenweem but formerly Senior Baxter Burgess in Edinburgh. He owned two lodgings in Edinburgh's High Street one of which was on the north side of the Street 'at the Anchor Close a little below the Cross Well'. It was in Anchor Close in Dawney Douglas's Tavern that one of the most convivial of the eighteenth-century Edinburgh clubs of literati and wits used to meet: the Crochallan Fencibles whose lively meetings Robert Burns attended during his visits to the capital in the years between 1787 and 1791.

Before leaving the eighteenth century, something must be told of Anstruther Easter's own club of literati and wits.

15
The Beggar's Benison

The Most Ancient and Puissant Order of the Beggar's Benison and Merryland was founded about twenty years before the notorious Brotherhood of the Friars of St Francis of Medmenham, but both were in the same tradition of gentlemen's clubs. The earliest known club was Le Cour de Bon Compagnie in the reign of Henry IV at the beginning of the fifteenth century. Like most subsequent clubs it was primarily a dining club. Sir Walter Raleigh was said to have founded a dining club which met in the Mermaid Tavern on the Thames, and in the reign of James VI and I Ben Jonson founded another, but it was with the institution of the coffee house in about 1650 that clubs began to flourish: literary, scientific, philosophical and political. After the Restoration in 1660 and through most of the eighteenth century the number and variety increased, many of them embodying the 'extravagance and often lawless fancies of idle young men'.

Most of the well-known clubs belonged to London and the south, but Edinburgh and Glasgow kept abreast of the times. There were respectable clubs of professional men which met in the capital during law terms; there were 'sad accounts of some secret atheistical clubs in or about Edinburgh'; convivial clubs like the Circulation which commemorated Harvey's discovery of the circulation of the blood [1628] by the circulation of the glass; Sweating clubs, as in London, the members of which in a state of intoxication sallied forth at midnight and attacked or jostled any inoffensive citizen they chanced to meet; and there were clubs actually called Mug House Clubs which were suppressed because of their disorderly conduct.

A few clubs survived to become respectable in the nineteenth century but most of them were eccentric and short-lived. All were convivial, but only Anstruther's Beggar's Benison survived long after Rakes' Clubs had melted away before the religious revival and ethical revolution of the late eighteenth century. The other distinction that the Order could claim was that it was the only club that was based on a pagan rite of an erotic, though school-boyish, nature.

Many of the minutes and written records of the Order were destroyed, possibly by Matthew Forster Conolly a few years before his death in 1877. The chest containing the remaining relics and insignia of the Order was removed from the town clerk's office by his son-in-law, Dr J. F. S. Gordon, incumbent of the Episcopal Church of St Andrews in Glasgow, an inappropriate custodian in view of the phallic nature of the Club's ceremonies and the uncompromising phallicism of some of its insignia. The ordinary member's medal is of beautiful workmanship, of silver gilt with Venus and Adonis, or it could be Adam and Eve, walking towards a bower, and the motto 'Be fruitful and multiply' on the obverse. On the reverse is Adonis and a sleeping Venus guarded by Cupid with the words 'Lose no opportunity'. A 'fine and rare copy of this curious badge' was sold at auction in Edinburgh in 1898 for sixteen shillings.

Some ten years after Conolly's death an antiquary, J. McNaught Campbell of the Kelvingrove Museum, borrowed the box of relics from Dr Gordon and then offered to buy it. From some surviving correspondence it seems that Dr Gordon was only too willing to part with the embarrassing collection. In October he writes to Mr Campbell: 'The Beggar's Benison articles cannot be but genuine and I have marked them at a low price'. He ends his letter: 'I desire to part with the entire hypothec [deposit] "box and dice",' in other words, lock, stock and barrel. A month later he writes again: 'Just take the Beggar's Benison in your own hands and do as you think best'.

McNaught Campbell showed some of the articles in a Glasgow Exhibition in 1911, the more respectable articles that is; there were others, he wrote, 'that it was obviously impossible to exhibit'. T. D. Murray, solicitor and son of the manse in Anstruther, wrote to McNaught Campbell at the end of 1911 that he had read of the Glasgow Exhibition and explained that he and some antiquarian friends were trying to get together some information regarding the Order. He was a relative of one of the last surviving members, he wrote, and one of his friends was the descendant of a member who was received into the Order in 1756 and they still had their diplomas and medals. Unfortunately he gave no names. He thought there would be much historical interest in any surviving minutes of the Order as 'many of the Jacobite lairds of the eighteenth century were members and it is well known here that the Society was used for political purposes (besides other purposes which you probably know of)'. And he adds: 'Of course you will understand that we are going into this matter merely for antiquarian purposes'.

Campbell had another enquiring letter from America. In 1897 an attorney-at-law in Philadelphia with the unusual name of Krumbhaar wrote to the Lord Provost of Glasgow to say that he had a parchment diploma of admittance of Andrew Ramsay, an ancestor of his, as a Knight Companion of the Order of the Beggar's Benison of Glasgow dated 1765, and he was anxious to learn something about the Order. From the wording of the certificate he understood that it was an association of gentlemen for social purposes, the kind of club one would have been proud to have been a member of. The Lord Provost asked McNaught Campbell to reply, with the advice that:

> possibly he could place the traditions of the club in a more favourable light than was disclosed to Campbell himself, or perhaps Campbell could charitably explain that the traditions never ripened into custom.

In his reply to T. D. Murray, Campbell wrote that he had strong reasons for doubting the genuineness of the 1892 *Print of the Order's Proceedings* 'for reasons which he could not put into writing'. These *Proceedings*, printed in a limited edition of 250 copies, were reprinted in 1982 with an introduction by Alan Bold. The book may be in part a late Victorian hoax, but included is a serious address given to the Society by James Lumsdaine of Stravithie in 1753, which reveals an enlightened attitude in its stress on the need for birth control in the interests of the woman's sexual satisfaction and of her protection from unwanted pregnancy.

The deal box and its contents were bought from McNaught Campbell in 1919 by Col. M. R. Canch Kavanagh, a member of the United Services Club, Edinburgh, and of the Conservative Club, Glasgow. He wrote a short résumé of the history of the Order to accompany the relics he had acquired, and he tried to get together descendants of the Beggar's Benison, and its offshoot, the Wig Club of Edinburgh, and unite them again into a revived Order. He constituted himself Sovereign Guardian and used the seal of Thomas Alexander, sixth Earl of Kellie, 'in the third year of my Sovereignty and in that of the Order 5922', that is 1922. There is no evidence that he succeeded in resuscitating the Order, though he says in a letter to an unnamed correspondent: 'I am not at liberty to say who are now members of my Society, but I can assure you that the social standard has not been lowered'. The deal box was bought from Col. Kavanagh by J. Gordon Dow, the antiquary of Crail, and after his death his niece and her husband donated the chest and its somewhat indelicate contents to the University of St Andrews.

According to the papers in the chest the Most Ancient and Puissant Order of the Beggar's Benison and Merryland was founded in Anstruther in 1732. Some claim for it a much more ancient provenance, but it seems likely that as frivolous clubs were then in fashion some local wit looked at the old and well-known stories of Anstruther and its environs to concoct a legend and a ritual. That wit was John McNaughton, last hereditary chief of Clan McNaughton and Collector of his Majesty's Customs at the port of Anstruther since 1728. He was a witness at the Episcopal christening of a shipmaster's son in 1737, representative Elder of Anstruther Wester to the General Assembly in 1763, and his fellow customs officer, Robert Hunter, named his son McNaughton Hunter after him.

Three stories in particular are claimed as sources of the Order. In the fourteenth century William Anstruther, known as 'Fisher Willie' because of his interest in and support of the local fishing industry, was credited with collecting a band of like-minded companions at the Castle of Dreel and organising a small fleet of armed fishing vessels to protect the local fishermen from English and Dutch raiders in the waters round the May. The importance of the story to the Order was the meeting, doubtless of a convivial nature, of local gentlemen in the Castle of Dreel.

The second story concerns the Isle of May. St Adrian was slain on the island by marauding Danes in about the year AD 870 and his tomb there was soon discovered to have miraculous powers and became a place of pilgrimage for barren women, an example of pagan fertility rites becoming attached to a Christian shrine. James IV and his queen, Margaret Tudor, visited the island on more than one occasion to receive, it was claimed, the Prior's special blessing, 'Be fruitful and multiply'. (One Prior, John Rowe, benefited from his own benediction to the extent of having four bastard sons):

It is with these lusty monks of Pittenweem, Col. Kavanagh writes, and their guardian Knights Templar of the Dreel, that the Society or Brotherhood of the Beggar's Benison undoubtedly had its origin. Its motto is the monkish blessing 'Be fruitful and multiply'.

And the motto adds that the Knights should 'Lose no Opportunity' to be so.

The third incident from which the Order is supposed to have arisen is that of the 'Gudeman of Ballengeich', James V [1512-1542], and the gaberlunzie woman who carried him across the Dreel ford when the burn was in spate. In return for a gold coin the sturdy beggar woman gave the disguised king her benison or blessing. 'The story is fictitious', somebody states flatly in the account in the deal box, either Dr Gordon or Dr Charles Rogers whose book *A Century of Scottish Life* is quoted. But fact or fiction, Col. Fergusson, in his book on Chancellor Henry Erskine, and Col. Kavanagh are both satisfied with the story and claim that there and then in the Castle of Dreel James V formed an order of knighthood with the beggar woman's blessing: 'May your purse na'er be toom And your horn aye in bloom', translated as 'May your purse never be empty, and your manhood never fail you'. The verse suggested the design of the seal of the order, those relics which were quite unsuitable for exhibition, a full purse hanging from a phallus with the anchor of Anstruther in the background.

Dr Charles Rogers maintained that the contrabandist clubs of eastern Fife culminated in Anstruther's Beggar's Benison. Several of the Knights were reputed smugglers but it seems unlikely that smuggling had any particular mysteries to contribute to the bawdy Order.

From 1732 the Order met twice a year, at Candlemas [in February] and on St Andrew's Day, in the old Castle of Dreel in a room which they called the Temple. When the castle was no longer habitable the Knights met at an inn in the Back-gait and latterly in Robertson's Hotel. At the Candlemas meeting of 1738 the seal was designed and the diploma, a sly travesty of a ship's licence, drafted by the Collector of Customs. Membership cost ten guineas, the diplomas three guineas, and a medal in gold five guineas.

A Code of Institutes was signed in 1739 by the thirty-two charter members in which they designated themselves Com-

G

panions of the Most Ancient and Puissant Order of the Beggar's
Benison and Merryland, whose 'laudable purposes' were
founded on the principles of 'Benevolence, Charity and Humanity'. That the business of the order should be carried on 'with the
greater decency and regularity' certain officers and dignitaries
were appointed: the Chief was to be named the Sovereign
Guardian and was to preside at all chapters, meetings and
assemblies, and all diplomas and writings were to be issued in
his name from Anstruther. The earliest known Sovereign was
'Sir' John McNaughton or McNachtane who was elected in 1745
and remained Sovereign until the year of his death, 1773. Another
Sovereign, 'Sir' James Lumsdaine, held the office for more than
forty years. From McNaughton's election until the dissolution of
the Order in 1836 there were only five Sovereigns and one of
them, an Earl of Kellie, resigned almost immediately after his
election. The second dignitary was the Remembrancer or Deputy
to the Sovereign who was to preside in the Sovereign's absence,
and the third officer was the Recorder who was to compose the
'Writings and Bye-laws relative to the business of the Order'. The
Code of Institutes was signed at the Beggar's Benison Chamber,
Anstruther Easter on the fourteenth day of September 'in the
year of the Order 5739 and in that of the Christian AEra 1739'.
The method of dating was taken from Masonic genealogy. The
Medmenham Monks parodied religious ceremonial, but the
Beggar's Benison was rather a parody of Freemasonry. The
Masonic Movement, like the Beggar's Benison, claimed ancient
roots in the Knights Templar, but had in fact been developing
alongside the social and convivial clubs of the seventeenth and
eighteenth centuries.

A Chaplain was later added to the dignitaries of the Order. On
May 27th 1767 the Rev. John Nairne, minister in Anstruther
Easter (a nephew of one of the founder members, Thomas
Nairne, surgeon in Anstruther) was constituted a Knight Brother
and Chaplain and held that office until his death in 1795. Col.
Fergusson quotes a letter from Nairne's grandson:

> From clergymen being amongst its [the Beggar's Benison's] members
> I am disposed to think it must have been a convivial club of distin-
> guished and clever men addicted to literature.

Nairne goes on to explain that probably the seal was the only
objectionable feature of the Order, otherwise his grandfather,

who was a respected parish minister for fifty years, would not have been a member of it. The Rev. John Nairne's successor as Chaplain, however, the Episcopal minister at Pittenweem and Bishop of Ross, the Rt. Rev. David Low, requested several years before his death in 1865 that in the records of the Beggar's Benison his name might be expunged from the proceedings of each of the forty anniversaries in which he had taken part, but Nairne's grandson may have been right. The conviviality of the Order may have become innocent enough well before the end of the eighteenth century, but by the mid-nineteenth century, when Bishop Low made his request, eighteenth-century clubs like the Medmenham Monks and the Beggar's Benison had a scandalous reputation, as the following incident seems to demonstrate.

In April 1982 a gentleman from Edinburgh came to the Fisheries Museum with a certificate which contained the name of Anstruther. The recently constituted Archives Committee of the Anstruther Improvements Association bought the certificate from him as it was a Beggar's Benison diploma dated 5764 [1764] in the nineteenth year of 'Sir' John McNaughton's Guardianship. It had been granted to Thomas Matthie, the descendant perhaps of the merchant who freighted the Pittenweem vessel that was driven into the end of the east pier in 1715. The gentleman from Edinburgh had been helping his wife redecorate an old house there which had belonged to an elderly aunt, a Miss Matthew, and he had found the diploma hidden under layers of wallpaper. It was obviously not something to leave lying around in a Victorian household.

There were thirty-two Knights of the Order and the founder members were all from the East Neuk of Fife. Several of the names are familiar: Charles Wightman the merchant, David Leslie, merchant of Crail and Anstruther, Alexander Myles, burgess of Kilrenny, described as a dour Presbyterian, whose descendants farmed in Anstruther Wester as well as in Kilrenny, Robert Waddell, shipmaster and shipbuilder, chief magistrate of his native burgh of Kilrenny, a zealous Whig, and Philip Paton, merchant and baillie in Anstruther Easter, father of the Collector of Customs at Kirkcaldy and grandfather of Admiral Paton and his brothers. There was an Anstruther of Anstruther, an Oliphant of Carnbee, a Lumsdaine of Innergellie, an Erskine of Cambo, an Earl of Kellie, and Anstruther's own Collector of Customs, John

McNaughton, 'famed for his gifts of song and story'.

Initiation or 'Collar Day' was always on November 30th. Each knight wore his medal, the Sovereign wearing his attached to a green sash or collar on which was printed at either end in gold a coronet and the words BEGGAR'S BENISON and SOVEREIGN. The proceedings started with dinner at 3 o'clock, followed by the initiation. An 'altar' with the pewter test platter was placed in the centre of the 'Temple' and the Initiate was led in by the Recorder and two Remembrancers to the sound of a small silver horn, which was a pun on the beggar woman's benison. All these items are still in the chest. The ethos of the Order was the pagan glorification of the phallus and the puerile initiation ceremony concerned its display and measuring. After the ceremony glasses engraved with the Benison seal were filled with wine and passed from Knight to Knight, with a hearty toast to the new member who was then required to read a passage from the Song of Solomon, with comments. There then followed an exhibition of some local Venus: at Candlemas 1734, the minutes record, 'one feminine gender of 17 was hired for One Sovereign, fat and well-developed', and at Candlemas 1737 'two girls 16 and 17 posed, exhibited and danced nude. Nothing inharmonious'. One might say it was almost respectable compared with the activities of the Monks of Medmenham. After the dismissal of the Venus the party carried on into the small hours of the night with wine, speeches and song.

Other wits joined the Order. John McNaughton was assisted by Thomas Dishington, town clerk of Crail, 'an individual hardly less gifted than himself', and Sandy Don, 'schoolmaster in those parts [Crail] . . . a fellow of infinite humour'. Several Earls of Kellie were members including the seventh Earl, 'Fiddler Tam', the violinist and composer. The special Bible presented to the Order by one of the Earls of Kellie contains on its flyleaf the names of twenty-nine Scottish peers, all of whom were members of the Order, including the Earls of Rosebery and of Crawford and Balcarres. 'Judging by the Records of the club that have been preserved' which he had himself seen, Col. Fergusson writes, 'it is difficult to say who, of any prominence in literature or society at that time, was not a member of the Beggar's Benison . . . It is emphatically said that almost every nobleman in Scotland had at one time been ballotted for as member'.

There were several public references to the club during its

lifetime: in the *Glasgow Journal* of May 16, 1765, there was an announcement of a meeting of the Glasgow branch at the Black Bull Inn on the 22nd of the month, and in *Ruddiman's Magazine* of 1768 there was a notice that on Wednesday November 30th 1768, 'being Collar Day of the Most Puissant and honourable Order of the Beggar's Benison the Knights Companion re-elected as Governor, Sir John MacNachtane, being the 24th year of his guardianship'. In Tobias Smollett's *Humphry Clinker*, published in 1771, there is a description of a dinner given by the cadies, or errand boys, to their patrons after the Leith races, and one of the toasts was 'The Beggar's Benison'.

When France joined the American colonies in 1778 in America's War of Independence, the following announcement appeared in the *Edinburgh Advertiser* on February 3rd:

> At a chapter here this day, the Knights Companion of the Order stimulated by a desire to promote His Majesty's service do hereby offer a reward of ONE GUINEA, with the Beggar's Blessing, over and above other bounty, to every able-bodied man within the kingdom who shall betwixt now and the first day of March next, enter volunteer into the regiment commanded by the Rt Hon. the Earl of SEAFORTH and in Capt. Robert Lumsdaine's company of the said regiment. To be paid at their chambers in Anstruther by James Johnstone there.
>
> From our chambers in Anstruther this 27th day of January 1778. Signed: Patrick Plenderleath, clerk.

The Captain was a member of the Lumsdaine family of Innergellie, James Johnstone was the vintner, baillie and town treasurer and Patrick Plenderleath was a writer in Pittenweem, town clerk and factor to the Anstruther family.

On the following day another notice appeared in the *Edinburgh Advertiser*:

> For the encouragement of all young fellows of spirit who wish to maintain the dignity of Great Britain, by serving the best of kings, the Knights Companions of the most ancient and Puissant Order of the Beggar's Benison and Merryland of GLASGOW, hereby offer a reward of FIVE GUINEAS to every able man who will enlist with their Knight Companion Sir Henry Wilsone, Lieutenant of the Glasgow Volunteers, until his number of men is completed.
>
> The money to be immediately paid by Sir William Elliot, Recorder

to the Chapter, upon producing a certificate from Sir Henry.
Given at our hall, this 20th day of February 5778.
GOD SAVE THE KING

Whatever the Order may or may not have been in 1778 it was certainly patriotic.

According to Prof. A. G. Cross there was even a mention of the Order in a French book, *Histoire Abrégée de Différentes Cultes*, published in Paris in 1825. From the prevalence of nautical imagery in the Diploma and Code of Institutes, the historian J-A. Dulaure thought that the Order was composed of naval officers.

A Chapter of the Order was founded in Edinburgh by John McNaughton when he became Inspector General of Customs there in the late 1760s. It was into the Edinburgh Chapter that the Prince Regent was inducted in 1783, and two years later a distinguished Italian was admitted a Knight Companion, Signor Vincent Lunardi, secretary to the Neapolitan Embassy and 'first aerial traveller in an English atmosphere' [near London]. He made an ascent in a hot-air balloon from Holyrood Park in Edinburgh in September 1785 and landed near Cupar. No honour was too great for the young, handsome, and successful voyager, Fergusson wrote, and the highest honour of all was the honour of knighthood of the Beggar's Benison 'bestowed upon him, as one who has carried his *jinks* to a height unheard of yet . . .'. A Scottish peer was supposed to have founded a Chapter in London, and as we have seen, Glasgow had its Chapter by 1765. But the existence of a more exotic branch has recently come to light.

In Col. Kavanagh's list of members of the Order and of its associated Wig Club is a surprising entry for 1819: the Grand Duke Nicholas and three of his staff. In February 1984 I received from Harry Watson, author of *Kilrenny and Cellardyke*, a copy of an article from the 1984 autumn number of the *Scottish-Slavonic Review* entitled *The Order of the Beggar's Benison in Russia. An Unknown Episode in Scoto-Russian Relations*, by A. G. Cross, Professor of Russian at Leeds University. An odd fact mentioned by Prof. Cross was the appearance of a photograph of a Beggar's Benison medal in a Russian book, *English Art in the Hermitage*, in 1979. The reason for the presence of the Grand Duke's name in the Order's Records and the mention of the medal is now explained.

It appears from Prof. Cross's article that there were already Rake-type clubs in Russia in the seventeenth century. In 1692 Tsar Peter I founded a Most Drunken Synod devoted to carousing, bawdy humour and sacrilegious acts. There was a similar club among foreign residents in the German Quarter of Moscow, and in Moscow and St Petersburg at the beginning of the eighteenth century there was the Bung College or British Monastery which included several Scotsmen. Since the sixteenth century Scottish mercenaries, merchants, craftsmen and tutors had settled in Russia, and since the building of St Petersburg at the beginning of the eighteenth century trading vessels sailed regularly between Leith and the new port on the Baltic. Several Anstruther ship-masters, including William Halson and David Fowler, made the journey.

In some papers in the Derbyshire Record Office in Matlock belonging to a British Envoy and Ambassador to the Courts of Catherine II and Alexander I, Professor Cross found in a notebook some pages relating to the Order of the Beggar's Benison. There is an account of the Admission of Knights which resembles the Anstruther ritual, without the 'grotesque humour', and there were one or two new Officers which emphasised the intentional parody of the Masonic Order. All the papers are full of the usual witty *doubles entendres*. This St Petersburg Chapter or Consistory, as they called it, was founded by none other than John McNaughton through his friend William Porter, a witty member of the British community there. The St Petersburg Consistory was founded in the year of McNaughton's death, 1773. His bawdy humour, at least, never failed him.

The Most Ancient and Puissant Order of the Beggar's Benison met for the last time on November 30th 1836, the year, as Alan Bold points out, that the word *Bowdlerise* came into the language. There was one brave voice against dissolution, that of Viscount Arbuthnot, but the last survivor of the Rakes' Clubs had to go the way of the rest. There had been one or two mishaps in its early days: the Candlemas Banquet of 1736 had not been agreeable 'owing to several Knights turning insubordinate', and two years later 'several members got combative', so stricter regulations were passed and the Code of Institutes agreed. It was expressly decreed that:

No Person, or Persons whatsoever shall be invested with the order of Knighthood aforesaid unless he or they are really, actually, and

truly possessed of these Qualities [Benevolence, Charity and
Humanity] and are of undoubted worth, untainted honour, integ-
rity and candour, and detesting litigiosity; neither shall any Person
be capable of being admitted that is convicted of cowardice, or that
is even suspected of being capable of ingratitude, malice, slander,
defamation, or other infamous thing or action.

Altogether the club had had a good run, just over a hundred
years. Its membership had encompassed Jacobites and Whigs,
Presbyterians and Episcopalians, lairds, merchants, peers of the
realm, smugglers and officers of customs. It had spread its
benevolence, charity and humanity to Edinburgh, perhaps to
London, to Glasgow and to Scottish expatriates and others in St
Petersburg, so perhaps the Most Ancient and Puissant Order of
the Beggar's Benison should be remembered not for its lewd
facetiousness, but for its long-lasting good humour and fellowship.

16
Melville's Manse and Neighbourhood

The Rev. James Melville came 'in the simmer seasone, in the monethe of July 1586, to teatche at the kirk of Anstruther, situat in the middes of . . . [four] congregationes', which he found 'a burding intolerable and importable'. Within three years he found ministers and stipends for three of them and leaving Anstruther [Wester], to the great regret of his parishioners there, he resolved 'to tak him self to Kilrynnie alean'. The nephew of the more famous Andrew Melville, who worked unceasingly to establish Presbyterianism in Scotland, James Melville was born in 1556 in the parish of Marytoun near Montrose where his father was minister, and was educated in Montrose and entered the course of 'Philosophie' at St Andrews in November 1571. He heard John Knox preach that year, and took his pen and little book to note such things as he could comprehend. In the opening up of his text, however, Knox was 'moderat the space of an halff houre' but when he 'enterit to application, he maid me sa to grew [shudder] and tremble, that I could nocht hald a pen to wryt'. When not studying he enjoyed singing, playing instruments, and 'archerie and goff'. He was a quiet-spoken, mild-mannered man who was often chosen as spokesman for the Presbyterian party in place of his fiery, forceful uncle.

On a piece of ground 'quilk the Lard of Anstruther gaiff frielie for that effect' the people of Anstruther 'oblesit them selves to big me a house', which was 'in Junie begoun, and in the monethe of Merch efter, I was resident therin'. The parish provided about three thousand sledges of stones and fourteen or fifteen chalders of lime, 'the stanes from the town, and lyme from the landwart'. He was so much in debt when the house was finished that he thought of leaving Kilrenny, but after bitter bargaining over the 'teinds fisches' the minister's stipend was finally fixed and with the young schoolmaster John Doig, his 'fathfull yok-fellow', undertaking the half of his burden in the parish, and the interest of his 'happie halff marrow' [his wife] in forwarding his calling, he was content to settle in Anstruther.

Two years after building his manse Melville secured an agreement with the lairds of Anstruther and Kilrenny and the magistrates and Council of Anstruther Easter for the erection of the burgh's own kirk. Money was raised by the freewill offerings of the parish and work began in 1631. The church was opened for worship in 1634, twenty years after Melville's death. It was another seven years before Anstruther Easter was disjoined, as he had wished, from the parish of Kilrenny, becoming the smallest parish in Scotland, 5½ acres, the boundary being coterminous with that of the burgh. The quaint steeple was added as an after-thought in 1644. The church was renovated in 1834 and the writer of the Goodsir MS regretted the removal of the old box pews and old carved oaken pulpit. The church was changed, he thought, 'into an ambitious imitation of the latest erected dissenting meet-ing house in the neighbourhood, exaggerating if that were possible the want of taste there shown', but Conolly thought it was 'one of the most neat and comfortable churches anywhere to be found'.

During Melville's second exile James VI and I, with whom he was always on intimate and friendly terms even though they disagreed about the best form of government for the Church, offered him in October 1606 a bishopric in Scotland through his emissary Sir John Anstruther, but Melville was not to be tempted. A year or two later while he was still in exile his wife Elizabeth died at about the age of 40 after twenty-five years of marriage. Against the wishes of his uncle who hoped that he would marry a friend, a widow nearer his own age, Melville in 1612 took as his second wife, the 19-year-old daughter of the deceased vicar of Berwick-on-Tweed, where he died in exile on January 20th 1614 'after he had spent a great part of his life in the service of God, and suffering for the truthe'.

His grandson sold the manse to the Anstruthers in 1637 and the Rev. James Nairne, son of an Elie shipmaster, was the first minister to re-occupy it in 1717 when it became the property of the town. The building is a typical crowstepped three-storey L-plan tower house with two vaulted cellars and a stair turret in the re-entrant angle. A two-storey wing was added on the west side of the manse in 1753 and a third storey in 1864. The most recent restoration was largely due to the initiative of the Rev. Charles Miller who came to the parish in 1973 at the time of the union of the Parish Church and the Chalmers Memorial Church. For the

The Old Manse, built by the Rev. James Melville in 1590 and beautifully restored in 1977.

excellence of their work on the restoration T. A. Murray & Son received a Saltire Society Award. The seventeenth-century rectangular doocot in the garden, with its crowstepped flanks and its 291 stone nesting boxes, was restored in 1977 with generous grants from interested bodies.

There was no other new building above the town after the completion of the manse and the church until the beginning of the nineteenth century. About ten years after Dr Goodsir's conversion of the malt barn in the Back Dykes a new house was built on the other side of Melville's manse.

John Clarkson, proprietor of the principal back house in the close on the shore, died in July 1815 'at a very advanced age'. He left the property to Mary Clarkson, then aged 16, 'natural daughter of the deceased John Clarkson, my eldest son', late Lt. Colonel in the East India Company, together with £1,000 sterling and £800 to her brother William when they came of age or married. On May 31st 1820 she contracted a marriage with Archibald Johnston, younger of Pittowie [a small estate near Crail taken into the airfield in 1940], son of Andrew Johnston of Pittowie, merchant and baillie in Anstruther Easter, and nephew of James Johnston, vintner. The family probably came to the town early in the eighteenth century from Leuchars. Archibald Johnston was Agent for the Bank of Scotland in St Andrews, a wealthy man owning land in the parish of Anstruther Wester, who bought and sold property in the burgh and lent money to house buyers.

A year before his marriage Archibald Johnston bought from David Rodger, corn merchant, and his grandson David Rodger, brewer, that malt steading by the Hadfoot burn which had formerly belonged to Mr James Halson. In the next few years he built a villa in the garden created by George Ayton. The architect is thought to have been George Smith from Aberdeen, then practising independently in Dundee and Fife. The principal back house and the malt steading must have been demolished at this time and the granary converted into a dwelling, coach house, stable and loft.

A close neighbour was his sister Rachel Johnston, a 'judicious and sensible woman', who in 1821 married the endearing Rev. Robert Wilson from Dunino, minister of the parish of Anstruther Easter for forty-three years. Natives of Anstruther in all parts of the world reminded the writer of the Goodsir MS of the story of the Rev. Robert Wilson's explanation to the two women sitting on the pulpit stair who could not find the psalm: 'Twa axes and a vow Tibbie wuman, twa axes an' a vow'.

Archibald Johnston did not live long to enjoy his new property as he died in 1829 at the age of forty-four. His wife continued to live in St Andrews where she died in 1870 and was buried with her husband and four of their children in the Cathedral burial ground. Their two sons, Andrew and Archibald, died in the same month at the ages of four and one, and two girls died at the ages of 18 and 19. Two other daughters lived to maturity.

William Ballantyne, retired baker, and his brother Alexander, a half-pay officer of the Royal Navy, rented Johnston's Lodge in 1841, and Philip Oliphant, writer and bank agent, occupied *Johnston Cottage* ten years later. Mary Clarkson or Johnston sold Pittowie to her late husband's cousin Captain Alexander Corstorphine in Kingsbarns, late of the East India Company, and in 1852 she sold the villa to George Darsie, tanner, and his wife, Margaret Johnston Walker, probably another cousin. (She was a

Anstruther Easter parish kirk, erected in 1634. The tower was added ten years later.

cousin of Rear Admiral Black from whom she received a legacy in 1853.)

The family of Dairsie or Darsie claimed descent from the D'Arcys of Normandy who received from the Conqueror lands in Lincolnshire and who later distinguished themselves fighting in Scotland under the Edwards. A branch of the family was granted lands in Yorkshire and created Earls of Holderness. In 1508 'Sir Anthony Darsye wes send in ambassadrie to the King of France . . . and the King convoyit thame to the Yle of May in the firth be sey'.

The lands of Dairsie in Fife were said to have been held by the Dairseys of that Ilk under the bishops of St Andrews until the family ended with an heiress, Janet de Dairsey, who married a younger son of Learmounth of Ercildoune in Berwickshire. The name Dairsie occurs in the Parish Register of Anstruther Wester from April 1587 when William Dairsie the shipmaster and his wife Grisell Balfour had a son Andrew and three years later a daughter Margaret. There was a 'Jhon Dairsy, alias Halye Jhon' who died in

Anstruther 'be west the Burne' in 1593 and in 1598 an Ande Dairsie, 'alias Holy Ando'. They were not all holy, however. A son of Thomas Dairsie was presented for baptism in 1598 by Thomas Richertson, elder, 'becaus the father had nocht com [to] the examination and Lords Table and was negligent in learning'. There were Darsie elders, stentmasters, town councillors, baillies and chief magistrates of both burghs until the death of George Darsie in 1919. By trade they were shipmasters, coupers and fishcurers, maltmen, tanners, and shoemakers.

The purchaser of Johnston's Lodge, like his father before him, was a tanner and his tannery, which he also used for fishcuring until the 1850s, was on the north side of the East Green. He exported cured herring to the West Indies and imported skins, usually through Leith, from Denmark and the Baltic, oak bark from Belgium, cod liver oil from Newfoundland and salt from Liverpool, and did business with Rotterdam, Hamburg, and London where much of his leather was sold. He was a manager of Anstruther Wester from 1853 until 1868 and died in 1875 at the age of 68, a man 'of a quiet and unambitious spirit . . . He was strictly upright and conscientious in all his actions'.

Of his four surviving sons, three went to join the family of James Darsie, a deceased great uncle, in America, and settled in Pittsburg. Their descendants still come to visit the home of their forbears. George, the eldest son, found his way to the Pacific, and so we come to the most exotic of the incomers to the property, formerly the principal back house.

The young George Darsie began his career in Liverpool either with his uncle John Rodger Darsie, a salt merchant, or with Stephen Williamson. Before long Darsie was in Valparaiso where Balfour Williamson had its first foreign trading depot and from there he went to Tahiti to the trading firm of John Brander from Elgin who had business connections with Williamson's firm. The American Henry Adams wrote that Brander's plantations produced 'coconuts by the million; his culture of pearls produced pearl shell for Europe by the ton; his ships transported all the trade of the islands; his revenue was vast and his wealth estimated in millions'. (When he died it was found that he had gambled a lot of it away.) He owned one steamship and about twenty trading schooners and one of his shipmasters was Capt. Leslie who ran away to sea as a boy and later married the daughter of Provost John Martin, the Kilrenny oilskin manufac-

Archibald Johnston's 'new villa', Johnston Lodge, built in 1828. The ballroom wing, the porch and the pillared gate were added in 1912. The property was restored by the National Trust for Scotland in 1973.

turer. George Darsie soon became manager of this vast concern.

In 1856 John Brander married *Tetuanui i reia i te Raiatea*, princess Titaua Marama, chiefess of Haapiti, then aged 14, the eldest child of the chiefess Arriitaimai and Alexander Salmon, a young English trader who arrived in the islands in 1841. They had nine children who were all sent to Europe to be educated, and two at least of the five boys were educated at Madras College in St Andrews. Henry Adams wrote that the princess spoke excellent English and was familiar with America and Europe; she visited Elgin with her husband in 1865. As 'first lady' of Tahiti (taking the place of her sister, Marau, who had divorced the alcoholic king, Pomare V), she entertained Queen Victoria's second son, Alfred Duke of Edinburgh in 1868. Miss Gordon Cumming, a visiting Scotswoman from Morayshire, wrote of a party in the 1870s:

> Yesterday Mrs Brander gave us a startling proof of her skill in organising, and of the resources at her command. At the Governor's ball it suddenly occurred to her to invite all present to a great native feast on the following day at her country home. At daybreak she started . . . preparations, on a scale which in most hands, would

have involved a week's hard labour. Messengers were despatched in every direction to collect fowls, turkeys, sucking-pigs, vegetables, fruit etc. etc. A party was told off to build a green bower in which to spread the feast. Glass, crockery, silver and wines had to be brought from the Red House [in Papeete] . . . She provided conveyance for everyone, from the English admiral and the French governor down to the smallest middy . . . her own stable could not supply the demand, so every available trap was hired, and plied to and fro over the three miles, till all the guests were duly assembled. You will allow that this was a truly Tahitian phase of hospitality.

John Brander died in 1877 and in 1878 the widowed Titaua Marama married her manager, George Darsie. With their children Georgina, George and Lieumonte, the two youngest Brander daughters, and John the Cook, they retired to *Johnston Lodge* in 1892. One subsequent guest at the house was the daughter of the last princess of the Hawaiian royal family and her husband, an Edinburgh merchant, the beautiful Princess Kaiulani of Hawaii who was admired by Robert Louis Stevenson; she died of pneumonia in 1899 at the age of 24. Princess Titaua Marama, who had adapted herself 'with consummate tact to her new surroundings, and endeared herself to one and all in our community', died at Johnston Lodge at the age of 55 in 1898.

George Darsie, junior, was educated at Waid Academy. He served with the British Army in the Anglo-Boer War and returned from Canada to serve with the Fife and Forfar Yeomanry in the Great War, dying of wounds at Soissons in May 1918. His brother Lieumonte, who in 1899 was a 'young man who is fast coming to the front' among local golfers, emigrated to America and lived to the age of 96, leaving four children the eldest of whom was named George. George Darsie, senior, 'one of our worthy townsmen', died in April 1919 and is buried with his wife in the parish churchyard, their pink granite tombstone on the south wall of the church puzzling visitors who wonder how a South Sea Islands chiefess should have ended her life in a small Fife fishing village.

The tall, handsome Georgina Darsie married the son of the manse next door, Thomas David Murray, solicitor. In 1912 they had new gates made for *Johnston Lodge* and a new front porch and added an elegant ballroom where Ina Murray gave lavish parties and rehearsed the children's concerts that she gave for local charities — often spending more than the concerts earned. Mary

Murray, 'a sweet little tot', introduced and concluded with recitations a children's concert in 1920 in aid of the Parish Church, and in which the future BBC Radio producer Charles Maxwell and his sister Enid, children of the town clerk, acted a little play. To raise funds for the War Memorial the following year Ina Murray and a committee of ladies arranged a *Bal Masqué*, a 'brilliant function', the *Observer* reported, for which the 'usual drab' Town Hall was transformed 'into a bit of Paris'.

The extravagance and generosity of Georgina Murray were more than her funds could bear and in 1926 she was bankrupt, but the following year her half-sister, Titaua Brander known as Paloma, came to her rescue. She married in 1900 the Rev. Andrew MacLachlan, minister since 1898 of the United Presbyterian Church in the Back Dykes. She was a pretty, friendly woman, a talented artist and musician and an accomplished linguist. Her husband is remembered with a *Financial Times* always under his arm — to some purpose. They lived in *Johnston Lodge* to an eccentric old age. Paloma died at the age of 82 in 1954 and her husband three years later at the age of 85. In his will he left £100 to a former servant, the late Katie Davidson who had been the Murray children's nurse and who was married in the ballroom in 1918 to 'Jeemes' Watson, the fisherman-painter; the capital from the sale of *Johnston Lodge* and everything in it belonging to his wife he left to the Governor of Tahiti 'with the £25,000 already paid' — by Paloma for an out-patients' wing to a hospital in Tahiti; and the residue of his estate, over £37,000, he left to the University of Glasgow where he graduated MA in 1895.

Lt. Col. T. D. Murray DSO devoted many years to the local Territorials (and bred bull dogs); he died in March 1923. Georgina Darsie or Murray died in England in 1979 at the age of 99. Their two sons were killed in the RAF in the Second World War.

According to a letter in the *Pacific Islands Magazine* of July 1960 from a George Darsie in America, probably Lieumonte's son, George Darsie of *Johnston Lodge*, the last of the Darsie family to live in Anstruther, came into his own title of Lord Holderness and Earl of Leirmonth (*sic*) on the death of his father in 1875.

After the death of the MacLachlans the house remained empty for more than ten years. There were suggestions that the Scottish Youth Hostels Association might be persuaded to buy it or that the Town Council should buy it for Council offices, and Mr Clarke looked at it as a possible hotel. The late Mr Band bought it in 1966 with the idea of making it into a motel and plans were drawn for the conversion of the ballroom into a restaurant, but nothing further was done. Then in 1970 a young surveyor from Edinburgh converted the old granary-coach house into two holiday homes, and interested the National Trust in buying the larger property, which they did in 1971. From their office in Pittenweem the Trust restored the sorry-looking villa and by the end of 1973 had converted it into three self-contained flats.

The next house above the old burgh, *Bellfield* in School Green, was built by the shipmaster and shipowner, Archibald Williamson, a few years before he died in 1847.

The first Free Church was built above the burgh to the east of *Johnston Lodge* in 1843. It was opened in October and 301 members of the congregation partook of the first communion. Gourlay wrote that this first structure was a modest building with red-tiled roofs which doubtless fitted inconspicuously into the pantiled burgh. The building was remodelled by John Milne of St Andrews at a cost of £600 and re-opened in 1860. It is interesting that most of the leading men of the town attended the Free Church, among others the Provosts William Halson Anderson and Walter Readdie, Provost John Martin of Kilrenny, the Darsies, the Williamsons (except latterly Mrs Williamson), and William Jarvis.

A further rebuilding was proposed in the 1880s, and when Stephen Williamson was informed he immediately offered £1,000 to the Building Fund, which was gratefully accepted. Of the total of £4,800 he eventually contributed £2,273 with a further £120 for twenty medallion windows. The congregation contributed £600, and the Church Extension Building Committee promised £200; the rest was collected by the Rev. Alexander McAlpine, Mrs Jamieson and Provost Martin. The old church was taken down and the foundation stone of the new one laid in October 1889; the architect was David Henry from St Andrews, architect of Waid Academy. The church was 'put up regardless of expense' and was opened for public worship on Wednesday May 15th 1891, free of debt.

At the service of dedication there was a large attendance from Edinburgh and from all over Fife but the church was only 'very comfortably filled'. 'There might be some regretfully turning back to the old place with its many associations', the Rev. Dr J. H. Wilson of the Barclay Church, Edinburgh, said in his sermon. The new building, with its fine steeple, handsome interior and

Princess Titaua Marama of Tahiti, Chiefess of Haapiti, and her second husband, George Darsie of Johnston Lodge, Anstruther.

generous provision of vestries, school rooms and kitchens, was out of character and overpowering in its size and situation.

In 1848 with Alexander Balfour from Levenbank, the son of a foundry owner, and with a distant cousin who later left the firm, Stephen Williamson had gone to Liverpool and three years later with financial backing from his uncle Alexander Lawson, a linen manufacturer in Kingskettle, the young men set up the firm of Balfour Williamson & Co. Ltd., shipowners and shippers of dry goods to South and North America. The firm, originally owner of three ships, among them the little brig *Medium of Anstruther*, 200 tons, which had been built for Stephen Williamson's father, often employed Anstruther and Fife mariners and sea captains.

The Company set up its first office in Valparaiso, importing cotton manufactured goods from Manchester and heavy linens and hessians from Dundee and exporting wool, nitrate and guano. Soon another office was opened in San Francisco and by the end of the century Balfour Williamson had offices along the entire Pacific coast of the Americas and with its various diversifications was one of the first 'multinationals'. New men on joining the firm had to sign a pledge 'to abstain from all use of spirituous or other liquors of intoxicating properties' even though, as the Company's historian, Wallis Hunt, points out, whisky, port and sherry were prominent among its consignments.

In 1880 Stephen Williamson was elected Member of Parliament for the St Andrews Burghs as a Gladstonian Liberal. He interested himself in the fishing industry and in the provision of navigation lights for the Forth, but was generally known in Parliament as the 'Member for Chile'. He was against the merging of the St Andrews District Parliamentary constituency into the County and was in favour of the re-union of the Church of Scotland and the Free Church and the disestablishment and disendowment of the Church. It was this last that cost him the support of academics and churchmen in St Andrews and lost him the election of 1885 when he and Sir Robert Anstruther tied for the seat: they both took their places in the House of Commons but neither could vote. The following year he followed Gladstone as MP for Kilmarnock and resigned from politics after his defeat there in 1895.

When the Chilean branch of the company was formally constituted in 1863, Alexander Balfour insisted that a proportion of the company's profits was to be allocated to religious and benevolent objects. (Income tax in 1863 was 7d in the pound.) Williamson gave generously to a local nursing fund and invested in a local steam fishing-boat company. The Waid Academy tower was paid for out of his gift to the school of £1,000, and on the death of his mother in 1882 he gave *Bellfield* to the Chalmers Memorial Church as a manse. This was in addition to large charitable donations to hostels, missions and churches in Liverpool and Chile.

In 1900 the Free Church of Scotland united with the United Presbyterian Church and four years later the congregation of the UP Church in the Back Dykes united with that of Chalmers Memorial Church. The Erskine Church, as it is still called, was built with nearly 400 sittings at a cost of £860 and was opened for worship in February 1852. The manse in Ladywalk (now *Brackness House*) was built in 1860. After the union the former church was used as a Sunday School and in 1938 the staff of the Labour Exchange in the High Street moved in. Forty years later the building was bought by a Manchester clothing firm, who had rented an outbuilding at the Anstruther Holiday Camp for two years, and it has since been known as the 'Shirt Factory', although the fifteen women employed full-time make ladies'

Thomas Chalmers Memorial Church was opened for public worship in 1891 and closed ninety years later.

blouses. Little change has been made externally, and internally the former church makes a well-lighted, spacious workroom. The history of the Stephen Williamson building, however, has not been so felicitous.

The congregations of the two Anstruther Churches declined after the Second World War and it was decided in 1973 that they should be united [the Established and the United Free Churches were re-united in 1929], but which church should be used? The two churches were used on alternate Sundays but an independent panel of arbitrators decided that the older church, St Adrians (now known as Anstruther Church), should be retained. The decision was not unanimously welcomed. The Church of

J

Scotland's Kirk Care Committee showed an interest in converting the Memorial Church into sheltered housing for the elderly, and architect's plans were submitted. Fife Region were so enthusiastic that they offered to pay the warden's salary and supply 'back-up' social services, but some of the former congregation opposed the scheme in the hope of re-opening the church for worship. The decision was finally taken out of the hands of the congregation and in 1982 the larger, newer (but more expensive to run) church was closed.

Once the decision was made the Chalmers Memorial Church was stripped of its wood and fittings, and the shell put up for sale. The Curator and Secretary of the Fisheries Museum produced a scheme for a boat museum, art gallery, theatre and restaurant but no funds were available. An Aberdeen construction company bought it in 1986 for conversion into flats and it has since changed hands again but nothing has been done. Meanwhile windows are broken and pigeons have taken over the steeple, and the once proud building steadily deteriorates.

Stephen Williamson died in 1903 and the following year his eldest son, Archibald, asked the Easter Town Council if they would grant the site of the horse trough at the head of the west pier for a memorial of his late father in his native town. He promised that the memorial would be a handsome fountain of granite from eight to twelve feet square and from fourteen to sixteen feet high. It was unanimously agreed to grant the site. Kilrenny welcomed the memorial but pointed out that Cellardyke was Williamson's birthplace, but as we have seen, Williamson had connections with all three burghs. Dr Wilson said, to applause, that it was very fitting to have a fountain 'which will last practically for ever'. But the huge red granite fountain, inaugurated ceremoniously in September 1905, was removed in 1939 when the west pier was widened. It spent some years in a Council store and ended its days in pieces on a Council tip behind Waid Academy. The extraordinary thing was that the horse-trough that was removed had been erected only a few years before to commemorate the late Queen Victoria's Jubilee; only one member of the Council objected. The engraved granite stone from Williamson's memorial fountain is now beside the old mercat cross on the west wall of the Cellardyke Town Hall, which was rebuilt by Stephen Williamson in the 1880s and taken over by the community in 1988.

Of the visible Williamson benefactions only the Waid Tower remains in constant use, but the family is commemorated in Anstruther Easter's first council housing estate, the first scheme to be built in the East Fife Burghs. On the birth of a son, Stephen, to his eldest son Archibald in 1888, Stephen Williamson bought the estate of Glenogil in Angus. The Glenogil Gardens Housing Scheme in Ladywalk was opened by the Rt. Hon. Sir Archibald Williamson, Bart., MP for the Elgin Burghs, on June 30th, 1921. [In 1922, when granted a peerage, he took the name Lord Glenogil of Forres].

Before the innovation of council housing schemes, however, other changes had taken place in Anstruther Easter.

17
Anstruther Easter in the Nineteenth Century

The East Green was probably common pasture in the early days — the monks of Balmerino were granted the right in 1221 to pasture four cows and a horse there — but later it may have been used for bleaching linen. Substantial houses were built there in the seventeenth and eighteenth centuries. On the south side of the Green in 1715 Andrew Waid and his wife Christian Darsie built a house which was the birthplace on June 18th 1736 of the town's future benefactor, another Andrew Waid. After a successful career in the Royal Navy and in business in Perth and Dundee, Lt. Waid made a will (in 1800, four years before his death), in which he planned an academy on his property in the Green 'to be called in all time coming Waid's Orphan Academy' which would train from the age of seven 'orphan boys in indigent circumstances' to qualify as 'useful seamen for the British Navy'. Waid served at sea when recruiting was chiefly by means of the press gang and proper training for naval seamen was negligible.

As most of Waid's legatees were long-lived, his money was not available until the 1880s, and by that time the Royal Navy had its own training scheme. Waid's legacy, about £15,000, was therefore put towards the foundation of a local secondary school, Waid Academy, which was opened on September 6th 1886. Among the dignitaries at the opening was Lt. Andrew Waid's nephew-by-marriage: Alexander Guillan, bookbinder in Tolbooth Wynd, who three years later celebrated his 100th birthday.

As the Dutch whaling industry declined, the British Government began in the 1730s to subsidise a British industry and up to the 1780s Scotland received almost a million pounds in grants. A little of that money came to Anstruther. Several local businessmen formed the Greenland Whale Fishing Company in about 1743 with Baillie James Johnston, vintner, as manager. The Company feued a piece of ground 'called the Forth' somewhere between Waid's property and the Brae to erect a boiling house. Two whalers worked for the Company, the *Rising Sun* and the *Hawk*, both of Anstruther, but Dundee and Peterhead were the

Seventeenth-century houses at the corner of East Green and Hadfoot Wynd, demolished in the 1920s.

whaling ports on the east coast of Scotland and Anstruther's venture could not compete and was soon dissolved, leaving behind a name, Whale Close.

Eighteenth-century houses at the west end of the Green survive with their crowstepped gables and pantiled roofs and, behind the front house, a corbelled stair turret over a 'through-gang' or pend, but many others, including Waid's house [No. 22], were rebuilt as the East Green became almost an industrial suburb. Inscribed on the pend arch of No. 26 is the date of its reconstruction, 1841, and the initials of Robert Todd, fishcurer; in plaster above the arch is a set of coopering tools. The business was carried on by his son John Todd, several times Provost of Anstruther Easter, who in 1862 had his own 'smart, good-looking schooner', the *Anne Walker*, to bring in salt. From the 1880s until the early 1920s the premises were occupied by Johnston Brothers, rope and sailmakers. Now that industry has gone from the Green the original 'cellars' have been for the past twenty years a first-class restaurant.

Across the road, in the small house which still retains the iron bar on which the forge door hung, was James Gow's smithy with facilities for brass-founding. His son ran his late father's business until about 1930. Further east was George Darsie's tannery from which East Fife shoemakers were supplied with leather. A sideline was the sale to plasterers of horse hair which was spread on the street to dry. Further east on the site of a row of 'dingy hovels' a gasworks was built in 1841 which supplied the three burghs until 1965; the wall surrounding the gasometer still stands. To the east of the gasworks on the site of an old corn barn by the Caddie's Burn (still an 'excellent granary' in 1856) was Oliver Thaw's large fishcuring yard which was gutted by fire in 1924. On the south side of the Green to the east of the Baptist Church was John Bonthron's cod liver oil factory and his son's Anstruther Ice Company. There was a small kippering shed in Whale Close and on the sea side of the Green the workshop and yard of marine engineers and shipbuilders.

There were once handloom weavers, a shoemaker, a tailor, a plumber and ironmonger, a joiner and undertaker, plasterer, slater and several engineers living and working in East Green. By the end of the nineteenth-century shops selling ready-made shoes and clothes gradually replaced the curriers, shoemakers and tailors but the shops, the works and a short-lived petrol station have gone. Now, apart from the restaurant, a tearoom, and a hairdresser (and gas company waste land), the Green is entirely residential. On the sea side are a builder's yard, solicitor's office, dental surgery, and in a seventeenth-century house a tavern; the only maritime business is the small office and warehouse of a fish merchant.

Known locally as the house of Maggie Lauder, of 'Anster Fair' fame, this 16th-century cottage next to the Baptist Manse was demolished in the late 1920s.

When the Tolbooth was demolished in 1871 the police station was moved to an early nineteenth-century house on the north side of the Green. Two cells of the jail remain with wooden bed-board and barred window. In 1904 the station was moved up to the former Free Church manse until a new station was built on the Crail Road in 1974. The *Old Police House* was divided into two flats and in the 1980s the jail at the rear was converted into a third flat, appropriately named *The Cells*.

In the late 1970s the North East Fife District Council decided to erect on the former fishcuring yard at the east end of the Green a Sheltered Housing Scheme of self-contained flats, for which a competition was set. The winning scheme, by the Dundee architects, Baxter, Clark and Paul, was named *Harbourlea* by Councillor Mrs Gardner and was opened in February 1982. The architects received a Commendation from the Civic Trust and an award from the Saltire Society. The great charm of the scheme is that it fits so well into the traditional architecture of coastal Fife, with pend, close and courtyard, varied heights and colours (in the past, for variety, ox blood was often added to whitewash), cutaway corners which once allowed the passage of pack horses through narrow wynds and vennels, and — a nice touch — the gutter or rone across traditional dormer windows.

'A Public Character' wrote to the local paper in January 1857 about the many improvements that were needed in Anstruther Easter and asked if there were any inducements for retired families to come and reside in the burgh. 'None whatever,' he declared. 'There are in the first place, no dwelling houses of a habitable nature to be had, and no disposition to build any.'

Between 1860 and '63, however, there were erected some suitable villas and genteel houses — there was a reservation in the deeds that the premises were not to be used for fishcuring — 'tastefully and judiciously laid out' on the 'Lands of Meadowshade in the Barony of Anstruther and the parish of Kilrenny': Union Place, built by Provost Robert Greig, and John Smith and David Cook, solicitors. William Jarvis, shipbuilder, Charles Ingram, fishcurer, and Thomas Lyall, shoemaker, lived in Union Place. No. 3 was bought by the Free Church Session for their Beadle, and No. 10 was bought by the Evangelical Union Church for a manse, which had to be sold in 1916 to pay the minister's salary.

The contemporary *Elm Lodge*, between Union Place and the UP Church, was occupied for many years by Dr Macarthur, general practitioner, who made his rounds on horseback. He died in 1897 and his wife, Rachel Macarthur, died in Edinburgh on November 26th 1936 fifteen days after her 110th birthday; had she lived a few days longer she would have lived under seven monarchs. Macarthur was followed by the popular and public-spirited Dr J. J. Wilson who was born in 1867, the son of the minister of

Cyclists in Rustic Place, c. 1900. The pointed gable of the Evangelical Union Chapel erected in 1833 is visible beyond the pantiled roof on the left. It is now a warehouse.

Dunkeld Cathedral. He came to assist Dr Macarthur in 1890 and practised in the burgh and surrounding district for fifty-five years. He was a town councillor for forty-five years, a prominent and active Freemason and at the time of his death in Elie in October 1949 the oldest member of the Kirk Session. 'There was practically no healthy activity amongst us', Dr Ogg said at a memorial service, 'which did not find in him an enthusiastic and generous supporter.' He particularly encouraged football and in August 1924 kicked off at the Anstruther Rangers Football Club's first match at Milton Park.

In May 1862 under the heading 'More New Buildings' the *East of Fife Record* announced that the Trades Box Society of Anstruther Easter was considering feuing their land 'known as St Ayle's Park'. Six dwellings were planned in the form of a crescent. The paper explained that the land was granted to the monks of Dryburgh by Henry de Anstruther 'for the safety of his soul and that of his wife Matilda', but it had belonged for a number of years to the Trades Box Society 'who are now consecrating it to a more beneficial purpose than perpetuating religious superstition'.

The first application for a feu was made by Mr Ireland, fishcurer, but John Martin, oilskin manufacturer and Provost of Kilrenny, built the first villa, No. 2, in 1874. The Baptist Church took No. 3 for a manse, the fifth in this part of the burgh. The tall semi-detached villas at the west end were built by the business-like Robert Williamson in Cellardyke who only built a house when he had a purchaser. One was occupied by a son of Robert Watson, another of Cellardyke's oilskin manufacturers, and No. 5 was from 1915 the home of Provost Thomas Abernethy Dalzell, ironmonger in Anstruther Easter.

A forbear, William Dalzell, was a customs officer whose daughter Janet in about 1703 married John Lyall, eldest son of the wealthy Robert Lyall in Anstruther Wester. John Dalzell was a tinsmith in the Easter High Street and he and his son Thomas, sometime manager of the Anstruther and Cellardyke Gas Company, were regularly elected West Anstruther's Town Plumber. Thomas Dalzell died on November 29th 1922, leaving a simple and straightforward Trust Disposition. He left his gold watch to his doctor in Edinburgh, £200 to a cousin in London, and advised his Trustees to allow Messrs Gray & Pringle to remain, either or both of them, as tenants of his shop in the High Street so long as they desired to do so. He directed that his estate, to the value of about £4,500, should form after the death of himself and his wife (his son must have predeceased them) a permanent fund to be known as 'The Provost Dalzell Trust' for improvements within the burgh of Anstruther Easter 'and within any larger burgh of which the burgh of Anstruther Easter may form a part'. Over the last few years the Tennis Club, the Bowling Club, Waid Academy's Former Pupils' Rugby Club (for their conversion of a derelict eighteenth-century High Street house into a clubhouse) and the Anstruther Improvements Association (for their Burgh Room in the Fisheries Museum and a Meadow Nature Reserve on the Dreel) have been grateful beneficiaries.

Dr Chalmers maintained that the Church should be closely associated with education, not that he and many of his contemporaries believed that education should furnish working people 'the means of abandoning their status', but that it should furnish them with the means 'of morally and intellectually exalting it'. In this developing neighbourhood around Melville's manse, the Free Church built a school in 1846 at the junction of the Back

In the background is the tower of Anstruther Easter parish kirk. The turret behind the man in the cart was removed from the town hall in 1920. On the left is the Murray Library, built in 1908.

Dykes and Ladywalk on the Lands called Meadowshade. It was opened in November with between fifty and sixty scholars. In April 1858 tenders were invited for the erection of a girls' school and the following year the adjoining school house was built. In 1867 the Boys' School with 226 names on the roll was the largest in the district. The Female School had about eighty scholars under a Miss Buick who taught the 'elementary branches' with knitting and sewing. 'The higher branches including Latin, French, algebra, history and geography etc' were taught by Robert Smith from Glasgow. The large gathering of parents and friends 'and many influential inhabitants of the town and neighbourhood' at the annual three-hour (sometimes four-hour) inspection of the school in March was 'much gratified with the successful teaching' and expressed 'unqualified approval of the result'. In reply to the presentation of an inscribed gold watch from the pupils Mr

Smith, the *Record* reported, said that the great thing with parents
in the town was to get their sons into shops, offices, or at some
trade, and they never thought of aspiring to higher grades; in this
he thought they were not altogether right. 'There was nothing he
more desired than to train some of them for these [great]
universities.'

The schoolroom was used each year for popular lectures and
for Gaelic church services for the half-dealsmen who came for the
summer drave.

As the School House in Tolbooth Wynd was 'presently keept up
by the party of Souldiers lying here attending the Customehouse',
the Town Council resolved in July 1718 that the house 'last
posesst by John Reid nixt adjacent to the kirkyard dyke' be taken
in tack from the Kirk Session for a school. The Session, who
contributed to the salary of the schoolmaster and paid for the
education of poor scholars as in Anstruther Wester, acquiesced.
By the beginning of the nineteenth century the school in School
Green was in a bad state of repair and unsafe for children so the
Council arranged with the Kirk Session in March 1811 to buy the
school, school house and garden and erect a new one, 'the Kirk
Session to add such money as they could spare'. The Session
advanced £53 and the work of rebuilding the school — the school
house had to wait — was slowly accomplished.

There were 150 pupils on the roll of the Burgh School in 1870.
The following year, on the death of Mr Greig the schoolmaster, an
advertisement required that his successor be qualified in the
ordinary branches of education, and in addition Latin, Greek and
mathematics; the school was commodious, and there was a good
Dwelling House and Garden, and its teaching was 'in the highest
degree satisfactory'. In 1873 the Free Church School was transferred to the School Board and the Burgh School was re-classed as
an Infants' School. There was an ex-6th class in the 1890s in the
East or former Free Church School 'which would have been bigger
had the school not sent so many bursaries to the Academy'.
The buildings of both East and West Schools were by this time
insufficient and inconvenient, so plans 'not the cheapest', of
Williamson and Inglis, architects in Kirkcaldy and Edinburgh,
were selected and a school at the west end of Melville Terrace was
opened in September 1901. The old Free Church School in
Ladywalk was sold to the Volunteers in October 1901 as a Drill
Hall (for some years now it has been a Community Centre) and

the old Burgh School was sold in November to William Brown, joiner in Castle Street (whose woodshed at the west end of the street was blown away in the storm of 1898), and it has remained a joiners' yard ever since.

Another school was built in Ladywalk in 1913 for cookery (in which boys who might go to the fishing were instructed), laundry and other manual subjects, but it did not last long. It is now the East Neuk Area Health Centre and the former Free Church schoolhouse is the East Fife District Council's Rate and Registrar's Office. The new elementary school became part of the Academy in the 1920s as South Waid. Since then Anstruther Easter has not had a primary school of its own; pupils go to the Anstruther Wester or Cellardyke Schools and then at the age of twelve on to the Academy.

When the Waid was built it was not alone on the heights above the old burgh. Across the road was the Clydesdale Bank (built in 1858 on the site of the Manor Place), some old houses and barns in the Loan, the railway station, and Mitchell's ropery to the south of the recently opened line to Boarhills. At the junction of the Loan and Station Road was a museum and picture gallery built in 1866 for Alexander Woodcock, surgeon in the Royal Navy and great nephew of Captain John Ballantyne R.N. Woodcock, a tall white-haired gentleman fond of children and dogs, intended to leave his splendid collection to the town, but he died intestate, and as Gourlay wrote: the 'untold treasures of this far-famed shrine of the muses . . . [have] gone like the dream of yesterday, the collection being dispersed in the autumn of 1887', the year of Woodcock's death. The building was then occupied by James Anderson's famous cleek factory (and is now a car showroom and dwelling house).

To the south of the school was the old 'smiddy green' at the junction of the new St Andrews and Crail Roads; Anstruther Farm, of which the early nineteenth-century farmhouse remains but the barns are giving way to a small private housing estate; and *Adelaide Lodge*, built in 1865 for William Murray, who came to the burgh from Leven as a young man in the 1820s and set up a drapery business in the High Street opposite Conolly's office. He later rebuilt the shop in a Victorian style. The 'General Drapery Establishment' was carried on after him under the name of James M. Duncan until 1987. *Adelaide Lodge* was built for the genial and popular draper, several times provost of the burgh, by his sons,

David and William Murray. In 1853, when still in their twenties, with a stock of drapery goods they emigrated to Australia, a destination sought at this time by many other young men from the three burghs. The brothers set up a business in Adelaide, hence the name of the villa, which so prospered that they soon opened branches in Sydney, Melbourne, Perth, Brisbane and other towns. The company by 1907 was one of the 'most profitable undertakings in Australia . . . and one of the largest employers of labour in the Commonwealth'. David was active in public affairs in South Wales, political, educational and religious, and died in London in 1907 at the age of 77. In his charitable bequest he left £4,000 to his native town for the establishment of a library and reading-room, which was erected in Shore Street the following year, in red Dumfries sandstone, by John Currie, architect in Elie. William retired to Anstruther Wester to live with his daughter Louisa in the *White House* until his death in 1920. Their sister Helen Pittendrigh bought Chalmers' birthplace for the town, and their nephew James Pittendrigh, a former pupil of Waid whose descendants are still associated with the firm in Australia, donated the Adelaide Challenge Cup to the school in 1914. The granddaughter of William Murray, senior, was the first in the burgh to own a car and his great granddaughter still lives in *Adelaide Lodge*.

Other substantial stone houses soon followed in the salubrious suburb above the old burgh. *Anchor Lodge*, opposite William Murray's house, was built in 1879 by John Currie, the Elie architect, for another highly-respected provost, William Halson Anderson, fishcurer and latterly farmer. Although he did not follow his forbears in a seafaring career, he was noted when a youth for his expert handling of small boats. In 1866, while farming at East Pitcorthie (and living at *Clifton Villa* in Anstruther Wester), he excavated for a shale oil works when factories in the district 'would have been a boon'. About thirty men were employed but the works were not a success and soon closed. Halson Anderson built *Anchor Lodge* when he leased Crawhill which he farmed until he was nearly eighty. He was provost of Anstruther Easter for twenty years, the longest-serving provost ever; he was a consistent Liberal, a member of the Free Church, and for almost fifty years an excellent Factor of the Sea Box Society. He died in 1907 at the age of 85, leaving a widow, Elizabeth Forgan.

In the 1880s and '90s those businessmen who did not build in Anstruther Wester built their new villas in Melville Terrace and Rustic Place along the Crail Road. William Goodall Readdie, for instance, coal merchant and manager of the gasworks at 8 Melville Terrace and his brother-in-law William Scott Bonthron, auctioneer, fishcurer and cooper at number 7. The architect of the terrace was John Currie.

The improving spirit was also felt down in the old burgh, and not before time, some thought. A correspondent complained to the local paper in November 1856 of the disgusting practice of rearing pigs and accumulating dungheaps in and around the most crowded parts of the town. Another complained about the High Street and more especially the road leading to Mayview [Ladywalk], 'one of our most public thoroughfares and fashionable promenades . . . During daylight one has to keep both eyes and nose elevated, and to pick his steps most gingerly, but at night . . . !!'

In his letter to the Editor in January 1857 A Public Character drew attention to the irregularity of the streets and houses:

> Can anything be more unsightly or absurd than the old, delapidated, granary and coal-cellar looking building that meets one in the face as he emerges from the bottom of Roger Street. It is called the Town Hall, but is a disgrace to the place. It not only stands in the way, but is one of the ugliest looking buildings to be met with anywhere. And then going a little eastward, you meet a row of small low-roofed houses, but for what reason and how they were placed there no one can tell. Pass on a little and you find the pavement completely obstructed by the gable end of a house which has no right to stand there; at last before you enter East Green, an old, delapidated house meets you fairly in the teeth, and one has certainly 'to pick his way most gingerly' before he gets into the right course. I have been specifying one locality; but every part of the burgh presents the same 'regular irregularity' and neither effort or exertion has been made (so far as I can learn) to remedy the evil.

The house which barred his entrance to the East Green was at the foot of Hadfoot Wynd in the middle of the road and was removed in 1862. The row of low-roofed houses was demolished at about the same time and the abutment on Shore Street was removed in the spring of 1866. The removal of the unsightly Town Hall took a little longer.

There was talk in 1862 of decorating and repairing the Hall but the *Record* suggested that the greatest improvement would be to have the unworthy building taken down and rebuilt. It was not only a disgrace to the town and an obstruction, but 'what was of more consequence so cracked and rent as to be dangerous. Patching it up would be a useless waste of money'. It stood well forward into Shore Street between Rodger Street and the foot of Tolbooth Wynd.

From an inscription on a coat of arms in the building, the *Record* wrote in 1871, it was built in 1668 at a time when 'parties built their tenements on such sites and with such materials as their whims [and topography] dictated at the time'. The Tolbooth had a main hall in its upper storey, access to which was by means of a 'most inornate and unsightly covered stone staircase'. It had a steeple which in 1707 was 'loose and failing soe that the bell cannot be rung'. There were some cellars or hovels where potatoes and guano were stored, a weaver's workshop, and to the east a Common House where butcher-meat was sometimes sold, a granary which was rouped as part of the Common Good, and a town officer's house in which at one time the school was held, and which at another time was used as a jail. The jail gate or 'Flemish yett' [most of Scotland's iron in the early days came from Flanders] stood for many years on the site of the demolished houses at the corner of Hadfoot Wynd and East Green until in 1986 it was removed to the Fisheries Museum to prevent further weathering.

The Tolbooth was adequate for a public meeting place when it was built but in a town of 'such public spirit and enterprise as Anstruther, whose meetings and assemblies have so increased of late years' it was no longer so. A public meeting was held in 1866 to discuss the building of a new and better hall but there was little encouragement 'when the trade of the place was at a very low ebb'. In May 1868, however, the Sheriff complained of the inadequacy of the hall for holding even his quarterly courts there, so serious thought was given to raising the necessary money and selecting a site on which to build. A joint-stock company was tried in 1866 but only £600 was raised, so the Town Council appealed for public donations and in a few months £563 was contributed by thirty-three subscribers. Various sites were considered and John Smith, writer, who was determined to find something suitable finally suggested Davidson's large fishcuring

Old houses in Cards Wynd, demolished in the 1920s.

yard in Kirk Wynd and Cunzieburn Street. He negotiated for the premises and a few other properties there and offered them to the town for the price he had paid, about £600. £1,529 was raised towards the estimated cost of £2,200, individuals contributing £802. £200 was raised by the inevitable bazaar. The architect was Mr Harris in St Andrews and the foundation stone of the new hall was laid in August 1871. Visitors came from Torryburn to Fifeness, 'the Dan and Beersheba of the county'; Crail made a holiday for the inhabitants to see the procession of 'merry masons'; flags were flown from every house and bands arrived at the station for a procession through West Anstruther. There was a short halt at Robertson's Hall [the *Commercial Hotel*]. The proceedings were opened by Grand Master J. White-Melville Esq. of Mount Melville.

Baillie Duncan from Crail hoped that Anstruther would have ample use 'for their very large hall', but Provost Todd did not think the size would be a fault: 'the people of Anstruther were sometimes blamed for aspiring to do too much, but he was of the opinion that it was better to do things right at once, and not by halves'. A West Anstruther correspondent to the *Record* a few months later chided Anstruther Easter 'for building a harbour that will never be finished and a hall that will never be filled' when there was no money to pay for either.

The coat of arms of Charles II on the west wall of the main hall commemorating his visit to the burgh in 1651 must have come from the old Tolbooth. After Amalgamation a table was made for the new Council Chamber from the Council tables of the three constituent burghs.

Several houses in Shore Street were improved or rebuilt in the '80s and two embellished with baronial turrets in the '90s. Houses were numbered in 1884 and streets improved but there were complaints of 'furious driving'. Litter constantly accumulating constituted a PUBLIC NUISANCE, and the Sea Beach was in a 'discreditable state' with OFFENSIVE DEPOSITS near the entrance from Shore Street.

Among the houses at the east end of the High Street rebuilt during the nineteenth century was the house bought in 1768 by William Tennant, landlabourer, which he rebuilt as early as 1801 as a house of two storeys. It was inherited by his eldest son Alexander Tennant, merchant and farmer in Anstruther Easter, and a close friend of Matthew Conolly's father. A well-educated man, he married Ann Watson in Cellardyke whose brother was a sea captain and lived in East Green. Their youngest son David was a schoolmaster at Dunino and a corresponding member of the Philosophical Association in St Andrews, and of the British Meteorological Society in London, but it was his second-eldest brother who achieved the greater fame: William Tennant, born on May 15th 1784.

From the burgh school William Tennant, lame in both feet from early childhood, attended the University of St Andrews for two years and then returned to study at home. For a while he was clerk to his brother, a corn merchant in Glasgow, but the business failed, and in Conolly's words 'the creditors, in absence of the principal, secured the person of the unfortunate clerk', but in his enforced inactivity William Tennant wrote *Anster Fair*. It was so well received after William Cockburn's publication that an Edinburgh edition followed in 1812. With the poet Capt. Charles Gray R.M., James Dow the schoolmaster, William Cockburn the bookseller and other local 'poetical wits', Tennant formed the Musomanik Society, whose members met 'to rhyme and scribble in what shape, manner and degree [they] will, whether [they] be pleased to soar in the épopée [epic], to sink in the song, to puzzle in the riddle, to astonish in the ode, or to amuse and make merry with the bouts-rimés' [end-rhymes]. The worthy Society, which included among its members [Sir] Walter Scott and James Hogg the Ettrick Shepherd, was Anstruther's nineteenth-century answer to the Beggar's Benison. Its 'joyous celebrations' were suspended in 1817 'in consequence of the separation and dispersion into life's tumults and unpoetical business of its principal founders and members'.

In 1813 Tennant was appointed schoolmaster at Dunino and continued his studies in the University library. Besides Latin and Greek he was acquainted with Arabic, Persian, Hindustani, and Coptic, 'and had no small proficiency in the Sanskrit'. After three years at Lasswade he was invited to Dollar Academy as classics master and in 1834 was appointed to the chair of Oriental Languages at St Andrews. Fourteen years later because of ill-health he retired to the house he had built at Dollar where he died on October 15th 1848. He was buried at his own request in Anstruther Easter's churchyard where an obelisk with Latin and Hebrew inscriptions marks his grave. He was of a serene and unruffled temper, 'a poet of mirth and cheerfulness', and was described by a contemporary as a 'mere apology for a man, but every inch a gentleman'.

Cunzie Street in the early years of the nineteenth century was described as 'the narrow winding rather unsavoury Back-gaite with its quaint old French aspect'. The 'causey' was crowned with flagstones, 'the sides being avoided by careful folk on foot', and each house had its outside stair, which with the flagstones were removed from Kirk Wynd and the Back Gait before the end of the century. Many of the old houses were demolished in the 1920s, the cleared space being named 'Cook's Circus' after the then town clerk.

By the end of the nineteenth century Anstruther Easter's

population was just over 1,000, fewer than in 1881 when it was 1,248, which was more than in 1851 when it was 1,161. The burgh had five churches, three banks, several insurance offices, and three hotels, one of which, the *Victoria* on Shore Street, was taken over in 1905 by the Post Office whose telegraph department did enormous business at the time of the drave and the winter fishing. Besides the factories, yards and breweries there were sail-lofts in Rodger Street and Wightman's Wynd and seasonal fishcuring on the piers and the Folly. Anstruther's water mill on the Dreel was working and there was a weekly corn market in the High Street. From the time of William Cockburn until the building of the Murray Library in 1908 there was a circulating library and reading-room in the town, and ministers, general practitioners and writers provided courses of popular lectures. Many of the working population still lived in one- and two-roomed houses and endured hardship when trade and the fishing were poor, but as the new building and rebuilding demonstrate, there was an air of prosperity up to the First World War about the almost self-sufficient burgh.

18
Anstruther in 1989

In its New Year message in 1935 the *East Fife Observer* thought that prospects for the future were bright: the proposed re-organisation of the herring industry with a ban on ring-net fishing in certain areas of the Firth of Forth, and the possible construction of the Forth and Tay road bridges would benefit industry and the East Fife fishermen in particular. In 1951 the *Statistical Account* could record two boatbuilding yards in Anstruther, two golf-cleek factories, two garages, two engineering businesses, two fish chandlers and one blacksmith. In 1989 all have gone. In their place is a Manchester 'shirt factory' in the Back Dykes, a locally-owned prawn freezing plant in the old corn barn at the top of Burial Brae, and a small factory on the older of the two industrial sites.

Above the Dreel and Anstruther Easter's former Bleaching Green the Scottish Development Agency's first industrial site was prepared in the late 1970s, grassed and set with trees and shrubs, but only one factory has ever taken up a place. A German firm, Dreher Automatic Systems Ltd, was launched in 1979 'in a blaze of glory'. About three years later eight workers were made redundant and the firm went into liquidation. In May 1983, however, former employees formed themselves into a co-operative under the name of Dreelside Engineering Ltd with two engineers, two third-year apprentices and a lady administrator. Five years later the firm, under another lady administrator, has seven employees and is still kept busy making hydraulic manifolds. A second industrial site was prepared in 1986 but so far no other factory has come to the town.

Even before the Second World War fishermen were discouraging their sons from going into the declining fishing industry and were putting them instead to apprenticeships on shore. Since the War the practice has continued and few sons now follow their families' long tradition at the fishing. The fisherman father (in Pittenweem) of the present Rector of Waid Academy was happy to see his son enter a bank, but the bank held little attraction for

225

the youth, and almost on impulse, at the age of 17, he accepted an unexpected offer to go to the Falkland Islands to be a peripatetic teacher for the next four years, which set him on a more congenial career.

Local working men are at a disadvantage these days as those in work have to travel beyond the burgh. During and after the War the Rosyth Naval Base was an important source of employment — as many as eighty in 1948 travelled there daily. Many others leave the town for employment elsewhere, as in the past, but a number return when the chance arises or come back when they retire. Women have rather more opportunities for employment in schools and shops, banks and offices.

Anstruther's main industry, a sideline a hundred years ago, is tourism. In the early days lists of visitors were named in the *East of Fife Record*. A holiday camp and a caravan park in Cellardyke, hotels in Anstruther Easter and Wester, and bed and breakfast and second holiday homes throughout the burgh, accommodate visitors from April to September, but as the Rev. Mr Anderson said at the opening of Robert Brodie's cleek factory in 1913, visiting is in some seasons very uncertain; one cold wet summer can have repercussions in the following year. Nevertheless, the town puts itself out to entertain tourists: the charming Sea Queen ceremony in Cellardyke; the Lifeboat Gala at the harbour in July (Anstruther has the only lifeboat station in Fife) which attracts as many as 4,000 visitors on a fine day; the Waid Centre with its small swimming pool and indoor and outdoor sporting facilities available to visitors and residents; the new East Neuk Outdoors Centre with canoeing and sail-boarding among other activities; and the Community Council's annual Civic Week.

Community Councils were established by law after the 1975 reorganisation of local government, as Anstruther's Council explained in the *East Fife Mail*, 'to ascertain, co-ordinate and express to local authorities the views of the community' about those matters for which the District Council was responsible. They were to relay suggestions and complaints regarding street repairs and maintenance of public works, rights of way, beaches etc. The Community Council is a shadow of the burghs' own autonomous Town Councils of the past but it is a useful channel for the expression of local views on local problems. Its call for some 'active and strong-minded assistance in this admittedly unrewarding job' goes to the heart of its difficulty, but it works

The Lifeboat Gala Day's Raft Race, July 1981.

hard, and among its many achievements are its tourist entertainments including an annual art exhibition in the Fisheries Museum, the proceeds of which, as of all its activities, go to charity.

The Council produces a useful and informative brochure for the tourist season each year, but once Anstruther had its own weekly newspaper, printed and published by successive generations of the Russell family at 25, Shore Street and then at 56, High Street. It was first published in 1856 as the *East of Fife Record* and from February 1914 as the *Coast Burghs Observer* until December 1915 when its name was changed to the *East Fife Observer*. At one time it was nicknamed 'Two-minutes Silence' because of its paucity of news. It declined after the Second War and was taken over by a Leven newspaper in 1967 and became the *East Fife Mail*.

There were 90 shops in the three burghs in 1951; now there are half that number. The town has a bakery and there are still several locally-owned shops, mostly in Shore Street, Rodger Street and the High Street. As in so many High Streets across the country the only new shops are estate agencies and building society offices, but the burgh has a new private art gallery (in Shore Street). Of Anstruther's cultural enterprises, the oldest is the Anstruther Philharmonic Society founded in 1892. A few years earlier A. J. Macarthur MD gathered around him a group of talented musicians who in 1873, in the newly erected Town Hall, gave as their fourth concert, with a choir of a hundred members, Handel's *Samson*, 'which was then', the Rev. J. A. Paterson wrote in a short history of the Philharmonic, 'for the first time in Scotland sung by a purely amateur society'. The Society has over fifty members and gives an annual concert early in the year. The Anstruther and District Amateur Operatic Society was founded in 1938 under the presidency of the late George Doig, chemist in Rodger Street, and apart from the war years has given annual performances of musicals ever since.

There is no dearth of active societies in the town for both men and women: Rotary and kindred societies, Women's Guilds and W.R.I.s, the Guizards Dramatic Society which gives a performance each year in the Byre Theatre in St Andrews, and two Improvement Associations, Cellardyke's which arranges the Sea Queen ceremony and Anstruther's which arranges a winter series of talks under the title 'Anster Nichts'. There are few Saturday mornings without a charitable Coffee Morning, and many Wednesday afternoons with charity Fashion Shows. There is no question, however, that the population is an ageing one — a second District Council Sheltered Housing Scheme, *Ladywalk* by the Bankie Park, was opened in 1984. Many 'strangers' retire to the burgh, but there is still probably a higher proportion of young families in the town than in the neighbouring burghs of Crail and Elie.

The town with its post-war housing schemes both private and Council — with the inevitable sixties' high blocks — is now many times the area of the three ancient burghs. There are several parks and open spaces: the historic St Ayles Park on which cattle grazed until the 1920s, and which public-spirited inhabitants saved from conversion into a car park in 1970; the pre-First World War Milton Park near the railway; Bankie Park where Provost William Readdie, coal merchant, used to graze his horses; and the latest, Dreelside, completed in about 1980. Miss Esther Chalmers,

Anglers on the east pier.

President of the Anstruther Improvements Association, suggested to Provost Pickford in the late '60s that a 'Pleasance' might
be created along the Dreel from the Old Anstruther Mill up to the
railway bridge. (The old unsightly mill itself was splendidly
restored and converted into flats by Alastair Reekie and the
National Trust in 1976.) The Union Harbour, however, is still the
living centre of the burgh, with its colourful row of small shops,
pubs, library and museum. Old photographs show a somewhat
grim Shore Street of gaunt grey buildings, but it was transformed
by colour washes in the 1950s.

In 1984 a plan was launched by a working committee of the
Scottish Institute of Maritime Studies at St Andrews to 'transform
the [Anstruther] Harbour into a major tourist attraction' and
in conjunction with the Scottish Fisheries Museum 'provide
facilities for the restoration and accommodation of historic craft',
and crafts, as part of a 'Heritage Trail' through the former Royal
Burghs of the East Neuk of Fife. As the scheme has developed,
however, the emphasis seems to be less on heritage and more on
tourism. But what Anstruther probably needs more than either (it

is doubtful if the burgh could cope with many more cars) is other highly specialised industries like the Dreelside co-operative, providing skilled and satisfying employment; the restoration of empty historic buildings in the town and the tidying up of waste places. And the complaints of a hundred years ago are still relevant.

Index

Figures in italics indicate an illustration

231